KU-494-244

LEEDS BEC
DISCARDED
70 0043276 8

£5.95
7A88

From The Women's Press Ltd
34 Great Sutton Street, London EC1V 0DX

Diana L. Eck is Professor of Comparative Religion and Indian Studies at Harvard University, and affiliated with the Centre for the Study of World Religions. She is the author of the critically acclaimed *Banaras: City of Light* (1983).

Devaki Jain, an economist, is Director of a women's research organisation, the Institute of Social Studies Trust, New Delhi, which does in-depth reviews of women in employment and in the informal and unorganised sectors. She is the author of *Indian Women* (1975) and *Women's Quest for Power* (1980).

Diana L. Eck and
Devaki Jain, editors

Speaking of Faith

Cross-cultural Perspectives on Women, Religion and Social Change

The Women's Press

First published in Great Britain by The Women's Press Ltd 1986
A member of the Namara Group
34 Great Sutton Street, London EC1V 0DX

First published by Kali for Women, New Delhi, 1986

British Library Cataloguing in Publication Data

Speaking of faith: cross-cultural perspectives on women, religion and social change
1. Women—Social conditions 2. Women and religion
3. Social change
I. Eck, Diana L. II. Jain, Devaki
303.4'84 HQ1154

ISBN 0-7043-4016-X

Reproduced, printed and bound in Great Britain by
Hazell Watson & Viney Limited,
Member of the BPCC Group,
Aylesbury, Bucks

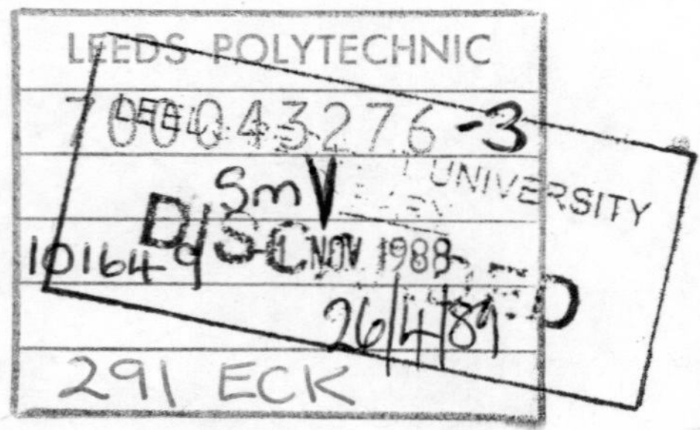

Contents

ACKNOWLEDGMENTS

There are many women and men who contributed in many ways to both the Women, Religion and Social Change Conference and to the publication of this volume. First, we would like to acknowledge the work of those who were involved over a period of nearly two years in thinking and planning toward this conference, and in the administration of the conference itself: Melanie May, a theologian, and the tireless Administrative Director; Fatima Mernissi, who was a visiting scholar from the University of Rabat during the planning period; John B. and Ineke Carman, Director and Assistant to the Director of the Center for the Study of World Religions; Dorothy A. Austin of the Harvard Medical School; Merry I. White of the Harvard Graduate School of Education; Constance Buchanan, Director of Women's Programs at the Harvard Divinity School; Frederique A. Marglin of Smith College; Karen Fields of Brandeis University; Susan McCaslin of the Center for the Study of World Religions; Kimberley Patton of Harvard University; and Elizabeth Dodson Gray of the Theological Opportunities Program. At various stages in the planning process Sylvia Marcos, Baroroh Baried and Nawal el Saadawi provided suggestions and critique.

Various institutions also provided support. The Harvard Divinity School and the Center for the Study of World Religions were generous with space and facilities. The Center's Luce Foundation grant for studies in Comparative Ethics provided basic conference funding. The President's Advisory Committee on the Status of Women made a grant with funds designated for women's projects by President Derek C. Bok. The Special Fund for Undergraduate Education joined with the Divinity School Office of Women's Programs to make possible the taping of the entire conference and the production of sets of tapes for students. International transportation and the participation of Third World women was made possible by generous grants from the Swedish International Development Agency (Karin Himmelstrand), The Lutheran World Federation (Eva VonHertzberg), and the Pathfinder Fund (Freya Olafson). The continuation of the work of the Women, Religion and Social Change Project at Harvard, including a colloquium series, the publication of a newsletter, and the preparation of this manuscript has been made possible by the support of Laura and Richard Chasin of Cambridge, Massachusetts.

We would especially like to thank the editors of Kali for Women, Ritu Menon and Urvashi Butalia, whose enthusiasm for this project inspired the two of us to undertake the publication of these papers, despite the pressures of time. Support for this project in India has been generously provided by the Norwegian Agency for International Development.

And, finally, we thank all the women and men who participated in the conference and whose voices and thoughts are an integral part of what is presented here. There are those who chaired sessions, those who participated in panels, and those who presented their own impromptu case studies, shared their own experiences, and asked searching questions—all of which created a whole much larger than what we can reproduce in these pages.

INTRODUCTION

Women, Religion and Social Change

These papers bring together and attempt to relate three of the most important topics in today's world — women, religion and social change. They emerged out of an international, inter-religious conference on Women, Religion and Social Change, held in June 1983 at Harvard University. Of the 26 women who made presentations from their own context and culture, 17 were from Asia, Africa, the Middle East, or Latin America, and nine from North America and Europe. The presentations were not meant to be formal academic papers by any means. They were, rather, "case-studies," which considered the particular questions and ways of thinking specific to the experience of women as they work for social change in their own cultures and religious traditions. The broad working question of the conference was, What is the relation of religion to the kinds of social change projects and struggles in which women are engaged around the world?

First, our focus was on **women**. What do women have to say about the relation of religion to social change? In our era, the subject of "women" has become a focus of thought and study as in no century or era ever before. There is concern for and discussion of women's roles, women's rights, women's votes, women's economics and women's studies. In virtually every area of social change, gender has become a category of analysis, which is to say that political issues, economic issues and development issues are thought of in terms of women's participation and their consequences for society. In fields of academic study in the humanities and social sciences, the use of gender as a category of analysis has changed not only the results of research, but the methods of research, the questions asked and the shape of the field itself. No matter how much or little ground has been gained, it is possible in the 1980s to attest to the fact that there is a rising women's consciousness that has produced in almost every part of the world something that can be identified as a "women's movement". It is not always called feminism, although in its plainest sense "feminism" is what this movement is about: listening to the voices of women, advocating the participation of women, caring about the rights and concerns of women, working for the welfare of women and transforming the world of women and men through the struggle of women for equality and for a just and peaceful society.

Second, we focussed on **religion**. In both its progressive and reactionary forms, religion has entered into and shaped almost every major conflict and crisis in the world today. On the progressive side, there are the movements toward the radical alliance of the churches with the poor and oppressed in Latin America and in Black South Africa. There are activist movements, reform movements, peace movements among Jews, Buddhists, Hindus. On the reactionary side, there is narrowness and chauvinism in every religious tradition, which easily allies itself with narrow and chauvinistic national and economic interests. There is the fundamentalism of the Moral Majority in the United States, and, as our Israeli participant reminded us, there is a fundamentalist "moral majority" in Israel as well. Moreover, fundamentalism as it is found in many other parts of the world, including the Muslim world, for example—takes on the quality of a crusade against western political, economic and cultural imperialism. It becomes an exaggerated and extreme, but nonetheless important, reassertion of cultural integrity and identity over and against the dominant exported world "culture" of the West.

Religion is both a problem (or *the* problem) where its structures of dominance have oppressed women, as well as a solution where its vision of liberation or equality has generated powerful movements for social change. The same religious tradition may be both a problem and a solution. Islam's vision of human equality, or the Hindu affirmation of women's power (*shakti*) may be sources of strength even when much of the tradition compromises women's equality or power. In the midst of a predominantly patriarchal theology, women's theology of liberation in the Christian and Jewish traditions may derive strength from the powerful image of the Exodus: liberation from bondage and setting forth toward freedom. Not surprisingly women committed to social change have a deeply ambiguous, or perhaps paradoxical, relation to their religious traditions, and women's movements for change have been both within traditions, and over and against traditions.

The English word "religion" is problematic as well. It comes from the Latin *religio*—"to bind". Religion is the bond of kinship which binds together, or binds us to God. It is not an establishment or structure, as much as a tradition or family in which we stand. However, in many cultures the English word "religion" is neither meaningful nor useful. In the Hindu world, for instance, *dharma* may be rendered as "religion" but it is also natural law, social law, social structure, right order, ethics and ritual obligation. In our planning and in the conference itself, we used the term "religion" alongside terms such as "values," "ethics," "tradition" and "cultural tradition" to give a sense of the range of phenomena we had in mind. As we put it in our conference prospectus, "We mean the word 'religion' to include those deeply held traditions and values which shape our ways of life, our ways of thinking and our hopes for change."

Social change too is a fact of life everywhere. The second half of the twentieth century is a time of accelerated change, change which has created unprecedented social crises. Lightning-fast changes in technologies, major changes in the structure and the mobility of families, and fundamental changes in values—all have created a perpetual crisis in consciousness, and the need for the perpetual redefinition of who we are. There is an ever-present, ever-widening gap between our consciousness, individual and collective, and the world we have created. This is nowhere more clear than in the expansion of military technology and the creation of nuclear weapons, without the simultaneous expansion of our capacity as experts and citizens alike to think rationally, carefully and morally about their possible "use". Nuclear weapons have imposed a new internationalism and interdependence that is far beyond what we have actually achieved as a human community. In fact, it seems clear that nations, far from recognizing the fact of internationalism and interdependence, are increasingly committed to nationalism and independence. Finally, along with the technologies of death, there are technological advances in genetics and the manipulation of life processes that pose unprecedented moral and ethical questions for all of humankind.

Religion and Women

The understanding of religion is significant, both for women and for the processes of social change. In order to understand, analyze and begin to change the situation of women, insight into religious issues is foundational, even for women who do not think of themselves as religious. The values and images of culture, the myths or stories it tells about reality, and the images and attributes with which it envisions the divine are of fundamental significance to the role, status and image of women in that culture. Whatever the divine, transcendent or revelatory nature of a religion may be for women and men of faith, its language is human language. A culture's religious traditions *are* its forms of expression, its processes of meaning-making, of image-making and of creating an ordered world, a cosmos. Moreover, that "idea" of an ordered world includes social and class relations, and gender relations. A culture's ethos or "world-view," includes the image or images of women, many of which have been created by men. We think through and with these images; so do our neighbours. They have been for the culture as a whole, even for "secular" participants in culture, profoundly influential in thinking about women.

It is little wonder, then, that some of the most important feminist work has come from those who rethink the tradition from bottom up—those involved in thinking through the very symbols and images with which we think. This is a task of cultural and religious image-making: What is a woman supposed to be? What is her image of herself? How does society absorb and react to both sets of images?

An analysis of women's situation in the world of the 1980s cannot rest with a catalogue of exhaustive facts and figures on women's wages, legal rights, professional opportunities and historical achievements. Important as these may be, women are not shaped by these things alone, but by the foundational ideas of society about women—ideas and ideals which are not only "in society," but in ourselves as well. There is no way forward but to take on a task which women have turned from, in part, because of the dominance of the "modern" ideology of secularism, and that is the task of looking clearly at the uses and misuses of religion.

During the past years, especially during the United Nations Decade for Women, women have come together in international forums to discuss a wide range of topics: women and work, women and education, women and development, etc. For the most part, the focus has been on the political, economic and social concerns of women. Nonetheless, what has often emerged from the discussion is the extent to which many of these issues are rooted in deeply held values and attitudes, or in religions. Little attention has been focussed directly upon the religious or value dimensions of various programmes of social change. While values, ideologies and religious images are crucial to the struggles of women in various parts of the world, both in negative and positive ways, both on the right and on the left, there have been few occasions on which women from a variety of cultures and religions have gathered to discuss the relation of religion to their concerns. Here that discussion has begun.

Religion and Social Change

Religion is not only important for an analysis of the position of women, it is important for understanding social change as well. Change takes place in the context of, or in rebellion against, a world which is shaped by a world-view, with its notion of human and divine order. Such a world-view may *not* be at the forefront of the minds of most people as they think about the political order, social injustice or family planning. Such precisely is its power. As a participant from Egypt claimed, the villagers and masses are not religious; they have to work too hard to make ends meet to think about religion. While women from Latin America strongly disagreed, the point is still worth considering. Many villagers, of course, might not think about it. And secular or western-educated intellectuals or policy makers might not think about it either. All the while that no one "thinks about it" at the consensus level as an active force in either village life or in policy planning, development and family planning programmes the world over run aground on what are essentially world-view issues—so foundational that one often does *not* think about them at the level of conscious decision making. Both "religion" and "women" might be seen as having been what Devaki Jain calls the "missing factors" in development.

In many parts of the world, it is a clear and greatly significant fact that religious institutions already provide the largest and most extensive network of grassroots organisations, with the possible exception of public schools. Despite the conservatism of some elements of religion, one can see the active involvement of religious people and organisations in major movements for social change the world over: the church-based anti-nuclear movements in Europe, especially in the Netherlands and West Germany; the South African Council of Churches; Gandhian ashrams and institutions in India; Koranic study groups of the Aisyiyah in Indonesia; and base-communities in Latin America.

Methodological Issues in Inter-cultural Dialogue

The process of thinking through and planning the conference on Women, Religion and Social Change was also a "case-study" in inter-cultural values. The day is long past when one might need to apologise for discussing "process" as a subject inherently boring. It is clear today that in any international or inter-cultural context, procedure is not simply instrumental, but fundamental. One cannot separate the process through which we plan and move internationally from the kind of world we hope to create.

Participation

The question of who participates in a forum or conference intending to address comparative or global issues is not simply an organisational matter, but an importat methodological issue. In North America, the issue of participation is persistently raised by women, as well as by Blacks and other minority groups, who are acutely aware that "who participates" shapes how the event will be structured, what will be discussed and, indeed, what will be concluded. At an international conference, the importance of the issue of participation is exponentially greater.

Participation is in itself an important ethical issue, especially in the relations between the dominant countries, East and West, and the South. In international organisations, for example, there can be no real recognition of interdependence in the community of nations if the only role acceptable to some participants is that of dominance, at the top of the hierarchy. In academic fields, too, there is a genuine sensitivity and concern among those in the Third World that western academics often assume a posture of dominance in their research in Third World countries, and do not give sufficient credit to their colleagues and assistants in the places of their research.

Without denying the value of western contributions to understanding the situation of women, it was clear to our international planning committee that in this context, and at this stage in the discussion of religion, values and ethics, it was essential to hear women speaking of, and out of, their own cultural and religious traditions. This may seem obvious, but it has not been so obvious that it has provided the starting point for very many international meetings. We say "starting point," because clearly dialogue and even cooperative, reciprocal research, is a goal. But we begin by listening to the voices of women who speak of and out of their own experience, in their own culture and traditions. A primary principle of dialogue is that those who enter into dialogue, across difficult political, religious and cultural lines, should be free to "define themselves," and not be defined by others. The issue of defining ourselves, as we shall see, is crucial for women—not only in relation to women of other cultures, but in relation to our own cultures, in which the definition of woman is often provided by tradition, laws, myths and images not of women's own making.

The participants in the Women, Religion and Social Change conference were from various fields of work—scholars, activists and policy makers. From the academic world came Elizabeth Amoah, from the Department of Religion of the University of Ghana and Veena Das, an anthropologist from the Delhi School of Economics at Delhi University. There was Chatsumarn Kabilsingh of the Faculty of Liberal Arts at Thammasat University in Bangkok; Masako Tanaka, an anthropologist from Meijo University in Japan; Kumiko Uchino from Keio University in Japan in the sociology of religion; Fatima Mernissi, a sociologist from the University of Rabat in Morocco; Elsa Tamez from the Seminario Biblico in Costa Rica; and Daphne Hampson, a theologian from the University of St. Andrews in Scotland.

There were also participants in other professional fields, working for change. There was Nawal el Saadawi, the former Egyptian Director of Public Health, a medical doctor and writer. There was Brigalia Bam and Bernadette Mosala, both South Africans—Brigalia working with an international union in Geneva, and Bernadette working for the Home and Family Life commission of the South African Council of Churches. There were educators such as Jean Zaru, a Palestinian Quaker who teaches ethics to Muslim and Christian children on the West Bank, and Elisabeth Adler, the Director of a Lay Academy in East Berlin. Shulamith Koenig, an Israeli, works with a civil-liberties group in Israel and the United States. Devaki Jain, an economist, works with projects on women and development in India. Radha Bhatt, a Gandhian activist, leads a women's ashram in the Himalayan foothills. Baroroh Baried, a scholar and professor from Yogyakarta is also the head of Indonesia's Muslim women's organisation, Aisyiyah. Julia Esquivel, an exiled Guatemalan teacher and poet, lectures and works for human rights in Central America. Sylvia Marcos of Mexico is a scholar and pyschotherapist, working with indigenous marginalised women. Jose Hohne-Sparborth is a member of a base-community active in the disarmament movement in the Netherlands.

From North America, case-study presentations were made by academic women such as Beverly Harrison in the field of Christian ethics at Union Theological Seminary in New York City; Sissela Bok in the field of moral reasoning at Harvard University; Carol Gilligan in human development and moral reasoning at the Harvard School of Education; and Judith Plaskow, a Jewish theologian of Manhattan College. There were also women active in roles of religious leadership, such as Judith Aronson, a Jewish educator in Los Angeles and Sandra Wilson, a Black Episcopal rector in Connecticut.

In addition to these twenty-six participants who presented case-studies, there were about thirty North American participants, both women and men, from several different religious traditions and perspectives, including those who work in the field of women's studies in religion; those who work in comparative ethics; and those who are foreign area specialists. For instance, Inez Talamantez, an Apache woman, now on the faculty of the Department of Religious Studies of the University of California at Santa Barbara, spoke powerfully of Native American traditions and of the importance of hearing the voices of those who have been marginalized in North America. And Peggy Cleveland, a feminist farmer in California, spoke of the need to look at the moral dimensions of food production and distribution the world over. Charlotte Bunch, a feminist activist and writer, spoke of the new international efforts to organise against traffic in women and female sexual slavery.

Several participants also came from international agencies working in the area of women and development, such as Freya Olafson of the Pathfinder Fund and Lois Leffler of the Lutheran World Federation, both sponsors of the conference. Students from the Harvard community and lay women in the Boston area churches from the Theological Opportunities Program of the Divinity School contributed long hours of volunteer work for the conference and were also invited to participate in the life and discussions of the conference.

The issue of participation is also an integral part of planning. Shaping the conference questions, writing the prospectus and carefully revising the prospectus—all were tasks that needed the perspective of women from several cultures and traditions. It was clear in our early planning discussions with Hindu and Muslim colleagues and friends that this could not simply be a conference conceived and planned at Harvard, to which women from around the world would be invited. It would need the participation of an international group of women in planning as well. Devaki Jain, Diana Eck and Dorothy Austin first discussed the conference in New Delhi. Fatima Mernissi came into the discussions with Jane Smith of the Harvard Divinity School, and Karen Fields of Brandeis University and Frederique Marglin of Smith College, both associates of Fatima since graduate school. Fatima later spent two months at the Center for the Study of World Religions in Cambridge as a visiting scholar, and joined in our planning team. Constance Buchanan and Corky White joined the planning group, and Melanie May, with a year's experience at the World Council of Churches in Geneva, became our chief administrator. Diana Eck visited Baroroh Baried in Yogyakarta and discussed the conference prospectus, and Sylvia Marcos and Nawal el Saadawi spent time with the planners on their visits to Cambridge.

Naming the Issues

The issue of "issues" is as significant as the question of who shall participate in the discussion. What are the key issues for women in different parts of the world, especially as they think about religion in relation to their work for social change? And who shall decide what the issues are?

The case-study approach adopted meant that we did not attempt to define the overarching "issues" in advance. Rather, we began with women from various cultural and religious traditions speaking out of their own experience. Beginning with experience, collective and diverse, the issues began to emerge. Rather than beginning with presumed issues and questions, the conference enabled us to see what the issues and questions are, as women struggle with religion and with social change today. The chapters of this book now reflect a stage in that process.

We did not, then, attempt from the distance of Cambridge to identify the ethical questions and issues faced by women in Ghana or India. The process of dialogue on religious values and ethics is better served by listening to how the questions are posed by those women themselves. The shift in methodology is like that which Carol Gilligan mentions in her presentation. Rather than supplying women with an "ethical problem" and asking how they would deal with it, Gilligan began by asking the women: What *is* an ethical problem? While we might have asked for a case study on the issue of dowry in India, we learned something quite different from hearing Radha Bhatt speak on the issue of fear and the growth of moral fearlessness among the women of the Kumaon hills. We might have asked for a case study on female circumcision, but instead we learned something about Ghanaian society by listening to the issue chosen by Elizabeth Amoah: the conformity imposed by witchcraft accusation against women in Ghana. What we have here is not a full or representative perspective on women's struggles with religion, but we do have an authentic beginning.

The intellectual point at stake here is an important one: who names the agenda, the topics, the terms? It is especially significant for cross-cultural studies of any kind, since there has been too unreflective a tendency to transfer the intellectual or social vocabulary of the West to other contexts, as if that vocabulary were normative. We have mentioned the difficulty we encountered at the start with the term "religion". But, similarly, "feminism," "women's rights," and "women's issues" are often incapable of translation, either linguistically or culturally, into a non-western context. Even powerful terms such as "justice" do not convey a universal meaning. We asked the two women from Japan, for example, to think about what might be closest to the western notion of "justice" in the Japanese context. They said it would be "harmony," a fact that both surprised and enlightened many of us. It is precisely in inter-cultural dialogue that we become most clearly aware of our own categories of thought.

The question of who defines what is a "women's" issue is especially important. Here the insights we gain from dialogue are essential. For the women with whom Radha Bhatt works, fear is a women's issue; for Fatima Mernissi, conformity, hierarchy and rebellion are women's issues. From Elizabeth Amoah, we learned that in Ghana, success is as much a women's issue as failure; women are accused of witchcraft for both. From Julia Esquivel and Elsa Tamez came the insight that, while women in Central America clearly bear a special burden of oppression and pain, the first women's issue is one that women share with men: liberation. Thus, there is an increasing sensitivity to the traditional categorization of certain subjects, such as reproductive rights, family and health, as "women's issues". No doubt they are important, but one might equally see the primary "women's issue" in the U.S., for example, as militarism, the primary "women's issue" in Botswana as water, the primary "women's issues" in South Africa as apartheid.

Case Studies: Beginning with the Particular

While the issues were chosen by the individual participants, the format of the conference was the presentation of these issues in a case-studies manner, loosely defined. The presupposition here was simply that religious ethics and values are most clearly seen at the outset by looking at the particular, and not at theories of religious and social ethics. The problems of cross-cultural ethical interpretation, the points of conflict between world-views, and the possibilities for moving forward together, are most clearly seen by the discussion of particular issues among participants of differing perspectives. Here misunderstanding, conflict and convergence become sharper and clearer. Case studies, in this approach, are not the last step in the work of comparative ethics to which finely tuned theoretical perspectives might be "applied"; rather, they are the first step from which theoretical perspectives may, in time, emerge.

This approach seeks to generate a "text" for studies of religious ethics and values in a comparative and inter-cultural context. An illustration of such a text is on the general topic of violence and non-violence, a transcript of which is included here as an appendix. In the first two full days of the conference, several case studies discussed violence or non-violence, in different contexts. Radha Bhatt spoke of the non-violent campaign waged by the illiterate women of the Kumaon hills to close the liquor shops and stop the spread of alcoholism. Brigalia Bam spoke of the systemic violence of the situation of Black women in South Africa, the most exploited and uprooted group of all under the apartheid regime. Bernadette Mosala spoke of the challenge of dealing with "families" in her work with the South African Council of Churches, when the migrant labour system and the resettlement policy of the South African government treat the Black family as a unit which can be forcibly torn apart and thrown in different directions for work and family life. Elsa Tamez of Costa Rica presented a case study of Dona Amada Pineda, a Nicaraguan woman who participated in the fight against the Somoza dictatorship. Julia Esquivel spoke of the suffering of the Indian people of Guatemala at the hands of the Guatemalan army: the massacre in Chiul, the rapes in Parraxtut village, the torture of Bethlemite nuns, and the "conversion" of Christian women of Central America to revolution. Jean Zaru from the West Bank spoke of the daily tensions of living under military occupation and of the oppression of oppressors and oppressed alike in the Middle East. Sissela Bok spoke of the systematic creation and expansion of zones of non-violence within which we agree to solve differences without recourse to violent coercion.

Thus, when we set aside a morning, mid-way through the week, for the direct discussion of the issue of violence and non-violence, we had already generated a considerable "text" of concrete experience. The subsequent discussion added to the cumulative text. An analysis of that discussion would be extremely fruitful in trying to define what violence is, to understand its various meanings—political, economic, social and interpersonal—and to see the flash-points at which the discussion of violence cross-culturally becomes very difficult or very context-dependent.

Conflict and Dialogue

One of the important methodological issues that emerged from the conference was that of conflict. As one participant asked, "How do we develop a methodology for dealing with conflict?" It is clear that conflict in inter-cultural dialogue is unavoidable in the microcosm of an international conference addressing sensitive issues; it is equally clear that such conflict is vitally important. It is precisely conflict that reveals the faultlines where world understanding cracks. For the cross-cultural study of religious values and ethics, and for the hope of progress in understanding, knowing where these faultlines lie is essential.

During the conference there were sessions filled with tension and strong argument. There was conflict, and at times angry conflict. There were radical disagreements. The session on violence and non-violence, for example, revealed fundamentally different pre-suppositions held by the Gandhian and pacifist women on the one hand, and the women from Latin America and South Africa on the other. The session on the Middle East also brought to the surface, in the microcosm of our conference room, the ways in which even liberal and like-minded Muslims, Christians and Jews, who basically agree on the situation in the Middle East, miss one another's points. The issue of racism and the scars of racism in North America, even and perhaps especially within the women's movement, came to the fore on several occasions. The continued marginalization of Native Americans became clear as we heard from the one Native American woman among us. These were not easy discussions. For many, they were discussions so difficult and painful that they had never been attempted.

In the midst of inter-cultural dialogue, conflict is important and unavoidable. However, conflict is not productive in and of itself. It is simply a cry of anguish, if there is no community context in which it can be pursued and resolved, or in which dialogue can be sustained. Here both the size and length of the conference were crucial. In a large international forum, or in a short two day meeting, serious conflict is, at best provocative, more often useless, and at worst destructive. In any case, it cannot be truly provocative. At a large international meeting, for instance, there may be a panel on the Middle East. Conflict is predictably produced, and at the end of a two hour session the participants and 300 members of the audience leave the meeting hall, angry or inspired, never to see one another again. In such settings, it is rare that conflict can be more than provocative, and it is likely that it will be destructive.

The insight we gained during our week together was that conflict was not only possible, but constructive, in the context of an emerging community. Those with whom we strongly disagreed were the same women with whom we shared breakfast and lunch day after day, and with whom we discussed one issue after another for an entire week. One could not engage in conflict and then leave the room with one's partisans; rather, one would engage in conflict and then have dinner with one's opponents. The time was long enough, the group small enough, that issues of enormous difficulty could surface and be discussed in the context of a developing community of trust.

As Nawal el Saadawi put it, "Out of conflict comes movement. This conference opened our eyes to many things, because conflict came into the open air, and we discussed it. We may disagree here, but at our next conference, we will agree."

Fatima Mernissi said with real conviction, "Here communication is possible. I am not talking about simple sorority. I am talking about my contact with Shulamith. We didn't understand each other at all. And she came to me later and said, 'We have to talk.' I'm talking about that. It is not a magic thing, and it is not easy. I am talking about the fact that this impossible dialogue here appears to be possible. It is not simple. I am not saying that now Shulamith and I understand each other. I am saying only that it is possible."

Perhaps the most important outcome of the conference was not only its contribution to the understanding of particular issues, but our affirmation and consensus that the process of dialogue is itself illumining and crucially important—important enough to elicit the continued commitment of the participants to ongoing relationship and dialogue.

DIANA L. ECK
DEVAKI JAIN

PART ONE

SPEAKING FROM EXPERIENCE: WOMEN IN THE MIDST OF CONFLICT

Introduction

In these presentations, women speak in their own voices, bearing witness to the experience of women in their own cultures. They come from areas of the world where social and political conflict has been relentless in recent years—Central America, South Africa, and the Middle East. In all these conflicts, religion has played a part both in buttressing long-held established interests and in providing the vision and commitment for radical change toward a better society.

As we entered into a wider discussion of the oppressor and oppressed, conflict and the resolution of conflict, violence and non-violence, we were intensely aware of the presence of these women among us, for whom such issues are not only posed at the level of ethical theory, but are confronted in the course of every day. For all of them confronting such issues has meant controversy and risk and for two of them it has meant exile.

Before she left Guatemala in 1980, **Julia Esquivel** was a primary school teacher, a poet, and a theologian who had studied in Costa Rica and Switzerland. She had been active in the ecumenical movement of the churches in Guatemala, and in the struggle for human rights and social change. In 1980 she was forced into exile by repeated threats to her life from the ruling generals. In exile she has carried on her work on behalf of her people as the director of the Committee for Justice and Peace (Comite pro Justicia y Paz). She has published in Spanish and English a collection of her poetry, *Threatened With Resurrection*. **Elsa Tamez** teaches at the Seminario Biblico Latinoamericano in San Jose, Costa Rica, and is a staff member of the Departmento Ecumenico de Investigaciones. She has written of the movement of the poor for liberation in Central America in her book, *The Bible of the Oppressed*. Both Julia and Elsa speak here of the experience of women, such as Dona Amada Pineda of Nicaragua and Victoria de la Roca of Guatemala, who have borne the weight of the suffering of their people, and of the many women who have played prominent roles in the work of liberation for the poor, and they speak of the relation of the oppression of the poor to the oppression of women. Recognizing our own oppression, says Julia, is part of the dynamic process of conversion—conversion to the struggle for social justice.

Brigalia Bam of South Africa, like Julia Esquivel, came as one in exile, now unable to return to South Africa. From 1973–79 Brigalia served as director of the programme on Women in Church and Society at the World Council of Churches in Geneva. Since then she has worked in Geneva with the international YWCA and with an international union. **Bernadette Mosala** works with the South African Council of Churches which has become an important voice for Black South Africans and, as a result, a target of harassment and continual investigation by the government of South Africa. Her portfolio in SACC is Director of Home and Family Life, a task of tremendous scope in the context of a system constructed upon "apartness," not only of races, but of family units. Under the migrant labour system families are separated—with workers living in dormitory conditions near the urban areas, and their families forced to live in the so-called "homelands" far away. Both Brigalia and Bernadette speak of the special burdens and insights of Black women at the bottom of the ladder in a society so rigorously hierarchical. They also stress the special vitality of these women in the freedom struggle in South Africa. Through large church-based women's organizations, through labour organizations, and through protest movements such as Crossroads, Black women play an increasingly active role in the movement toward social change.

Jean Zaru has lived her entire life in Ramallah, originally Palestine, and since 1967 a part of the militarily occupied West Bank. She is an Arab, a Quaker, and a Pacifist. For many years Jean and her husband have had a major role in the life of the Friends Boys School in Ramallah, where Jean teaches ethics to both Christian and Muslim boys. She has been a member of the Central Committee of the World Council of Churches and is a Vice-President of the World YWCA. **Shulamith Koenig** is an Israeli, born of Polish immigrant parents in Jerusalem. She has a degree in engineering, but now works as International Coordinator of the American-Israeli Civil Liberties Coalition, and the Israeli organization, Kol Kore, "The Summoning Voice," concerned with civil liberties and democratic action in Israel. Both Jean and Shulamith are actively involved in education and concerned with the cycle of humiliation, hatred, oppression and violence that is perpetuated in children and young people who have lived their entire lives in an environment of mistrust and hostility. Both speak of what Jean calls "affirmation as a strategy," and what Shulamith referred to as the urgency of being "pro" rather than "anti" toward both sides, as a route to breaking the cycle of negation.

In all these contributions, experience was the starting point for our attempts to understand the linking of religion and social change, and to think together, across cultural and religious lines, about fundamental moral issues. Our point in these case-studies was not to ask, How can we understand this situation from the analytical standpoint of an outside observer? Rather, we would ask, How can we understand this situation from the standpoint of someone, one of our sisters, deeply involved in the situation, struggling to change it, and committed to her religious tradition as a source of change? We cannot hope to understand a "situation" without understanding a single person who lives in that situation. Understanding one or two is at least a beginning, if only a beginning.

Speaking directly out of such experience of tension and conflict was often difficult. This is most evident here in this section, and certainly in the discussions that followed these presentations, because the experiences and contexts from which these women speak have been filled with both the pain of suffering and the rage for justice—for themselves, their families, and their people.

While it is clear, as Jean Zaru has said, that the oppressor is not freer than the oppressed, even so we hear too often only the oppressed charged to speak of their oppression and their yearning for change. Too seldom do we hear the oppressor—whether man, class, or nation—speak with anguish of that mutual captivity of oppressor and oppressed. As Brigalia Bam put it, "It is hard to talk about suffering. It is humiliating. When people ask you to describe what it is like to live under the system of apartheid, you feel you are undressing in public. I have never listened to a white South African woman talk about what it means to be an oppressor."

The sessions in which these presentations were made were charged with emotion and, at times, with conflict. Both the emotion and conflict became a source of deeper understanding. North Americans heard the chilling experiences of those on the receiving end of American economic and military policies in Central America. Jews and Arabs listened as best they could to one another. Those committed to pacifism—Hindu, Buddhist, or Christian—heard the voices of women whose experience was that armed struggle was often necessary.

The primary and most urgent issue to emerge from these presentations and the contexts of discussion in which they were set was the issue of violence/non-violence. Each of these women spoke from a situation that is both overtly and covertly violent. In discussing violence and our responses to it, it became clear that violence—in all our situations—is much more than simply the bearing and use of arms. There is the systemic violence of economic exploitation which crushes the hope, even the life, of the poor. There is the violence of social oppression, which attempts to dehumanize the "others" be they Blacks, tribal peoples, Palestinians, or Jews. That same violence often attempts to dehumanize women. There is the violence of human rights abuse inflicted upon those who have been stripped of their freedom or self-determination, who have been imprisoned without trial, who have been tortured, who have disappeared. And, of course, there is the violence of war—of open warfare, of guerilla warfare, of increasing global militarization, and of the nuclear arms race.

The issue of violence/non-violence emerged repeatedly in our discussions. Here "beginning with experience" was essential, for solutions to the problem of violence are not principled and theoretical, applicable to all contexts. As one participant put it, "I noticed that in violence/non-violence there is a slash. To me this means that the two are closely related. One of our achievements here is to have been able to see that truth is a very complex thing." For example, Radha Bhatt, a Gandhian from India, asked how structures of injustice can truly be broken down. "If you put a seed in the ground, the outside husk in time falls away and the shoot will come through. But if the shoot is not strong, the outside husk will not fall down. Non-violence works that way to my mind. If the people are strong, the structure will fall down by itself." However, Julia Esquivel from the experience of Guatemala posed the question quite differently: "Violence or non-violence is not the question for us in Central America. It is, rather, can we live or not? We are either going to live or be exterminated. We are like the woman who has to use every means possible to save herself and her children, or be exterminated. Our people organized to use non-violent methods, and the response to all these methods has been death."

Christian Women and the Struggle for Justice in Central America

Julia Esquivel

Many women's identity as Christians has led them to make a commitment to struggle for social and political change in Central America. Those of us who, through our experience, have come to understand the need for real and profound change in the Central American social and political structures, and who want to commit our whole lives to this task, have undergone severe, painful and often profound changes in our own lives and personalities. We have lived through experiences of death and resurrection, like that of the Pascal mystery. All death is painful. It is separation. It is rupture. It is being buried. On the other hand, resurrection is life; it is hope.

To be able to reach a place where, little by little, we become more and more involved with the people's struggle, we have had to die to our own social, cultural and religious prejudices. We have had to bury mental and social stereotypes imposed on us by cultural domination. If it were not for the revolutionary and popular struggle, whose main objective is gaining acceptance of the humanity and equal rights of the poor majorities, we women would never have been able to live such an internal exodus. It is our commitment that allows us, as women, to become involved in a constant process of change towards the New Woman. She is embodied in Mary, Mother of Jesus, who placed her life, body and soul, at the service of an utopian project: The Kingdom of God.

The terror, the persecution, the massacres; the total lack of respect for women who are poor and for those committed to the poor—these have generated increased strength, creativity, and determination in the hearts and lives of Christian women who have decided to commit their lives to social change. Who are these women? They are the poor—workers, peasants, tribal women. And with them are some middle class women who have chosen for the poor. They have found in the poor their brothers and sisters. They have found in the poor the face of God.

We ask women from the developed nations, for whom it must be extremely difficult to understand our experience, to try to understand and to identify with our people's suffering. For it is the *people*—women, children and men—who have been condemned to oppression, humiliation, servitude, and now to torture and genocide. It is the people who have demanded that we all change our ways and change our lives to bring about the liberation of the oppressed and oppressor alike.

It is difficult to know whether women, children or men are enduring the greatest suffering at the hands of the powerful, the Guatemalan army, and the Reagan administration. But we can affirm that women who are poor, and particularly Indian women, are enduring a double quota of pain to achieve their own liberation and that of an entire people.

The Testimonies

Perhaps many do not know that in Guatemala genocide is being carried out against indigenous peoples. In the last year, the Committee for Justice and Peace received evidence of 12,000 native people who were murdered by the army.

This paper is based on the very real experience of poor women, particularly peasants, in my country today. It is relatively easy to say that we, as women, endure a double quota of suffering and pain for the liberation of our peoples. But it is hard to really understand what this means if we do not hear concrete testimonies. The following is an example of such a testimony, received by the Committee for Justice and Peace.

> The massacre was committed by the civil defence patrols of the village of Chiul, municipality of Cunen in Guatemala. The patrolmen were forced by the army to kill their neighbours in the village of Parraxtut, municipality of Sacapulas, on December 22 and 23, 1982. This is what happened.
>
> On Wednesday, December 22, the captain of the military base located in Chiul ordered his secretary to transmit the order to the auxiliary mayors to round up all the civil patrolmen in the village. It was a big village, with close to 400 houses. In two hours about 350 men congregated,

ranging from 16 to 65 years of age. Chiul is on the highway which goes up to the Cuchumatan mountains, at the crossing to the highway to Alta Verapaz. Because it is located at a strategic point, the army has a large base there, with a thousand soldiers. They were in special training at the time, and that is why this "job" was turned over to the civil patrolmen.

The captain ordered the men to go to the village of Parraxtut, which is about one and a half hours away on foot, while an equal number of soldiers rode ahead with the officer in a military truck. Parraxtut was a village with 350 houses. The soldiers ran around and forced the people to gather. When the patrolmen from Chiul arrived, they gathered the rest.

Once all the people had been congregated, the officer ordered three groups to form, men, women and children. Then he ordered the civil patrolmen to begin to kill the men, and handed them weapons to do so. "You are going to kill all of these people because they are guerillas," he said. The officer then ordered them to shoot all the men who were in the plaza. The women were still alive. The officer ordered them to be separated into two groups, those who could "make it," and those who could not, in other words the young from the old. The younger women were given to the soldiers to be raped that night, and the others were massacred by the civil defence patrolmen from Chiul. The first group was locked inside the courtroom, and the second in the school and church.

Meanwhile the children were able to escape to the mountains, because the army was too involved with the men and the women. The following day, the officer ordered the soldiers to bring the young women out. He then told them to separate out the prettiest. The civil patrolmen were ordered to kill all except for two. The patrolmen who told this story spoke of the deep anguish which having to kill the women caused them. But they had to do it or be killed themselves.

One of the women who was still alive knelt in front of the officer's secretary and said in her Quiche language, "Please, tell the officer to give me two bullets." She was a widow, and her children had been murdered as well. The officer asked the secretary to translate. When he heard what she wanted, he roared with laughter and shot her twice. She did not die right away, and twisted on the ground in agony. The officer, enraged, took her clothes off, her *corte*, her Indian skirt, and then shot her for the third time, and she died.

The other woman was put in the truck with the soldiers, and taken to the base. The officer probably had chosen her for himself. The children, who had got lost in the mountains, finally found a place to hide, the older protecting the small ones, although not all survived the escape, for the area has very cold temperatures. The bodies of some of the children were found in the following days.

The civil patrolmen walked back to their village. They did not say a word during the whole trip back, walking in deep silence. The witness said, "Who knows what each one of us was saying to God." He let it be understood that God would understand and forgive, but still they were dying of guilt and shame.

When they arrived in their homes they broke down and wept. They wept for several hours. "We were filled with feeling," he said. They had killed their own brothers, and they felt impotent. They were ashamed to tell their own wives of what they had done. The women had been waiting for them through the night, and believed that the army had killed them.

This is an abstract of a report given by a witness who fled from Chiul. The repression, suffering and pain which the poor, especially poor women, are enduring in Guatemala are beyond description. Indian women, and peasant women in general, do not even have the basic right to live. From early childhood, sometimes from the age of 5 or 6, they acquire responsibilities imposed by penury and war. Even in "normal" times they do not have access to education, and only a small percentage ever learn to read and write. They never even learn about their human and constitutional rights. In many cases, they do not speak Spanish, and this too limits their ability to communicate and express clearly what they think, feel, and desire. They do not have access to social welfare programmes, nor to health care. Their very existence symbolizes the words of the Apostle Paul when he speaks to us of the madness of the Cross: "God has chosen what the world condemns as foolish to embarrass the wise. He has chosen what the world considers weak, to embarrass the strong. God has chosen the common and despised people. He has chosen those who are seen as nothing in the world to bring to nothing those who are proud, so that no one may boast in the presence of God. (I Corinthians 1:28.)

The Conversion

Until very recently Christian women in Central America were still repeating religious formulas without questioning their true meaning. Middle class women can see poverty, give alms to beggars, become involved in charitable projects and repeat the Our Father endlessly, and yet remain indifferent to the concrete problems and the profound structural causes of the miserable conditions in which most of our people live.

This is why conversion to the God of the poor is essential to begin to understand why there cannot be true peace without justice. It is not enough to be a woman, and as such oppressed and relegated to a secondary position. The real face of God is one of suffering, of a God who suffers when he hears the cry of the oppressed. Most women who call themselves Christians allow themselves to be imprisoned by the cultural, economic and traditional patterns that the consumer society imposes on them. They view themselves as Christian because they comply with certain Sunday religious practices.

Wealthy women believe they have the right to demand luxury, overabundance, even the superfluous—at the expense and exploitation of the poor in the Third World. Although it may be hard to believe, this type of woman exists even in our societies in Central America. There are women who torture other women, and who keep servants whom they treat like dogs.

Poor women, peasants, Indians, servants, and factory workers can also believe that their life is normal, and that it is God's will that they live, or rather survive, in the way they do. For centuries, most poor women with children have accepted the fact that their children die of malnutrition. To the question of how many children they have, peasant women might respond, "Five. Three dead and two living," or "Seven. Five dead and two living." These women also need to become acquainted with the face of a God for whom all people are equal, a face which is not visible in consumer societies and those called "developed".

For women, poor or not, the encounter with the real God is a realization that we are accepted by Him as daughters. It means encountering the God of the poor, and realizing that we are Jesus' sisters. It means remembering that He very clearly told the doctors and professors that all nations will be judged by the treatment they give their smaller brothers, the poor, and that He Himself is one of the poor. He demands of us pity, clemency, fraternity and service through each poor, weak or oppressed person we encounter. (Matthew 25:31–46, Isaiah 58.)

When we women of faith begin to open our eyes to our human dignity, and to our brothers and sisters, the true meaning of Our Father, Our Daily Bread, and The Promised Land is revealed to us. We discover ourselves as destined to live a human life together, along with our brothers and sisters in Christ, the world over. We can no longer passively accept a life of enslavement, and even less the role of the oppressor or accomplice in a society which subverts God's will for all men and women.

But we women, liberated from our blindness, become dangerous. Many people would prefer to have a woman who is dependent, submissive and fearful, a complete follower of established traditions and cultural patterns.

The Recognition of Our Own Poverty and Need

The first step towards the Christian woman's new awareness is seeing that she herself has never been recognized as a person. This first look inside herself—at her own dependence, her own oppression, her own misery and lack of freedom—is a necessary step in the conversion which will give her strength to choose another life, not just for herself, but for her brothers and sisters as well.

In becoming aware of the "other," she sees herself more clearly. All women, and particularly poor women, are a scandalous symbol of social oppression. For Christian women to commit themselves to the struggle for social justice, we need to see in the "other," poor as she is, our sister. For many a middle class woman the first stage in the process is understanding the injustice which oppresses the majority. Once she begins to open her eyes and becomes sensitive to this reality, the reality of the oppression of the poor, she also begins to see herself. These two steps—seeing our own poverty and really seeing the poverty of the poor—can occur simultaneously, or one after the other.

Renunciation and Involvement

The next stage in the process of awakening is acquiring the ability to give up a personal life project for a communitarian one. To understand this we have to see that many of our dreams as women are imposed from outside ourselves. Society, as it is presently structured, imposes models of happiness which are often imported from the developed nations or which flow from local social and cultural traditions.

Apart from those who have committed themselves to the revolution of society, few women have a life project which is truly their own, an authentic project. Generally they allow themselves to be swallowed by traditional patterns, such as marriage or other forms of strictly personal life. In Central America, the woman who has undergone a "conversion" to the poor and to the project of their liberation, can no longer make choices which are isolated from the society in which she and they live. Her life project can no longer be purely individual, isolated from her people. Her entire life is involved with the pain, struggles, risks and goals of her people.

There are many examples in the Scriptures for Christian women to follow. Mary, the young peasant from Nazareth, is a paradigm for all women who have faith and hope for a new society in which human life is the most sacred value. Engaged to an artisan, Mary was preparing herself for a married life. But the intervention of the God of the poor superseded that dream and project for something larger, a plan for her own people and for all of humanity. The Magnificat, emerging from the depths of Mary's soul, reveals clearly the depth and intuition which Mary had about this project.

The option the Christian woman takes in the struggle for a new society, rules out egocentrism. This option is a continuous voluntary, joyful offering of her own life for the common good. Romans 12:1–2. invites us not to go along with the current and the established ways of the world, but to take it and transform it, and to keep a clear mind open to God's will in today's context. Jesus says, "I beseech you, by God's mercy, to present your bodies as a living sacrifice, holy, and acceptable to God. Be not conformed to the world, but transformed by the renewal of your mind, that you may do what is good." Mary's acceptance of God's project of transformation for her people was like a sword piercing her heart until the real meaning of her life, as an active participant in the history of Israel, was revealed to her. Her example leads us to reflect on our own deep motivations for participating in the struggle for women's liberation.

Christian Women Who Struggle for Justice: Bearers of Life

Christian women who struggle for justice and real peace are true combatants—against death. Death wears many faces in our countries. It appears as malnutrition, as abject poverty, as exploitation, repression, counter-insurgency and even as "development" and population control.

All of Guatemala is embodied in that woman, writhing on the ground from two bullets, in the tribal village of Parraxtut. Guatemala is a woman, who has been raped and violated, who has nothing because of those who have power, that is those who have money and those who have weapons. This means that we in Central America do not have time to struggle only for women's rights; our struggle is the struggle to live, to survive.

In Guatemala, a religious woman from the Bethlemite order, Victoria de la Roca, was kidnapped by a squadron of soldiers who violently broke into her convent in the district of Esquipulas and took her away. After a month of cruel torture she was condemned to be shot. The officer in charge of the operation placed her in front of the squadron and invited the soldiers to rape her. She was wearing only a nightgown and a robe and she said to them: "I am a virgin because I am a religious; my body is consumed by cancer and I am weak; I have helped the resistance, because I have loved life. Whomever wants to abuse me, here I am." And she opened her robe. No one dared to touch her. The officer, infuriated, ordered his soldiers to shoot. She was executed without a trial and without counsel because she loved life.

The death of Victoria de la Roca is a challenge to hundreds of women like myself who want to follow her example. Like her, many other women have offered their lives as martyrs and as workers in the daily battle against death. Among them are Clemencia Azmitia, Rosario Melendez, Ligia Martinez, Sebastiana Mendoza, whose lives were completely involved in the project to create a new society—more human, more just, less cruel. I would like to share with you some of the thoughts of one of these women. Ligia Martinez was assassinated by the Guatemalan army on October 3, 1981. These were taken from a tape sent to a friend living in another country shortly before her death:

> I go on because I know that my people really need my work. I am truly dedicated to my work, and am satisfied and happy with it. When I become involved in my work my life changes. I feel great. I forget about my own worries and I am at peace. Before I know it the time has passed, and I await a new day to be able to continue working. . .weeks go by and I don't even feel it.
>
> I am involved in the struggle. I understand what the people's project is. I feel part of this project, and have opted for this project. I am ready to offer my life for it. But sometimes I go into crisis because of my own internal struggle, because of the tremendous tasks and risks, and because I **WANT TO LIVE**. The situation we are living, with such acute repression, makes me feel like an ant, defenceless. I want to **LIVE**, and one never

knows at what moment one will fall in the hands of the security forces. One can be caught not only in an activity, but at any moment.

(Guatemala, June 1 and 2, 1981)

These are testimonies of conversion—the conversion of women who have moved from being served to serving others. These experiences of giving one's life to service, with hope and faith in the struggle, are some of the riches emerging from our poverty as Central American women, who face death in the backyard of the United States. These experiences can be summed up as taking the option to make the Pascal mystery of death and resurrection our own.

Women have become involved in a variety of ways and at various levels in the struggle for a new society. Women are involved in legal work, in social work, in prophetic roles, and in combat. In the area of law, there was Marianela Garcia Villas, murdered by the Salvadorean army while she carried out an investigation of violations to the right to live. She travelled all over the world speaking out against injustice and crime. And there is Yolanda de Aguilar, a labour lawyer, whose husband was killed in an "accident" after winning a case involving a strike. Her 16 year old daughter was raped by the Guatemalan police, and she herself was kidnapped by the army when she entered the country to re-affirm her identification with her people's struggle.

There are Christian women, especially nuns, who accompany persecuted Christian communities which have been sentenced to die. Women who could have chosen a life of comfort, secure in their own status and prestige, have chosen the path of Christ next to people who are being pursued by the army, who are in constant exodus, hiding in ravines and forests. These women give their people hope. They make themselves present in moments of anguish and pain, as did the women who accompanied Christ to the Calvary, and who announced His Resurrection. And there are prophets among our women. There are many poor women, peasants, who are raising their voices so that the world can know of our people's suffering and recognize us, their own brothers and sisters. These women are the Living Word, because their life is living testimony, a symbol of the pain and the agony and the hope of offering one's life. This life is an urgent cry of the Spirit which calls on us to reveal ourselves, to take a stand, to see ourselves as sons and daughters of

God, as brothers and sisters. The most well known among them is Rigoberta Menchu, an Indian woman whose brother was burned alive in the square of Chajul, Quiche in Guatemala. Her father was burned alive in the Spanish Embassy, which he and others had occupied peacefully to draw attention to repression in Quiche, and her mother was tortured to death in Uspantan, Quiche.

There are many other women like her whose words are like nails in the flesh, words of the wise, as the Scriptures say. Their names cannot be mentioned, from fear of repression.

Finally, there are many sensitive Christian women, of all ages, who love life, but have been forced to take up arms to survive and to struggle for the survival of their people. There is an example in the Scriptures which confuses those who have never confronted the brutality of repression carried out by governments in countries struggling for their liberation. The Old Testament Book of Judges (Ch.4), speaks of the time when King Jabin oppressed the people of Israel and forced them to submit through military force. It speaks of his 900 war chariots, which played the same role as U.S. military aid to El Salvador and Guatemala today. For twenty years the people of Israel suffered such oppression, as our people endure today. It was the prophet Deborah, a woman, who called on the Israelites to form an insurgent army. And it was another woman, Jael, who welcomed the captain of the oppressing army into her tent, and as he slept killed him. The Song of Deborah celebrates the victory.

In Guatemala, I know of a 17 year old Indian woman, the mother of a month old baby. As many Indian women she cared for her plants, crops, and herbs which gave her and her people sustenance; she respected her elders. I have seen her contemplating her child with tenderness and grief, an orphan whose father was murdered by the army. She was a combatant who knew what it was to take up arms to defend her life. When her time came, Oshe left her companions and walked for six days through the mountains to give birth to her child, a preserver of her race.

This woman is a symbol of what we must be. We must combat the project of death which looms over humanity, disguised as development, consumerism, anti-communism. We must defend the life of the Creation, because all of humanity is waiting in anguish for the day in which all men and women can really live as brothers and sisters, and administer the resources of the world for the common good.

Amada Pineda: A Woman of Nicaragua

Elsa Tamez

Although I do not know Amada Pineda personally, she is constantly on my mind. I think of her physical and psychological fortitude—her tenacity as a fighting woman; her capacity to resist the hardest blows a woman can receive. She is from Nicaragua. She was raped seventeen times; five of her nine children are dead; her husband was tortured; and she was insulted by relatives and friends for taking a path they considered unfit for a woman: to fight against the Somoza dictatorship.

Amada Pineda is not only an individual woman. In her the marks of many Central American women are present, and in many Central American women she is present. Amada is a living testimony of the experience of women who participate in the birth process of Latin America, bringing forth a new woman, a new man, a new society.[1]

The Testimony of Amada Pineda

Doña Amada is thirty-eight or thirty-nine years old. She is the director of AMNLAE, the Nicaraguan Women's Association. She is a peasant, poor like the majority, married for some twenty years. She has had nine children. One died at birth, another of pneumonia, another of measles. Still another infant died in torrential rain as she was fleeing Somoza's National Guardsmen. Another son died at seventeen, assassinated together with a companion of the same age.

[1] The written testimony of Amada Pineda is taken from *Todas Estamos Despiertas: Testimonios de la Mujer Nicaraguense*. Margaret Randall, ed. Mexico D.F.: Ed. Siglo XXI, 1980, pp. 120–137.

two children, and a woman. In spite of these hard blows for a mother, the power of Amada's resistance not only sustained, but strengthened her.

Amada was persecuted, accused of being a subversive and a communist. She was finally captured. She could have escaped to the mountains, but she did not want to leave her children alone and at the mercy of the Guardsmen. Her captors beat her in front of her little children.

In prison, Amada was raped seventeen times in three days. Her words of protest tell of the experience:

> When they came to rape me, after various times, I could not endure any more. I rebelled and said to the official: "Who do you think I am?" I said to them, "Did you seize me in the Red Light District, or am I a prostitute? I am a married woman. I have my children, and all were fathered by my husband. And even though it is true that we are now separated, that does not mean that now I am going to become a prostitute, just like that. So, do me a favour and tell the rest of your soldiers not to come in this room where all of us women are."

After Amada left prison, she went to a doctor because she wanted to make sure that she was not pregnant, since she did not want to have a child by her torturers.

Amada's husband was a union leader, and later on he too ran into the same fate of torture and prison. Amada related that there in prison the soldiers told him how all of them had raped her and that she had venereal diseases. Amada was very upset. She describes how it was when she met her husband again:

> When we were able to be together again, I was afraid, as they had said so much to him against me. I thought he was going to start bothering me. But he said, "You're really stupid. Why? This happens to all women in this struggle, to every wife of the men who fight. Look at the case of Doris Tijerino," he tells me, "and of other women. No," he tells me, "I don't understand why you feel ashamed." Because I felt pain from all that had happened to me, all of this gave me a trauma. I felt as if all this had left a bad smell that I couldn't get rid of. He helped me a lot.

For Amada, understanding and support also came from the peasants. She said:

> I think the peasants are the ones who most understand this type of problem for the wives. At least all the comrades I know were able to

comprehend the barbaric treatment their wives had received, and they stayed together and fought afterwards with more courage.

During the final insurrection, Amada left some of her children with her mother-in-law and others with relatives. She stayed in Managua, in the neighbourhood called Bello Horizonte. There she fought along with other women, using everything they could muster.

> In Bello Horizonte we fought with what was there. Everything that they threw at us, we gathered it up. The mortars, the bombs that the airplanes dropped. When they mined us, we looked for them, took them apart and threw them back. They would set up explosives and we would return them. Even a 500 pound bomb, we pulled it out with a lot of work, because it made a big hole in the soft ground. We succeeded in pulling it out, divided it in half, inserted explosives, and put one part of it on the bridge of Bello Horizonte, and the other half we sent to another spot. In that house we were mostly women, but we did what we could.

Amada participated fully in Nicaragua's revolution to change the unjust structures of oppression that produce poverty, unemployment, alienation, and repression. Her participation helped her to recognize women's right to equality as well. Her life, dedicated first to the fight for social change, and now to the reconstruction of Nicaragua, has taught her what it means to be fulfilled as a woman and as an active agent in working out the history of her own people.

In relation to her being a woman, she says the following:

> My father always said that, being a woman, why would I want to get involved in all this. Because for men at that time, the man was the one who could do everything. The man was the one who could fight, who could study. That is why they did not let us go on with our studies, because they said that someday we would get married and spend our time doing household chores, so why do we need to know anything else?

After this experience of fighting and suffering, which enkindled dedication, courage and love, Amada has a new vision. She says:

> Now all this has changed. Women have shown that we have the right to participate, perhaps even more than the men themselves. In the insurrection we demonstrated this: there were women who ran away from their parents, and went to fight. Very young women and girls. We were always shunted aside and marginated, but now more than ever before we do not want things to be that way any longer. We want to join the

struggle. Sometimes it is even necessary to struggle in opposition to our own husbands. Because there are times when a husband wants to have you stuck at home, with four walls around you, without going out, just taking care of the children, feeding them, washing and ironing, doing all the household chores.

This summer, Dona Amada decided to go to the place where they killed and buried her seventeen-year old son, to bring "at least a few bones, or whatever," and bury them in the cemetery.

Other Amada Pinedas

Women's solidarity has, in Amada Pineda, a living testimony of the experience of women who participate in the birth process of Latin America. The feminine and feminist body-spirit of Amada shows the marks of many other women who want to be protagonists of history. There is the mark of Mónica Baltodano, a Commander, who had her first child when she was hiding in the mountains. She nursed him for two months, gave him up to her mother, and after the triumph of the Revolution three years later, saw him again. There is the mark of Gladys Baez, another peasant woman, one of the first to participate in the Sandinista Front, a woman imprisoned more than twenty-five times, declared past recovery because of the electric shocks inflicted to her head. Today she is coordinator of a communal cooperative organized by her and the peasants. There is the mark of Dora Téllez who, at the age of twenty-one, participated in the taking of the National Palace in 1978. There is the mark of Nora Astorga, today vice-minister of Foreign Affairs, who took revenge in her bedroom on the torturer and rapist of hundreds of women.

In the body of Amada there are the marks of the women of Cua, who were savagely assassinated by the armed forces of Somoza. There is the mark of the Christian love of Sister Marta, and many women religious who helped in so many revolutionary tasks. In the body of Amada is also the mark of each mother who lived, and still lives, with the anguish of the absence of her child, waiting to find out whether her son or daughter is alive or dead. There is the mark of the popular battalions, guarding the borders to defend what has been gained.

And also in the body of Amada are the marks of Marianela Garcia Villas, a Salvadorean woman, president of the Human Rights

Commission, assassinated by the Salvadorean armed forces; the marks of the women religious of Maryknoll and other Salvadorean women religious assassinated for defending human rights; the marks of many Salvadorean women, mothers, grandmothers, daughters, who suffer in the nightmare of the war. In the body of the peasant, Amada, are also the signs of the Guatemalan indigenous women who are raped, tortured, missing, imprisoned and killed—in Jilotepeque, San Metabaj, San Martin Comachac, and el Quiché. And there, in the body-spirit of Amada Pineda, is the poetic mark of our sister who always is in solidarity, Julia Esquivel. In the eyes of Amada are Julia's tears that refuse to dry up until her people take hold of the reins of history.

Women's solidarity has in the body of Amada a living testimony of the experience of women who participate in the birth process of Latin America, bringing forth a new woman, a new man, a new society.

Women, Struggle and Faith

Life and death—this is the situation of Central America. There is death because, except in Costa Rica, one child in ten dies from malnourishment before completing his or her first birthday; because the unemployment and underemployment runs at more than 50 per cent of the economically active population; because inflation is accelerating and basic food staples become unattainable for the poor, who are the majority; because illiteracy climbs in some regions to 50 per cent or 75 per cent; because there are so few health centres; because when the people raise their voice in protest, they are imprisoned, tortured, or assassinated; and because external aggression is a constant menace.

But, at the same time, there is also life—because a people has now taken hold of the reins of history and endeavours to create a better life for the majority; because many people, both women and men, have become conscious of the situation of death and have opted to participate in the search for life. From every drop of shed blood come many seeds of life, full of hope. For these reasons, I say that there is life in confrontation with death.

Central and Latin American women cannot embark on a struggle for their rights if they do not first consider the lives of the majority of their sisters. History has taught us that, in many cases, women have become conscious of belonging to an oppressed and marginated sector of humanity only when they begin to participate in the struggle to improve the lives of the majority, who are poor. Because of this, we in Latin America begin with women who are doubly oppressed by class and sex. We believe that we must work for equality starting with women who are poor, since working form this perspective tends simultaneously to change economically oppressive structures as well as male chauvinistic structures.

Our struggle of death and life takes place in a religious atmosphere, and so we confront the gods in this struggle. There are gods of death and the worshippers of death, who commit genocidal atrocities, more repulsive than a man or a woman can bear, the ultimate symbol of such gods of death being a knife buried in the womb of a pregnant woman by a member of the armed forces, killing both her and her child.[2] At times such an atrocity is even carried out in the name of Christ. It would seem that this fulfils what Christ told his disciples before his death of the appearance of anti-Christs. (Jn. 16.2)

The great majority of Christians, however, worship the God of Life, and in Him look for freedom and justice. In Latin America a great many Catholic and Protestant martyrs have given their lives for a new life. Priests, pastors and believers have discovered the hidden face of the crucified Jesus in the faces of the unemployed, in the faces of the hungry and those suffering from disease, in the death of the innocent, in the suffering of the tortured, in the eyes of the mother whose child is missing, in the burden of the prisoner, in the weathered faces of the indigenous person, in the tired face of the Black person and the woman worker. They have also discovered the face of the resurrected Jesus in the hands of the fighter; in the hands of the mason who builds for all; in the hands of the peasant who sows the field; in the minds of those planning a new life; in the legs of those who walk from one end of the globe to the other, proclaiming, like prophets, the massacres committed against God's people. They have discovered His face in the smiles of children; in the eyes of those in love; and on the lips of those who sing to the God of Life in the churches. They have seen His face in the emerging process of liberation. Here in the people they have discovered

[2] This is a frequent occurrence in El Salvador and Guatemala, as it was during the time of Somoza in Nicaragua. Testimonies of this type are found in *Boletin Internacional de la Comision de Derechos Humanos de Guatemala*, No. 2, pp. 21–34.

Jesus, endeavouring to bring forth a new humanity. In all of this, they are searching for a new mode of perceiving God, a new mode of being a church, a new mode of doing theology, and a new mode of being a man or being a woman.

History challenges us, at times with cruelty, to experience faith anew under these circumstances. It calls us to seek new roads, because the traditions which have been practiced for centuries ultimately do not lead forward today. As Christians, we believe that Christ speaks in everyday life, but how do we decipher his Word? If we listen, then little by little, the devotions, the prayers and the songs of the people of God who are discontented with the land of death, become dense, pregnant with content.

Many times in these songs of life and hope, a woman envisions what the life of the community should really be. And then she looks at her own life, and the way others relate to her. She sees the church, its structures and its hierarchies, and understands that her role there as a woman is not what it really should be. She sees the necessity of realizing her full potential, of discovering a new mode of being a woman, in harmony with the Latin American process of liberation.

In Latin America, after the opening of Vatican II, and from the time of the Medellin Conference (1968), what we call Ecclesial Base Communities or Popular Christian Communities started to form. These consist of groups formed around parishes, meeting to discuss the problems of the neighbourhood or of the country, to reinterpret the Bible in the light of today's reality, to sing and to celebrate. They worship in very creative ways, without rigid structures. On the Protestant side, small local churches have similar characteristics.

In these communities, women find ample space for participation. It is a space not only larger, but more significant, than the church traditionally assigns them. In these communities many women not only participate actively, but acquire real leadership roles. These communities, which are increasing in all of Latin America, are not another church opposed to the traditional church. On the contrary, they appear within the same church, showing a new mode of being a church, renovating and transforming, converting the church of Christ into a more human church, more evangelical, more on the side of the poor.

In Nicaragua, the Ecclesial Base Communities played and still play a very important role in the revolution. The same is true in El

Salvador and in Guatemala. This is really the persecuted church, because it endeavours to express and experience the Christian faith from the context of life versus the context of death. And this church has generated Christian martyrs for the cause of a new life.

Within this ecclesial experience of liberation, a new theological discourse is simmering. It is a Latin American theology of liberation, accompanying the journey of common people, through all of the risks and joys of the road, toward a new life. I am not going to discuss this theology, but I would like to emphasise that Christology is fundamental: Jesus Christ is seen as God incarnate, in solidarity with the poor, the one who brings forth full and abundant life.

This understanding of Christ in solidarity with the poor has also led women to see Christ in solidarity with women. There are many reflections that have come forth concerning the special pact Jesus has with women, as found in the Gospels. Jesus' life exemplifies a new attitude toward woman: a woman is recognized and respected as a person in herself; she is dignified; and she participates in society and in history as a transforming agent of action.

Conclusion

I have spoken of the Central American woman, struggling for structural changes, struggling at all levels, not only in the battlefield. I have taken the testimony of Doña Amada Pineda as an example of the many women whose testimonies inform us of the necessity of looking for a new mode of being a woman in our convulsed Latin America. I have looked to the testimony of such a woman because of the massive and significant participation of women in the Central American struggle, which in itself is an innovating fact of our history.

I have spoken of women's solidarity, because women of all ages have struggled and suffered together—giving birth to their babies while in hiding in the mountains; suffering the torture or death of their children; seeing their children die of hunger or sickness; being the objects of rape in prison; being touched and humiliated by the murderous hands of the armed forces.

I have spoken from the perspective of poor women, who are the majority. Without change in the structures of economic injustice, women cannot bring about a new mode of being. Thus, we in Latin America prefer to speak about a double struggle of women and the poor—part of the global process of liberation. In most cases women have become conscious of their oppression as women, beginning with struggles for housing, wages or transportation.

Finally, I have spoken of the liberation that is taking place in the churches, with the growth of the Ecclesial Base Communities. In this new mode of being a church, women have found the possibility of a new mode of being for women. They have found new inspiration, when they read and interpret the Bible from the perspective of the poor, from the perspective of liberation.

I have spoken about what I daily see, hear and feel in Central America. And I say, Let us be in solidarity, as women on the margins, with the many Doña Amada Pinedas of my people. They are a living testimony to the birth process of Latin America, which struggles to bring forth a new woman, a new man, a new society. I do not know Amada Pineda personally, but some day, when I meet her, I will tell her how much she has taught us with her life, and I will give her a hug and a kiss in the name of all women of good will.[3]

[3] In a letter dated December 28, 1984, Elsa wrote: "I met Amada Pineda this year in Nicaragua, and I told her about my case-study presentation of her. As I said, I gave her a kiss and a hug. We were in a base community, and I did this publicly.

Priorities for Women in South Africa

Brigalia Bam

The peoples of contemporary South Africa are indeed like all other nations. We are peoples of diverse origins, languages, social systems and technologies. But such diversities and cultural divisions do not necessarily divide people as they have done in South Africa. In Switzerland or the United States, for example, there are people of different origins, but they are able to live and work together. On the contrary, South Africa is rigidly stratified. It is the purpose of the government to define and enforce this stratification. The stratification and division is caused, fundamentally, by exploitation and oppression. My comments here will be based on the Black community; I will not try to speak generally about all the women of South Africa, although some of the ways in which women are oppressed will apply even to the privileged white women of South Africa.

The Theology/Ideology of Apartheid

Religions in South Africa, like Judaism, Islam and traditional religions, of which most people are a part, are a very strong political influence, but the official theology of the Dutch Reformed Church, which has been essentially a state church since the beginning of this century, has deeply influenced all the societal structures in South Africa. The dominant feature of this official theology of South Africa is its famous national ideology of apartheid. Apartheid is not just racism, for there is racism everywhere in the world and there are victims of racist societies everywhere. But South Africa is unique because this "racial segregation" or "political separate development," as they like to call it, is really a policy of racial supremacy. And it is interesting to note that this term, apartheid, was invented by an Afrikaner theologian, inspired by the early days of Nazism in Germany. The policy of apartheid started in the 1940s. This is an important fact of history, and unless we can understand it, we will never be able to understand South Africa today. This system in South Africa is really a religio-political system, and there lies the whole justification of apartheid.

Although South Africa has a population today which is over 94 per cent Christian, and this is something about which South Africa boasts, it is important to know that the Christian population consists of two conflicting systems, with very different values, representing very different forces. On the one hand, there are the forces of the representatives of the oppressors who believe they are justified in trampling the fundamental rights of the people of South Africa, in attempting to suppress them and in keeping them under perpetual servitude. These groups are represented by the ruling Nationalist Party which has been in power for 35 years, since 1948.

The other force is represented by the masses, the Black people who are the majority, who are struggling to survive under the yoke of white oppression. The Blacks in South Africa are in the majority, they comprise over 75 per cent of the total population. Of this 75 per cent women are in the majority. The whites constitute 17 per cent. The so-called coloureds, the people of mixed parentage, are six per cent and the Asians, two per cent. I go through these figures because there is now a bill which has allowed Parliament to give new power to these other racial groups. Thus, the policy of continuing to stratify all the racial groups continues and gathers momentum. The government is now trying to win over the support of the Asians and the people of mixed race, while still ignoring the rights of the majority Blacks.

The Black women of South Africa are the most exploited group in the whole set-up of the apartheid system. They are devalued both as Blacks, and, within their religious traditions, as women. Liberation includes liberation from some oppressive norms and values which stem from traditional African religions as well as from Christianity. Many of the undesirable traditional remnants of male-female relations have survived precisely because Christianity has, in some ways, reinforced them. For example, in my own tradition of the Xhosa people, women could not be "ordained" to participate in ceremonies which bring the ancestors back to earth until after menopause, when they attained a certain amount of purity. But then, of course, in the Anglican tradition women could not be ordained at all, before or after menopause!

Ours is a patriarchal society. Women face the experience of discrimination in job opportunities and at work, and discrimination in legal rights such as the right to inherit land. Sometimes people tend to be very generous toward African societies in their treatment of women, but not all African societies have had the privilege of having women as dominant groups. In South Africa, in addition, women have to fight the system of apartheid. The Black women, like all Blacks, have no right to vote. I do not know how to vote, because according to the government anyone of our colour is not intelligent enough to vote. But young people of eighteen years old, if they are white, can vote, because they are of a superior race. What this means is that the largest group in all of South Africa—Black women—have no way of participating in any political process or any decision making process. They are not permitted to make fundamental decisions about their own lives.

Blacks in South Africa have to carry passes. They are not just identity cards: all the information about a Black person is written in this book. If you are employed, it is written down who has employed you. If you leave employment, then the employer must sign it. Through passes, the movements of Blacks are controlled. And you must, as a Black, carry your passbook no matter where you go, because the police have a right by law to stop Black people and arrest them if they are not carrying the pass. That is why in South Africa the highest number of arrests are of people who are arrested because they are not carrying their passes. It took me a long time, after I had arrived in Switzerland, to liberate myself from my pass. I still carried it; I did not trust the Swiss police. At last, I began to be liberated from this vestigial oppression by my passbook.

And then there are all the laws that go with the apartheid system, laws passed by votes to make repression "legal". The apartheid system has had so many laws that have been repressive. Sometimes if one is altered, you hear the argument that things are improving in South Africa, and if we continue to invest and exert influence, this system of apartheid will ease itself out. The country will become wealthy, and the system will correct itself. This is an illusion. If people say this when you are working to support us in our struggle, do not believe them. They simply want to make their profits.

Women, Religion and Social Change in South Africa

It is probably religion, which dominates the lives of the Blacks in South Africa, that has made women increasingly more aware of their situation as Blacks and as women. In our society women are still considered the custodians of public and private morality. They are, as in other societies, the main agents of socialization and the carriers of culture from one generation to the next. And, of course, women are the greatest supporters of all our religious institutions, especially the church.

For those who have had a chance to visit the churches of South Africa, the very large and very faithful Black women's organizations will doubtless have been impressive. The question is—how can we use these organizations and women's religious convictions for change? This is a very important question, for church women's organizations are among the largest in South Africa.

The discontent of women has always been present in South Africa. We have inherited a great tradition of activism from women over the last one hundred years, and a lot of women's organizations and movements have appeared and grown. As early as 1906, women were great political activists, although there is almost never a record of their activities. There were women already in the 1920s who were involved in the development of the trade unions, and in the 1950s, in the campaign against apartheid, women were at the forefront of the movement against carrying passes. Again today, the women of South Africa, like women everywhere, are asking questions about themselves. "Who are we, and what does it mean in South Africa to be a Christian, to be a woman, and to be Black?" For a long time in the system and organization of the churches, women were required to be passive and humble, and had to take the inferior role. Those things went unchallenged. But the effect of the humiliation and dehumanization of the whole society under apartheid has forced more and more of us to stand up and ask these questions. It is not only a few articulate women who speak out: ordinary women in rural areas ask these questions and demand an answer to injustice. In the face of an imposed ideology—that African women are inferior because of their colour *and* because of their gender—the Black women of South Africa are experiencing an important liberation of the spirit.

We should remember that we have women *now* who are paying a price, a heavy price. Several women in South Africa are now under a ban which means, in some cases, that you cannot leave your house, you cannot go to an educational institution, you cannot write for publication. And under this ban we have women like Winnie Mandela, who is well known internationally, Priscilla Ajana, Deborah Machoba, Shiela Weinberg, Albertina Sisulu and many others some of whom are serving sentences. These are women who have taken a strong political stand, and it is important to understand the things they stand for and to continue to support them.

Among women's organizations, church women continue to grow strong. But the Black Women's Federation, which was a very important body, unfortunately was banned in 1977 along with other organizations, because the government in South Africa will not allow the Africans to organize themselves. Among white women there are organizations working within the country, like the Black Sash.

There is now a new active group in South Africa: the trade unions. They are the real force that is on the cutting edge in the country, and there are five women leaders of trade unions. In 1981, when the government was harrassing all the trade union leaders, seven women were arrested along with the men, women who were, in their own right, leaders and organizers of trade unions. This is an important move. Now, for the first time, we have also been able to organize women domestic workers, and there are over 800,000 such women in South Africa. They have no proper working hours, no security, no minimum wage, but in the past few years they have been able to organize themselves. In addition, out of the 214,000 women who are employed in the industrial sector, there are over 70,000 Black women who are beginning to organize themselves. They recognize their power: that they can organize within the working plant. It is through these trade unions that political organization and political education is going on.

It is perfectly clear that the Blacks in South Africa will bring about change, and women will be a part of that change. One of the most difficult things for us, at this point, is to have a vision of the kind of society we want. At present we are concerned about the system of apartheid: to destroy the system. But how do we create a society in which women and men and young people have justice, and recognition, and dignity? And how do we in South Africa—as women, and as Black people—liberate ourselves from our own poverty, and also liberate the whites from their wealth? Because even the elite are trapped.

International Issues and Priorities

There is first the question of the fundamental commitments of Christianity. The National Party in South Africa claims that apartheid is necessary to defend western Christian civilization. The basis of a great deal of Christian opposition is the rejection of this claim. I think, however, that we should examine whether there may not be some truth in this claim. Apartheid is the development of certain western assumptions concerning human identity, concerning authority, concerning freedom, wealth, success, and the Christian tradition has in my opinion, been captured, coopted and distorted to support these assumptions.

The second matter I would like to look at is the question of "How?" How can we bring about change in South Africa? I will not use the word "peaceful"—"peaceful change". I do not see *how* we can bring about peaceful change in such a violent and repressive society. This is a problem. The change cannot come about through the little groups that we organize as women—doing welfare, doing service, and so on. It has to come by changing the existing unjust political and economic structures. These economic structures cannot be changed in South Africa unless the western world helps us to change them. While the agenda for change is going to come from us, from within the country, it is only through solidarity on the question of economic structures that we can bring it about.

The third important question which is posed all the time to women is "How do we liberate the Gospel together?" The issue is how to liberate religion from the limited realm assigned to the churches. This has launched a debate on the mixing of religion and politics. Before I had a chance to work abroad, I thought that this was the obsession of the South African government, which wanted to maintain its own system by saying that religion and politics must be absolutely separate. But I found that even in Switzerland today, this debate is absolutely alive. When there was a discussion on the Swiss banks not giving loans to South Africa, again the catch-phrase was that we must not mix politics, economics and religion.

The women in South Africa are subjected to this all the time when, as Christians and as women, they begin to organize not only around welfare issues, but political issues as well. The institution of the church is not always supportive, and people begin to make the distinction between what properly is "religion" and what is not. The churches are happy as long as we collect money, as long as we take care of Sunday schools, as long as we run soup kitchens. But the minute a political action is taken by women there are very few people who will encourage them. This also was the experience of church women in West Germany who have been on a successful boycott of South African fruits for the past four years. We must all ask how to free ourselves from oppression within our own institutions. And we must have an integrated understanding of religion. The division of life in South Africa into "religion" and "politics" and "economics" is not possible, because our very existence integrates these commitments, and the domination will not end unless we can, as women, enter into the active political arena. There is a heavy price to pay, but I hope women will not give up the struggle.

I see today two priorities for us women on a universal level. The first is the priority of Peace and Justice. We all have our own concerns when we talk about peace. When I, as a South African, talk about peace I am concerned with the nuclear capabilities of South Africa, I am concerned about the hostility of the government to the frontline states, to the bombings that go on in Angola. My friends in Switzerland and in Germany are concerned about the nuclear arms race. The women in the villages of South Africa are talking about poverty. So when we speak of Peace, we must see it in its broadest form as linked with Justice. This is our priority.

The second priority is Liberation. How do we liberate humanity—women and men? As we begin to discover those who oppress us, we have the responsibility to liberate them as well. As women get positions of power, how do we use our power? And with liberation as our concern for humanization, how do we continue to help to humanize our societies as women?

Assault on the Family in South Africa

Bernadette Mosala

The family is not only the nucleus of society but, more importantly, the powerhouse of society. Any nucleus that is not alive cannot be referred to as a nucleus. In our traditional, primitive society the importance and power of the family was a given, hence family life was very sacred. This, on another plane, may also explain the origins of our extended family concept which was a commitment religiously adhered to by every member of the family. Anybody with whom you had a blood tie was truly part of you, and this was communicated to the young through the life style of the family.

The family is a powerhouse for social change because in any given family, under normal circumstances, will be found the ingredients and agents for social change, e.g. teachers, ministers, politicians, engineers, etc. Society needs the participation and cooperation of these people for its sustenance and upliftment and, of course, for change. Therefore families themselves, each with a certain measure of commitment, would be well poised to work for and bring about change in society.

In any given family, in addition to various agents of change, there are the usual generational layers of society—the adults, the youth, the children, the women and the men. Such a situation also provides an ideal vehicle for social change, as it moves from generation to generation. Change moves back and forth between the generations in a two-way street fashion, thus giving the family the dynamism no other institution can have without a heavy network of structures that sometimes encumber society rather than facilitate social change. These layers within the family are meant to ensure continuity from generation to generation.

We are talking about the family as a powerhouse, with a dynamism that is both self-generated and self-sustaining under normal conditions.

But if we have no families worth the name, as is beginning to be the case in South Africa, then how do we ever begin to speak of the church or religion and social change? For me the family *is* the domestic church. If we speak of a weak church we are invariably speaking of weak families, and, similarly, if we speak of a rotten society we shall be saying something about family life. So I see the family as that which underpins both religion and society.

In my country, which claims to be Christian, family life among Blacks is perpetually under assault by the government. In 1969, a government official, speaking of the migrant labour force, said, "This African labour force must not be burdened with superfluous appendages such as wives, children and dependants who could not provide service." Family was a "superfluous appendage".

The Crossroads programme, which has received a certain amount of international publicity, was a protest movement about family life. Women in Transkei, the largest of the so-called "homelands," wanted to live with their husbands, who were working in Capetown. Eighty-five per cent of the Black labour force in Capetown is migrant, that is 56,000 men who are required to live in single sex hostels. Only 12,000 Black workers in Capetown have the right to live there with their families. These women, whose husbands were classed as migrant workers, left their homes in Transkei to go to a stretch of sandy, barren land with but a few bushes in Capetown, where they put up shacks of cardboard, rusted corrugated iron, and bits of plastic. That was Crossroads. They were rural women, some of whom had come to an urban area for the first time. They were harassed, their shacks destroyed. Some were put in jail, not once, but several times. Their offence? Living with their legal husbands "illegally". But they have been tenacious in maintaining Crossroads, which has become a symbol of the brutality of the migrant labour system.

More people are saying, along with these women, "We want to live as families." But somebody with muscle and power is still saying, "No." When a man lives in a single sex hostel for 49 of 52 weeks in a year, with his wife and children somewhere in some godforsaken rural area, where is family? Is it in the hostel? Or in the rural areas?

This situation which has undermined family is brought about by the obnoxious migrant labour system that boosts the economy of South Africa and produces untold dividends for the foreign investor to live comfortably with his family elsewhere, pretending he is not aware of all or part of all these atrocities, or at best salving his conscience by believing that pulling out would hurt the Blacks more than the whites. Economics tends to be something impersonal and remote, but one does not have to be exceptionally intelligent to know that the migrant labour system destroys family life. One overwhelming example of the destruction of family life is the practice of what is euphemistically called "resettlement". It is really being uprooted, sometimes from the place one's family has lived in for generations, and being forced to live in a Black "homeland" elsewhere. You cannot imagine what it does to family life, to children and women in particular, because forced resettlement usually happens while men are in the cities. And in the "settlements" the support systems of family life, such as schools, health facilities and sanitation are totally lacking. Even basic necessities, such as water, may be miles away. Life is lived in perpetual day to day anxiety about when, and if, the next support cheque will come from the husband working in the city.

I have not the space here to analyze the split personalities that resettlement produces in the family. These men and women find they now belong to two worlds and they cannot fully identify with either. The men are strangers to their wives, children and homes. In the three weeks they visit home each year they get a visitor's welcome and treatment. Everybody endeavours to show his/her best behaviour until the father goes back, without having grappled with those issues of his home that he alone should address. Eventually, this becomes a way of life. It is like travelling in neutral gear, without engaging. This absence of an authentic interaction within the family is bound to have a cumulative effect on it, and because the migrant community is so massive at present, this very difficult pattern of family life hits a good portion of the Black society. Simply put, there are no models of family life available for a growing child. There are no roles or models of what it is to be mother, father, wife or husband.

In the urban area, on the other hand, the migrant cannot participate because he does not belong. He is viewed with suspicion and contempt by urbanites and he, in turn, views them with suspicion and contempt, but for different reasons. He experiences a kind of transferred aggression, as it were. But the question is, where exactly does he place his commitment in such a situation? It is little wonder that desertion and broken marriages are common.

Another important social issue that causes a great deal of concern to the church is the number of people who must marry simply for legal convenience. Very often a widow finds she has to marry in order to keep the house she has been living in—even before she has emotionally come to terms with her widowhood. Will there be any form of family life in a case such as this? Has a "family" such as this any chance of being the powerhouse I have referred to earlier?

In 1977, a survey we did in the Home and Family Life Division of the South Africa Council of Churches showed that illegitimacy was then in the fourth generation in Soweto. I don't know what the position is today, but we are already talking of three generations that have no access to free education, social welfare programmes, or to agencies helping single mothers and their children. They have none of these benefits, and do not know what family life is—they are people who have no pass books, no education, no skills, no job, no home, and no rights anywhere, urban or rural. They have no idea of what it is to be a member of a family. They will inevitably grow up to form non-family relationships and beget children, and so the cycle begins all over again.

In such a situation, where is the dynamic powerhouse of the family? What social change can such a "family" bring about—a change from what to what? Where is the domestic church I spoke of? The base line is wrong; and the rest is programmed, as it were, to go wrong. Social life is the dynamism of living, I think. Under normal circumstances, it is inevitable and natural. But because of the distortion of human relations and social arrangements, this dynamism is often deliberately frustrated, and we are forced to focus on "social change" as though it were something apart, something outside the process of dynamic living.

Religion in whatever form is central to human living. Men and women need to hold on to something, to be rooted in something. That religion may be expressed overtly or tacitly, and their religious belief may or may not be formalised in a coherent manner. Therefore, religion is the thread that runs through family life, both as a base and source of stability, and as a force for change. In this manner religion, with a belief in a supreme Creator, holds together and in tandem both family life and social change, crucial aspects of human living.

May God's Peace, Mercy and Blessings Be Unto You

Jean Zaru

In the search for peace in the Middle East, some people begin with the Camp David agreements, others with a new status for Jerusalem. Still others see peace primarily in the withdrawal by Israel, in whole or in part, from lands occupied by it in 1967. Many others start by speaking of the withdrawal of Israel from Lebanon. We who are Palestinians begin with the loss of our lands and our rights. There are about four million Palestinians, half of them uprooted and forcibly thrown out more than once, and the other half subjected and oppressed and strangers in their own land.

Chaim Weizman, later to become the first president of Israel, once remarked, long before the establishment of the Jewish state, that the world would judge Zionism by the way the Arabs of Palestine were treated. It was a wise utterance, but half a century was to pass before the world gained a clear picture of the relationship between Jews and Arabs in Israeli occupied Palestine. The increased awareness of the injustice suffered by us, and the results of that injustice in terms of discrimination and spiritual and material hardship, has been one important factor in bringing about a reappraisal of international attitudes towards the Arab-Israeli conflict.

There are several reasons why all of us, from whatever country we come, should be concerned with this conflict and work towards peace in the Middle East.

1. The Arab-Israeli conflict is potentially an explosive situation which could be a threat to world peace. It now affects the lives of millions of people in the Middle East. If it widens, it could affect the lives of tens of millions of people elsewhere.

2. Several governments support Israel militarily, politically and

financially. Each individual has the right, if not the duty, to know the facts in order to judge whether the support which his or her government is extending to Israel is given for a legitimate cause, and whether this support will, in the long run, benefit either the citizens of Israel or the cause of peace.

3. The Palestine Question has been on the agenda of the United Nations since 1947. Many resolutions have been adopted and nothing has been implemented. Therefore every individual has a responsibility directly or indirectly for the action or inaction of his or her government.

4. The present-day struggle for human rights all over the world, for us and for others, is a struggle in which all people must engage if we are to be faithful to the demands of our religious values.

5. In Judaism, Christianity and Islam, the concept of the divine nature existing in harmonious relationship with human nature and the natural order has been a dominant one. The teachings of these religious traditions helped underpin the belief that human beings have rights. Created in the image of God, our value comes from this likeness. God's nature is loving, free and just. God's purpose is to liberate human life from inhuman conditions, which exist because humans of free will have chosen behaviour that disrupts the intended harmony of peace, justice and freedom for all.

As a Palestinian Quaker woman, a native of the Holy Land, I have been confronted all my life with structures of injustice. As a Palestinian, I have lived under military occupation since 1967. As an Arab woman in a male culture, I have no equality with my brothers. And as a pacifist in an area of military conflict, I am often misinterpreted as being passive or submissive or accepting of injustice.

The structures of injustice—political, cultural, economic and social—have been at work in a destructive way throughout our community and have caused much spiritual as well as physical suffering for many, including myself. I have often thought about this: If there is that image of God in every person, why is there so much evil and darkness in the world? Why is it so hard for us to see that image of God in others?

My inward struggle was reflected in my outward action. I became increasingly sensitive to and aware of the suffering, which reflects the evils which plague the human race. But my struggle also opened me to God's redeeming love and activity.

Involvement in any action takes an effort, and there is always a price to pay. The question is, am I ready to pay the price, to share the suffering of others? Suffering for me is bearable, if it is for the cause of liberation, if it helps us to find a new community with each other and with God. I do realize that those who operate the structures of oppression are dependent upon the people they oppress, and are equally in need of liberation and God's grace. Yet, it seems to me that too often the will and strength to end the oppression comes from those who bear the oppression in their own lives, and very rarely from privileged and powerful persons and nations.

But where do we begin? If the Children of God wherever they are, are created in the image of God, then they are our brothers and sisters! What do we do to preserve the dignity of their lives? What do we say to the arms race and nuclear weapons? What do we do when in the name of "national security" scarce resources are used to buy weapons instead of combatting poverty and hunger? Can arms bring security, or keep peace? What do we say when these arms sales, promoted by industrialized nations, are often used for internal repression, violation of human rights and wars within and between countries? What do we do when our style of life, or our silence, is the cause of the presence of war-without-arms where the victims are millions of people who are dying from hunger and poverty?

What about social justice? Can there be peace between the starving and the affluent? Between the oppressor and the oppressed, occupier and occupied? Are we concerned when the Bible is abused in a pagan way to worship all kinds of false gods—money, material wealth, race, and other idols? What do we do when individualistic interests are often justified by quoting Biblical passages out of their historical context?

I believe that all of us, in our particular countries, are called to conversion: to be converted to the struggle of women and men everywhere, who have no way to escape the unending fatigue of their labour and the daily denial of their human rights and human worth. We must let our hearts be moved by the anguish and suffering of our sisters and brothers throughout the world. But how can we bear the pain, and where do we look for hope? What really can we do to solve our present political chaos and the crisis in the world, and to stop wars of all kinds?

First of all, let us take a look into ourselves, for the outward situation is also an expression of the inward state. It requires great self-denial and resignation of ourselves to God to be committed to peace and to non-violent action to bring about change. Such non-violence may have no immediate positive effect; it may even lead to seeming defeat. Whether successful or not, it may well require suffering. But if we believe in non-violence as the true way of peace, we must make it a principle not only of individual, but of national and universal, conduct. And we should try to do so without any feeling of moral superiority, for we know how soon we may stumble when we are put to the test. We may talk about peace, but if we are not transformed inwardly, if we still want position and power, if we are motivated by greed, if we are nationalistic, if we are bound by beliefs and dogmas for which we are willing to destroy others, we still cannot have peace in the world.

Living under military occupation has made me go through deep self-searching, and I have been confronted with three loyalties. The first loyalty is to Christ, who calls us to love our enemy. The second loyalty is to our fellow-men or women in need or trouble, to aid them in whatever way we can. The third loyalty is to our country, to love its people and its way of life. This loyalty prevents us from being willing to aid our invader. In our situation, no one can set the rules for us to follow, but what we can do is to testify that, in our experience, the spirit of God leads us into the truth and gives us the needed guidance in every situation.

We have gone through circumstances of great privation, anxiety and suffering. All these seemed at times to weaken our sense of dependence on God. But when I know that wherever I am, whether in affluence or in poverty, whether I have personal liberty or not, God has a service for me to render, I feel a sense of both hope and joy.

I call myself a Quaker or Friend, and Friends throughout history maintained a testimony for peace. War, we say, is contrary to the mind of Christ, and it is laid upon us to live by virtue of that life and power that wins through love and not war. This is not an easy testimony for it has three aspects.

1. To refuse to take part in acts of war ourselves.
2. To strive to remove the causes of war.
3. To use the way of love open to us to promote peace and heal wounds.

But how can I interpret this pacifism to my children and my students, when we are all victims of violence? How can I have peace within when I worry so much about life in general and the lives of my family members? How can I have peace within when others label my people as terrorists and justify our oppression by quoting the Bible?

When I have peace within, it is not because I approve of the violence around me, and it is not because I sit in silence and accept the many injustices around me. It is only through inner peace, however, that I am liberated to help my people. It is when I have the strength to endure, and the strength to attempt to love all women and men that I really feel that peace.

I see things differently now, having lived these years with the reality of "occupier" and "occupied". I know the oppressor is not freer than the oppressed. Both live in fear and do not have peace. No government, no army, no country, no leader is going to give us peace. What will bring us peace is inward transformation that will lead to outward action. Peace will come when we are peaceful, when we are at peace with our neighbours. And such peace means not the absence of action, but the absence of hatred. Peace is not only the absence of war or force. There is no peace when I treat others as nothing. When I think evil or hateful thoughts, when I lie or offend others, I violate their basic human dignity. I am being violent.

It is not easy for us to think of the sacredness and dignity of all life when our own dignity as people, as Palestinians, is not recognized. But perhaps through the hurt, the pain, the wounds, we may realize our real power and become agents of change for the better, rather than agents of change to transfer power from one group to the other. It might be a dream but it is my human right to dream and to work towards the reality of that dream.

As our shrinking world makes us all near-neighbours, we should be aware of two facts about our nature as peoples of this world. One is that we are very different from one another—in colour, in life-styles, in cultures and beliefs. The other is that we are exceedingly alike. There is a tremendous range of common needs and desires, fears and hopes, that bind us together in our humanness, and the well-being of each is crucially related to the well-being of others.

Through the ages people have engaged in a universal search for ultimate meaning in life, but they have turned this search into a struggle, into wars unto death to gain dominance for one particular ideology, religion, or nation. Our age of unparalleled advancement in education, science and technology has also been an age of enormous violence. Meanwhile, the need for an imaginative understanding, simple trust and creative cooperation has never been more urgent. Maybe the time has come when we should unite in certain common affirmations of life.

1. A pledge of honour and respect for every race, culture, religion and individual, without exclusiveness.

2. The recognition of the claim of every individual upon the resources of the earth for the necessities of human survival, and the moral obligation of the more fortunate to share with the less fortunate.

3. The right and responsibility of every individual to use his or her talents, energies and resources for the benefit of the community.

4. A commitment to the search for universal values, however differently expressed, in order to enable the individual and the community to overcome greed, power and self-seeking.

5. The affirmation of the "presence" of a spirit of hope and compassion available to all, by which our lives may be more whole, more creative, more harmonious, as we draw directly upon that power around us, and within us, and within all life.

We cannot live a single day without saying "yes" or "no" for death or for life, for war or for peace, but the choice is ours. There is no compromise in this matter. To postpone or evade the decision is still to decide. To hide the matter is to decide. To compromise is to decide. There is no escape from the decision, and this is our challenge.

A Jewish Perspective from Israel

Shulamith Koenig

For many years I was deeply convinced that I was one of the lucky few in this century to live and experience humanist ideology and to participate in the creation of a land based on such humanism. I am an Israeli woman, born in Jerusalem in 1930, the daughter of Polish immigrants who came to Israel in 1919. They came to fulfil the call of a Jewish humanist tradition, deeply believing that they would create a place on earth in which human dignity would be the fundamental political guideline, and where they as Jews would never be denied such dignity again.

I will always remember how easy it was for my generation. The experience of Israel was indeed a spiritual experience. We were not dealing only with "real politique": to gather the exiles, or to create a homeland for the Jews, or to have a government with our own taxes and administration. All these were a mere necessity for us, and a small part of a wider vision: to renew our lives with dignity which results in spiritual elevation, to harness a force which we were now free to express, to create a people-oriented society, all of which was taught and repeated to us in one important sentence: "You shall love your neighbour as you love yourself." We were taught that the heart of the Jewish tradition is this: that Judaism is not a religion or a dogma, but a way of life, "*Dat Chayim.*" We expressed our spirituality in dance, in song, in marching through the land, in making up new Hebrew words, in planting trees, in celebrating our traditional holidays as holidays of freedom, where human dignity had succeeded in overcoming violence and destruction.

The phoenix that rose from the ashes collected its historic memory to assert that the essence of Jewish spirituality is social responsibility. We were speaking the language of the prophets; we were their children, and in this deep sense, the children of God.

But the words were stolen from our lips and our mouths dried painfully. We were afraid to use words that could be used for power, stripped of their meaning, and spoken without human spiritual commitment. In the air all around us were the painful realities of the past, yet there was at the same time that feeling of spiritual elevation, a yearning for a vision that comes out of real and painful experience. And indeed we felt the vision was real: that humanism could be a modern spiritual answer to religious bigotry, an answer to fear and mistrust, to the humiliating acts in which we are all engaged and of which we are all victims. This for me was growing up in Israel. A new Jewish child making a promise to the world.

In the early fifties when I travelled to the U.S. to study engineering, I had the opportunity of hearing Erich Fromm lecturing on the prophets of Israel—Isaiah and Jeremiah. He spoke of superconsciousness and transcendence. I remember sitting in a large hall at the New School, students hanging from the rafters. As he talked, I was overwhelmed with the words of the prophets I had known by heart from childhood. These words were my politics and the politics of my parents. I wanted to get right up there and cry out loud with excitement, "He's talking about *my* prophets!"

Having been born in Jerusalem, and having been called Shulamith, was very important for me. To be born on the Shabbath was even more significant. I was born on the Shabbath in Jerusalem, and was called Shulamith—the feminine symbol of the land of Israel. In the Songs of Songs, King Solomon praises a beautiful woman "the Shulamite," and invites her to come that all might "look upon her". The Shulamite is a woman from Jerusalem. Jerusalem was called Yerushalem: "and the people will see peace". And so my parents, who did not leave Europe from personal persecution, but because of the knowledge of possible persecution, came to settle in Jerusalem, away from anti-Semitism. And when a daughter was born, they called her Shulamith. I knew from the day I was born that there was a mission for me and for my generation: the last generation to slavery, and the first generation to freedom.

A long tradition of yearning was put in the words of our poet Byalik, who declared our generation "last for humiliation, first for freedom". We felt like revolutionaries in all senses. Revolutionaries searching and creating new ideas. Israel has created the kibbutzim, a new human experience. We have revived an ancient language. We have read the Bible in Hebrew, and we have read it to give us strength, knowing that we, too, are the people who have passed forty years in the desert. Now we were here to create a new state with a new image. It was a love story. A fantastic love story. But as we all know, so often in love we do not see whom we hurt in the process. Zionism was such a love story, and it made one very big mistake: Zionists said that we were a homeless people coming to an empty land. We were indeed a homeless people, but it was not an empty land. There were people who had lived there for hundreds of years after the Jews were exiled. Indeed, we had come back to our home. We had come back from Europe because no one wanted us there. But it was someone else's home as well.

Zionism had one other misperception. Their leaders could not foresee the tragedy of the Holocaust. In the pogroms in Europe, all told, 1600 people were killed. In the biggest pogrom in Kishinev 81 people were killed. Of course, 1600 was an enormous number; it was tragic. But it was not six million! not twenty million! Who could foresee that there was so much hatred against humanity? For the Holocaust was not a crime against the Jews alone, it was a crime against humanity. Zionists, like everybody else, could not perceive that there was so much hatred in the world, that people could be herded like animals into concentration camps, that they could be exterminated in gas chambers, and that human beings could be made into soap, and human skin into lampshades. Nobody could have foreseen that. Nobody still can believe it really happened.

Before all this happened we were nation-building in Israel. We were very excited and idealistic in the process. There was one man in Israel, however, who *did* call our attention to the fact that Israel was not an empty land. His name was Martin Buber, and he was joined by his friend Yehuda Magnes. Already in the twenties and thirties they had spoken about a bi-national state, saying that the only way we could live and see our aspirations achieved would be to realize that this land belongs to two people now, and its nationhood can be worked out only through a bi-national state. Neither of the two nations could listen. Till this day we know we must each self-determine ourselves.

When we were children, we did not study the Bible as a religious document, not as a dogma. We were taught: "not a religion, a way of life". I would like to recount two personal stories about the meaning of that phrase to me as I grew up. As a child, I remember the Day of Atonement, Yom Kippur, which to my mind is the greatest humanist statement in our religious calendar. The Sages tell us about Yom Kippur: "On this day, God forgives you for your transgressions toward Him. However, God will not forgive you your transgressions against your fellow man or woman, unless your fellow man or woman forgives you first." And my father, a man who grew up in the Yeshiva, and my mother who knew the Bible well, although both were secular humanist Jews, used to go out every year between Rosh Hashanah and Yom Kippur, a period of ten days. They would go from neighbour to neighbour, from relative to relative, from associate to associate, and say, "Please, if I have wronged you in any way this past year, please forgive me." And once a year my parents would go to Synagogue; this was on Yom Kippur. That day they came to ask forgiveness from God. But not before, because "*Derech Chayim he*." For them, Judaism was "a way of life".

Another story: every morning, religious orthodox Jews put on phylacteries for morning prayer—a tiny box that the man ties between his eyes on his forehead, and connects with a long leather strap to his hand. In the box are the Ten Commandments, and the man says, "Let my hand remember what my head knows." I am recounting it as it was told me as a child. But my father used to say, "I don't have to go through this formal act. Every morning when I get up, I look in the mirror and say, "Daniel, you better remember what your head knows." So what we were given to understand is that the whole mass of ethical and moral values, everything that lies between the traditional Jewish 613 do's and don't's was going to be the deed of the day. Everything we did was a springboard to ethical and moral issues. "*Tikun olam*,"—"work for a better world". Everything we did was to create a model society which we constantly tested against the moral and ethical values of our tradition. We were dreamers.

This brings us to the creation of the state of Israel. Even before the war of Independence, we had fallen into expediency and pragmatism. Still, the Independence Day was a moment of great elevation. On May 15, 1948, we declared our independence; I would like to quote the part of this Declaration that has to do with a Bill of Rights:

> Israel will foster the development of the country for the benefit of all its inhabitants. It will be based on freedom, justice and peace as envisaged by the prophets of Israel. It will insure complete equality of social and

> political rights to all its inhabitants, irrespective of religion, race, or sex. It will guarantee freedom of religion, conscience, education and culture.

The unfortunate thing is that this document which was supposed to become the preamble of our Constitution and the infrastructure of our Bill of Rights, was never legally adopted! We have no Constitution and no Bill of Rights! There was a religious clash. Orthodox clericalism, which unfortunately can be found in all established religions, did not allow the non-religious and humanist Jews to adopt a Universal constitution. They still don't. They said, "Yes, you can adopt it, provided you say that all these Universal laws will be in the spirit of the *halachah*." Now, the *halachah* is a body of very strict laws that was supposed to be timely, but in the course of 2000 years it got terribly antiquated, for we did not have a state to modernise old Biblical concepts. By this not being adopted, today we have an Israel in which women are in many ways second class, and Arabs are second class. We have tremendous ethnic problems. But there is one thing that we do have, and that is freedom of speech. Many other personal freedoms are slowly being taken away from us in a very non-Jewish way, in the name of Jewish religion. Dogma, not life!

Israel is starting to drift away from its goals, by not teaching its children what inalienable rights are. The first Americans who came to New England, came wanting to speak Hebrew, because Hebrew was the language of the prophets, and their prophecy the first preamble to democracy. Paradoxically, we the Israelis, a people who came from 102 different countries, have no constitution. We had but one thing truly in common: getting out of persecution and humiliation into freedom. But, alas! the transition from persecution to freedom is difficult. It was a divisive, even polarising process in Israel. It was a painful process, which is still going on.

Moses held the Jews in the desert for forty years. He knew what he was doing. He would have the generation of people who had known slavery die, and take into Israel the people who had experienced freedom, who had experienced the rule of law, the rule of the Ten Commandments, who had learned to respect one another as equals, who had learned the dignity of the individual. Psychologists today tell us, though we have known it in some ways for many hundreds of years, that when someone grows up in a society with the mentality of oppression, whether he was oppressor or oppressed, it takes enormous power and strength to change that mentality. Moses knew, God knew, that those people who knew slavery could not work the deed of liberation.

In practice, we could not do in Israel what Moses did in the desert. We had people from 102 different countries, each bringing fear, paranoia, stereotypes and superstitions. There were European Jews, Oriental Jews, African Jews, American Jews. How do we make this one cohesive people? Teach them to speak Hebrew. Tell ourselves that Judaism is a social commitment.

I think of the words of T.S. Eliot, at the end of the poem, "Summit of Heaven," where he says, "Where is the Word we lost in words? Where is the knowledge we lost in information?" I say, "Where is the word 'dignity' which we lost in all the words we have been saying about Israel? Where is the knowledge which is godliness, in the midst of all the dogma that is superimposed on us?" How can we, the people of peace, make peace in the Middle East?

In Israel today, we have religious coercion. In Israel today, there is one religious interpretation which is "official Jewish religion," no reform or conservative interpretation allowed legally! No separation of Church and State. Jews who fought for the separation of Church and State all over the world, Jews who in the United States are fighting the Moral Majority and who protect vehemently the dignity of a pluralistic society, these people are supporting a moral majority in Israel. Then again, people say, "You must keep the unity of the Jews." But for those of us in Israel who demonstrated against what is happening in Lebanon, against the atrocities that continue to occur on the West Bank, for us the question is, "What does it mean to speak of the unity of the Jews?" On one side we are called anti-semites; on the other side, we are called Jews.

Those of us who lift our voices in protest in Israel have decided that there is one thing on which we stand firm and will not move: the teaching of our prophets, the moral and ethical values of our lives. The dignity of the individual must be coupled with social commitment. If the existence of the community contradicts the dignity of the individual, social commitment has no value. For the sake of the community, any community, individual dignity cannot be sacrificed. The two go together—the protection of the community and the protection of the individual, both individuals inside *and outside* the community. If we cannot protect both, we have denied the message of our prophets. With these agonizing questions, the Israeli-

Palestinian issue lies heavy upon us. How do we break through the impasse, and bring about change?

How can we equate the dignity of the individual with Palestinian self-determination, with the inevitability of a two-state solution, with the realization that Israel can be democratic and Jewish, an enlightened state for the Jewish people who wish to live there, as well as giving full equality to its minorities?

Those of us working for change in Israel have realized that we need to educate our young for such change. We know that a country is as good as its education. We have demonstrated in the streets. We have been called traitors. We have had tear gas bombs thrown at us. We are doing all we know how. And we know that, finally, education is the most important. We must educate our children, our teenagers, to understand what the dignity of the individual is. We are launching a programme in Israel to put civil liberties on the public agenda and prepare a curriculum for groups of 400 teenagers, Arabs and Jews, girls and boys, each year. The school programme is called Education for Democratic Leadership. Its premise is that it is not enough to live in a democratic country, and it is not enough to enjoy self-determination oneself. One must understand the need of self-determination for others, and work for it. Israeli women must understand the need for self-determination of the women on the West Bank. Belonging to feminist groups in Israel is not enough. It is a long road to go, but we must start in our humanist Jewish tradition and the promise we made to the world.

Finally, let me say this. Today in Israel there are 8,000 women who signed, two weeks ago, a manifesto to get our young men out of Lebanon. What happens in Lebanon or on the West Bank is not only tragic for the people of Lebanon and the West Bank. It is also a shameful tragedy for young Israelis who have to be there, and whose lives are distorted by the violence they perpetrate. A young Israeli soldier may shoot at an Arab child (so do Palestinians, at Israeli children). If he refuses to go to Lebanon, he goes to jail. The one thing I beg of Jews, of Christians, of Palestinians, and all Third World people: please do not trade atrocities. Each one of us can produce a bigger and bloodier atrocity. And often our communication becomes the destructive trading of atrocity. The minute we trade in atrocities, we avoid the real issues and undermine the reconstruction of trust. We women must assist in breaking through the vicious cycle of humiliation, fear and mistrust. As difficult as it may be, let us learn to be "pro" not "anti"—pro-Israeli, pro-Palestinian. We are both wrong; we are both right. Taking sides only enhances polarisation.

In 1925, our national poet Byalik wrote, "Satan did not invent, yet, the revenge of the blood of a little child." He said it about the suffering of the Jews in the pogroms. And in the war in Lebanon, even before the events in Sabra and Shatila, we spoke that sentence out loud, which had come originally out of our own sufferings, against our own leaders, Sharon and Begin. The poet did not say, "the blood of a Jewish child". Just the blood of a child. A Christian or a Jewish or a Muslim child. An Arab or an Israeli child.

All my life I was very proud that I was a Jew, a woman, an Israeli, a mother. Today, there are times when I am ashamed. I need to work together with my sisters from around the world to find a way forward. My question is this: How do we stop humiliating one another? How do we turn from the experience of humiliation, and yet not go on to humiliate others? How do we break the cycle?

PART TWO

CHANGING TRADITIONAL ROLES: RELIGION AND THE IMAGE OF WOMEN

Introduction

In this section, women discuss some of the images of women prominent in their own cultures—as mother, as wife, as witch, and even as rebel. From experience, we know that many of the issues with which women struggle—the control of fertility, the responsibilities within the family, the inequality of wages, the distribution of economic and political power, the rampant spread of militarism, the resistance to women's leadership—are deeply rooted in age old cultural presuppositions about gender. What is a man, and what is a woman? Such images of woman, or of man, are foundational. We carry them in the very structure of our consciousness. They are shaped by and are part of the centuries' long cumulative traditions of our religions and cultures. Even people who think of themselves as secular "think" with these images.

What images of woman do we think with? do men think with? do men and women of other cultures think with? For many women these images may well be man's images of woman, and we well know the extent to which we have been "colonized" by those very images. They become our own images of ourselves, and often in moving toward change, we confront within ourselves the dominant woman-images of the culture.

Nancy Jay, a sociologist at Harvard Divinity School, recounted that she had once been held in Boston's Charles Street Jail for her protest of the United States invasion of Cambodia. She said, "I learned from that imprisonment that it was nothing compared to my internal imprisonment. Oppression is not 'non-existent', simply because it is internal." It is tragically true that women have undergone brutal experiences of imprisonment or detainment in Latin America, South Africa, and elsewhere. It is also tragically true that women have been imprisoned, silently, for generations, by a culture's definition of who they should be.

The definitions are well known. According to the Hindu Laws of Manu, for instance, a woman must never be independent, but in youth be dependent upon her father, in maturity upon her husband, and in old age upon her sons. St. Paul writes that woman is the glory of man, while man is the image and glory of God. As the head of every man is Christ, the head of every woman is her husband. (I. Cor. 11). The point here is hardly to rehearse such definitions, which can be found in all our religious or cultural traditions, but to raise the question of whose definitions they are. Self-determination, that is, who we consider ourselves to be, is a fundamental principle of the relation of nations, the relation of people of various religious commitments, and the relation of women and men.

One of the major questions to emerge from these presentations is, "Who defines women?" Are we to be defined by the religious tradition, or one interpretation of the religious tradition—its images, scriptures, legal systems? Are we to be defined by cultural expectations, by family roles, by the power of the women-images projected by advertising? Or will we take our own self-definition seriously?

Masako Tanaka teaches anthropology at Meijo University in Nagoya, Japan. She received her doctorate from the University of Rochester with a thesis on *Kinship and Descent in an Okinawan Village*. Her papers in anthropology include work on maternal authority in the Japanese family. Here Masako looks at the myth of the mother in Japan, and the tenacious power of that myth even in a time change. Even highly educated women are seen as "pretty flowers" in the workplace; they tend to leave employment at the time of marriage, and have tended to accept rather traditional cultural definitions of wife and mother. The dynamics of traditional gender relations make the woman and mother all-competent in the domestic realm, and the man virtually helpless; in the public realm, however, the man is all-competent and the woman silent and virtually invisible.

Witchcraft accusation is part of the history of women in Europe and North America. Women who departed from the norms and conventional images of society were accused of being witches. **Elizabeth Amoah**, who teaches religion at the University of Ghana in Legon, looks at witchcraft accusation among the Akan. In this traditional culture, women are considered to be more vulnerable to witchcraft than men, and they are more likely to be accused of witchcraft to account for any deviation from the cultural norm: too much education or success, too many children, too few children, too readily influenced by her in-laws, too resistent to the family of her in-laws, etc. In her several case-studies of women accused of witchcraft, Elizabeth considers both cultural definition and self-definition—what others say of the presumed witches, and what the presumed witches think of themselves.

Fatima Mernissi is a sociologist, working at the Research Institute of the University of Rabat in Morocco, who has written widely in Arabic, French and English on women in North African Muslim culture. Her book, *Beyond the Veil*, has been an important contribution. Here, in the Muslim context, she raises the question of cultural sanctions against women who do not conform. She examines "women's rebellion" in the Muslim tradition—a phenomenon apparently significant enough in early Islam to have generated a word for it: *nushūz*. Fatima asks, Why is women's rebellion such a threat? Hierarchy depends, she says, on submission to order. In the Islamic tradition, the notion of submission is underlined because the term Islam means "submission" to God, and Muslim, the one who submits. To change, innovate, or rebel as women, to refuse one's submission to men, threatens not simply the stability of the hierarchy, but the very notion of hierarchy, which is dependent upon submission.

The power of traditional gender images is clearly seen in the presentation by **Elisabeth Adler** who is the Director of Evangelische Akademie, a lay church academy in Berlin, in the German Democratic Republic. Elisabeth has had a long career in international work with churches, including work with the World Council of Churches Program to Combat Racism. Her case-study here emerges from a seminar at the lay academy on women's attitudes and ambiguities about professional life in relation to personal life. The situation in East Germany is an important one, for there women have full equality under the law and participate fully as professionals in everything from industry to parliament. The issues for women are not in the realm of rights and opportunities, but they still exist in the realm of self-identity and self-image. This points clearly to the power of the images we carry with us, images with which we will wrestle long after the more tangible goals of social change have been achieved.

All these presentations make vivid and concrete the various

images of women and men shaped by our cultures and traditions, and in the slow process of being reshaped by women and men throughout the world. The picture here is partial. To it we could add the stories of those women in India whose value is calculated by the size of their dowry; those women in Latin America whose image is shaped by the culture of *machismo*; those women in Iran who have taken a traditional image again to assert a cultural self-identity independent of the West; those women in the United States who see nothing of themselves and their values in the rising male military culture. Demythologizing or debunking our images is not the answer. For images cannot really be replaced by "facts". Images function within our minds at a much deeper level. Images can only be replaced by new images, and new self-definitions, generated now with the full imaginative participation of women themselves.

The Myth of Perfect Motherhood: Japanese Women's Dilemma

Masako Tanaka

Whoever travels to Japan, particularly those from the more "emancipated" western societies, must notice that there are relatively few women in responsible positions. To be sure, women are visibly at work in offices, factories, shops and stores; but most of them are considered and treated either as "pretty flowers" who soften the otherwise rather drab male world of work, or as handy and docile assistants to male workers, or as the performers of the lowly tasks men themselves disdain to take up.

Statistically, more than one in two married Japanese women today works outside her household, and almost all young women graduating from high schools or colleges find employment outside their homes. Article Fourteen of the Japanese Constitution stipulates that no one shall be discriminated against on the basis of sex, as well as of race and creed, and throughout the lengthy educational process which for 95 per cent of the young population lasts for twelve or more school years, girls are given basically the same education as boys. Their performances are judged only on the basis of individual achievement. And many college professors acknowledge, sometimes reluctantly, that girls usually perform better.

Even so, these young women are rudely shocked when they begin to look for jobs. They realize, to their chagrin, that few companies give them a chance even to sit for the entrance examination. Employment is even more difficult. Most companies, if they need female workers, prefer employing high school graduates who are expected to stay on the job long enough to be profitable for the companies, and short enough to allow them to hire, in time, another bunch of fresh "pretty flowers". College educated women who start their careers four years later, they say, quit too soon or stay too long for the interest of the company. Since jobs assigned to women are, in any case, subsidiary to men's work, the need for career-oriented, experienced female workers is minimal.

Although today the number of women who continue to work after their marriage is growing, Japanese society generally expects women to leave the job upon the birth of the first child, if not immediately upon marriage. Women themselves, including those college-educated young women, accept this as inevitable, if not desirable, for they believe that the woman's place is ultimately in the home. Her primary responsibility is to her home, particularly to her children. Whatever else she does, she must first discharge this primary responsibility.

Such an attitude is reflected in a recent opinion survey sponsored by the Japanese Government and conducted in 1982 in six countries (the Philippines, the U.S.A., Sweden, West Germany, England, and Japan).[1] According to the survey, 72 per cent of the 1294 Japanese women questioned, between age 20 and 59, were reported to agree generally with the statement that the married woman should be more concerned about her family than about herself and should conduct her life accordingly (see Fig. 1). By comparison, only 6.1 per cent of Swedish women, 9.9 per cent of British women, and 17.6 per cent of American women agreed with the statement. Although 41.1 per cent of the West German women, and 57.5 per cent of the Filippino women subscribed to the family-centred view, the Japanese women were by far the most family-conscious.

Perhaps correlatively, Japanese women, more than any other group, believe that boys and girls should be disciplined properly according to their sex. As is clear from Fig. 2, 62.6 per cent of Japanese women subscribe to the differential discipline of girls and boys while in other countries the majority supports the equal treatment irrespective of the child's sex.

In addition, the same survey found 71.1 per cent of the Japanese women agreeing with the "traditional" division of labour, according to which "woman keeps house while man works outside". "Traditional," however, is something of a misnomer, since in the

[1] Bureau of Women, Prime Minister's Office (Sori-fu) "Fujin mondai ni kansuru kokusai hikaku (Comparative study of women's problems in six countries)" *Gekkan Yoron Chosa* (Public Opinion Monthly) Vol. 15–6, June 1983, published by the Office of Public Relations, Prime Minister's Office, Japan, pp. 50–98.

Fig. 1

"The woman, after marriage, should be concerned more about her family than about herself, and should conduct her life accordingly" (%)

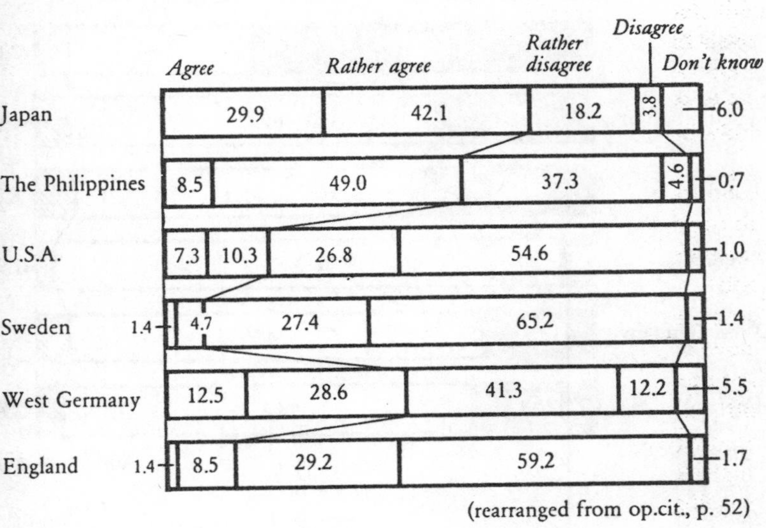

(rearranged from op.cit., p. 52)

traditional agricultural or small-business economy of Japan, both men and women worked. It is only since World War II that the majority of married women became *sengyo-shufu*—housewives whose only task is to keep the house and care for the family.

It is not at all surprising, therefore, to find that only 21 per cent of the Japanese women continued to hold jobs after marriage. As shown in Fig. 3, in all other countries but the Philippines, nearly half or more of the women continued working after they got married. Against this general trend it is quite striking to note that as many as 45.8 per cent of the Japanese women quit their jobs upon marriage not by the wish of their husbands but by their own inclination.

Why do Japanese women, who must be one of the most highly educated female groups and live in a highly industrialized modern society, so readily sacrifice their own pursuits for the sake of the family? Do they find pleasure in this act of self-sacrifice, or is there

Fig. 2

"Do you believe boys and girls should be disciplined differently according to their sex, or should be treated equally?" (%)

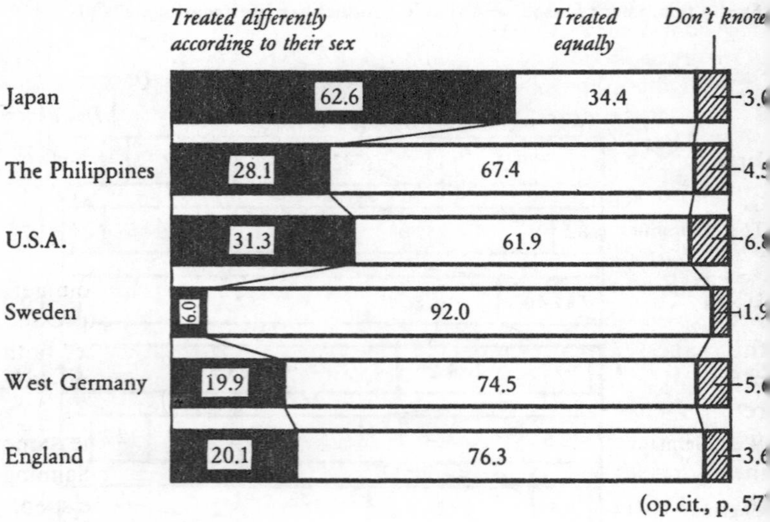

(op.cit., p. 57

anything they gain by self-negation? To answer these questions, it seems necessary to investigate the popularly held view about the male and female roles in this society.

In "traditional" Japanese ideology man and woman are thought to have distinct heaven-sent roles to play. The two roles are complementary and believed to be sex-determined. Very simply put, men work (usually outside the household) to earn a living, while women stay at home and take care of the family, which might include aged parents-in-law and dead ancestors, as well as children. A competent woman is expected to keep the household in perfect order, both physically and emotionally, without the help of the other members, specifically the husband. On the other hand, a truly manly husband is supposed to concentrate on his work, completely free of mundane household chores and worries. Neither man nor woman is supposed to interfere with the other's business. The following recent popular song, *Kampaku Sengen*, "A Man's Declaration to his Bride," illustrates this well:

Before I take you as my wife
I have something to say to you.
It may sound a bit harsh to a bride,
But this is what I really feel—so listen!
You must not go to bed before I do.
And you must arise before I do.
Be a good cook, and a beautiful wife.
Well, at least try as best you can.
Don't forget, a man has his work.
Without it our home can't survive.
I know there are things only you can and must perform.
Mind your business, and don't interfere with my work.
Do not nag; just follow me where I lead.

Amazingly, it was not the older generations, but the younger, who loved the song. And although some feminists duly expressed their annoyance, irritation and despair, younger Japanese, both men and women, seemed generally to feel that such a husband-wife relationship is quite proper.

In this connection, it is interesting to note here that the same international survey found 79.4 per cent of Japanese women claiming that they have the final say in how family income should be spent, while only 11.5 per cent of West German women, 22.2 per cent of Swedish women and 36.5 per cent of American wives claimed to have the same privilege.

The Japanese woman may not be treated as a responsible person outside the household, but at home she is completely in control. Her actual and/or moral authority in the family and the stable status accorded in the society at large as wife-mother is quite enormous, and is in radical contrast with the image of a working married woman, who is often conceptualized negatively. It is acceptable for an unmarried young woman to work outside, but many people still think that the married woman who continues her career does so only at the expense of her husband and children, and that she is selfish in pursuing her own interest. Under these circumstances, it is easy to understand why many highly trained Japanese women retire from their jobs when they marry and concentrate on home-making and raising children.

Of course it is true that women are accorded a certain respect as mothers and wives in most other societies; but in Japan there are

Fig. 3

"When you got married, what did you do with your job?" (%)

	Never held a job	*Quit job of own will*	*Quit job at husband's objection*	*Continued to work*	*Other*	*No answer*
Japan	26.7	45.8	2.6	21.4	2.9	0.6
The Philippines	55.4	13.2	11.7	16.4	0.3	3.0
The U.S.A.	34.0	9.3	3.2	49.1	2.2	2.3
Sweden	9.0	19.4	1.3	56.5	0.8	13.0
West Germany	10.1	21.1	8.4	49.0	2.3	9.1
England	5.6	13.5	2.5	72.9	2.6	2.8

(rearranged from op. cit., p. 71)

Fig. 4

"In your household who has the final say about how the family income should be spent?" (%)

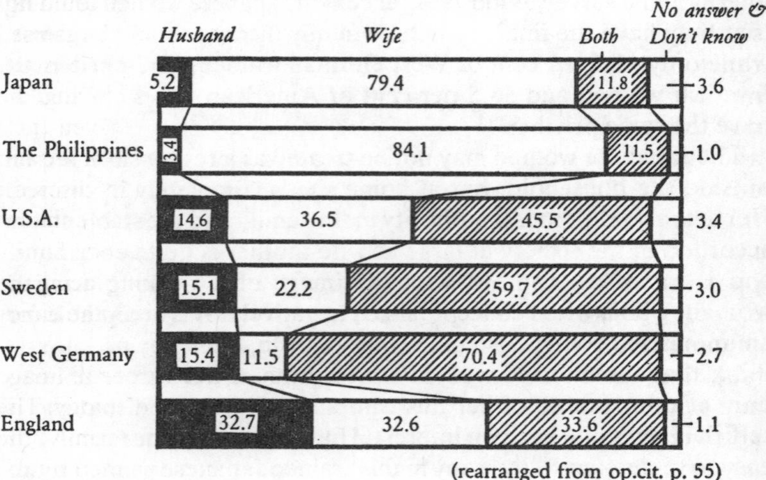

(rearranged from op.cit. p. 55)

some distinctively Japanese factors to be considered. I can point out just three here.

The first is the widely held sexual division of labour, due to which a Japanese man is normally raised with no training to take care of himself. He does not know how to cook, wash clothes or clean the house. And when it comes to caring for babies or for sick persons, he is said to be all thumbs. No efficient or kind woman wants to let him perform these chores.

Such ineptitude may be a very convenient excuse on the part of the man. In part, it is a genuine excuse, but it also has some real truth. The husband may behave like a lord demanding his wife's services, but this dependance makes him an entirely helpless person, as dependent as a baby is on its mother. No wonder all male-female relationships in Japan take the form of the mother-son relationship. The Japanese man knows it and accords his wife high respect, calling her "mother" just as her children do. Paradoxical as it may sound, such male dependancy seems to be one significant reason for the Japanese woman's high social standing as the housewife.

A second distinctively Japanese factor to take into consideration is the lack, in our culture, of the "Creator God". In other religious systems where a powerful personified Creator God is recognized, it is he who is responsible for the birth and the continued existence of individuals. By contrast, in Japanese common culture (I should not say "religion" here because Buddhist, Shintoist and other organised religions have their own theories about these matters), it is the mother who gives life and sustains it by feeding and giving the needed care. In former days, the rather impersonal Heaven (*ten*) and Fate (*un* or *en*) were believed to control these matters of life and death, but now highly educated Japanese people generally discredit this theory as a mere superstition. One result is to greatly enhance the mother's position as the life-giver. The wider practice of family planning has also contributed greatly to that direction by placing the choice of whether or not and when to have a baby right in the hands of parents, particularly in the hands of the mother.

A final specifically Japanese factor in thinking about the image and status of women in Japan may be related to the *ie* ideology. The *ie* is the traditional Japanese family. Unlike the nuclear family, the *ie*, once set up, is supposed to continue forever, succeeded by the eldest son or his substitute generation after generation. Ideologically this is an extremely patrilineal pattern. But for our concern here, the important thing to note is that it is the woman who enables this patrilineal continuity to exist at all. Without her, man cannot beget the all important heir and thus cannot carry out his sacred duty toward his ancestors. Neither will he be able to become an ancestor himself after his death.

To sum up, the Japanese woman, while treated unequally, even poorly, in public, does enjoy a high moral standing due to the structural position she occupies in the household as the life-giver, the sole care-giver, and the link with the past and future of the family. She thus has a very high moral standing as mother and wife, and she can wield her authority as long as she does not overstep this assigned boundary. But she faces a great dilemma: for what is expected of her is diametrically opposed to the principles of equality and individual dignity.

The liberation of the Japanese woman may not be achieved until she is ready to give up the privileged security of being the mother-wife. The Japanese have not really incorporated the Judeo-Christian concept of the "individual" with the capacity and responsibility to decide for himself or herself. It is not that we lack the concept of self; it is just that in our tradition it is conceptualized quite differently.

The self in the Japanese sense may be defined only in relation to others: who you are, who you are talking to, what is the occasion, what is your status and that of the other to whom you are talking (sex and seniority being the two most significant general determinants). Without all this information, one cannot behave appropriately in Japanese society. Thus, in a traditional setting, a woman's life may be hard, but it is not impossible for her to be truly "herself," defined in relation to the others whom she loves, and by whom she feels needed. Here I put the situation as positively as possible. It is also true, however, that even this relational "self" is threatened in the industrialized urban situation where families are isolated from community and kinship networks and where women's functions are diminishing. In addition, many women, full of energy and time, do not feel fulfilled by simply taking care of the family, with all the mechanical and institutional help now available. For better or worse, many Japanese women have already begun to walk in a new direction. We do not know where the path leads us, but somehow we have to find new meaning and self-respect in our rapidly changing situation.

Women, Witches and Social Change in Ghana

Elizabeth Amoah

In Ghana witchcraft belief and accusations are generally associated with women. At traditional shrines and in the new Ghanaian spiritual churches, those most often suspected and accused of being witches are women. It is the aim of this paper to examine the relation of the roles women play in the community to the accusation of witchcraft.

In Ghana, women do not constitute a homogenous entity; they come from different social, economic, educational, religious and ethnic backgrounds. Thus, for the purposes of this study, four categories of women were identified for a preliminary analysis: (*i*) those who have attained a high level of western, formal education, (*ii*) those who are successful in large businesses, (*iii*) those who are involved in market, trade, or small-scale business, and (*iv*) those who are social failures. In conducting this research, I visited spiritual churches and traditional shrines, to witness the proceedings and hear the confessions of suspected witches. In addition, I collected the conventional wisdom, expressed often in proverbs, that convey traditional attitudes toward witchcraft.

Belief in witchcraft has been and still is an aspect of the indigenous religious beliefs and practices of Ghana. Witchcraft is known in Akan as *bayie*: an external spiritual power which can manifest itself in various forms and which, it is believed, can possess a person. The general belief is that *bayie* is usually used for evil and destructive purposes: the destruction of human life, especially of children, and the destruction of property. *Bayie* is used to promote the interests and success of those who have it, at the expense of others. In a typical traditional Ghanaian society, the operative ideal is that the group's interest should supercede that of the individual. In such a system, *bayie* is evil because it is an anti-social phenomenon, used in most cases to promote individual interests.

Women are the focus of witchcraft belief and accusation, for despite the matrilineality of Ghanaian society, it is still male-oriented. In every sense men are considered superior to women, so that women depend upon them for their existence. This underlies the Akan proverb: *Obaa ho ye fa, na efi ne kunu*—"The beautiful woman owes her beauty to her husband." It is interesting to note in this proverb that *obaa* and *oyere* are respectively, the Akan words for a woman and a wife. The proverb is about a wife's dependance on her husband, *kunu*. Under normal circumstances, therefore, the word *obaa* used in the proverb should have been *oyere*—"the beautiful wife owes her beauty to her husband." But as the proverb stands, one gets the impression that *obaa*, a woman, is synonymous with *oyere*, a wife. And, indeed, in a typical traditional Akan society, to be a woman is to be a wife. A woman's identity is recognised in terms of her status as a wife.

Certain social practices reinforce the belief that a man is superior to and more intelligent than a woman. For instance, in most of the deliberations concerning the welfare of the community, women are left out. If men are present, the views of women are not needed; it is said, *Obaa de onim nyansa ben*? "What wisdom has a woman?" It is precisely because women are considered unintelligent that their views are rarely sought in decision making.

It is true that women have held the position of queen-mother, the maternal relations of the ruling chief, and in a few cases have become chiefs or rulers. Still, the importance of their roles was generally overshadowed by that of the male chiefs. Even in her important role of nominating the next chief, her decision was not final but had to be acceptable to all before her candidate was installed as chief. Like other women in the society, the queen-mother played the traditional role as wife and mother to the community. She would organize the man, especially in times of crisis, such as during a war. She would make sure that customs and traditions, especially those concerning women, were preserved and taught properly. Women occasionally became chiefs in cases where the ruling family realised that there were no competent men within it to assume the role of chief.

In a traditional society, women were considered weak, both physically and spiritually, for it was believed that they have light or weak *sunsum*. *Sunsum* is one of the spiritual elements present in a human being, and is believed to be transmitted to children through the father. It yields certain personality traits, such as bravery, and sometimes acts as a protective aura for the individual. Because women have weak *sunsum*, they are said to be easy prey to outside spiritual powers and influences. This belief in women's special susceptibility accounts, in part, for the frequency of witchcraft accusation against women.

Given what has been said of women's position, it is no wonder that in traditional Akan society there was a strict division of labour based on sex and sometimes on age. Domestic and housekeeping duties were assigned to women, as were the tasks of bringing up children. Planting food crops and maintaining the farms after the men had cleared and prepared the land was women's work. Selling the surplus food and selling fish was women's work, and at times women would provide for their needs and save capital by small scale trading in locally produced goods. Finally, some women, especially those who had reached menopause, performed religious functions as mediums, priestesses, diviners, and medicine women.

Formal and western education, industrialisation, urbanisation, and new kinds of trading in foreign goods have added new roles to the traditional roles of women. It is in the light of these new roles that the four categories of women were selected for this study.

Group 1: Women with a high level of formal western education

Four women were selected for this study. Since the author falls into this category, her own case will be presented in this group of women, for whom educational attainment itself may become the cause of witchcraft accusation.

Case 1

Age:	34 years old.
Family history:	The fifth of ten children, born after a set of twins. Traditionally considered to be tough, with a strong personality. The other brothers and sisters had a minimum education, a few up to polytechnic.
Education:	A doctorate degree at the University.
Occupation:	Presently a University Lecturer.
Marital status:	Unmarried.

Children:	Lost one, a few miscarriages.
Other views of her:	1. She is a witch because she is Tawia (someone born after twins). She is a witch because she is the only one of the ten children who could study up to a University level. In other words, she used her witchcraft to collect other people's intellects and added them to hers to be able to achieve what even men find difficult to do, that is, obtain a doctorate. 2. She is a victim of witchcraft. The witches from her extended family are preventing her from having husband and children, and this explains the loss of a child and a series of miscarriages. The witches envy her educational achievement, so they will make sure she does not have a nuclear family of her own.
Her own views:	She does not accept the accusation of witchcraft. Her present educational standard is to be attributed to her effort, and to encouragement from friends and relatives.

Case 2

Age:	32 years.
Education:	University degree, with a Master's degree in Law at Harvard Law School.
Occupation:	Legal Adviser in an oil company.
Marital status:	Unmarried.
Children:	None, but has tried to have children outside marriage.
Other views of her:	Her parents are not worried about her not being married, but they want her to have children even if unmarried. Her aunts are also worried about her not having children, and they advise her to consult diviners or spiritual church leaders because they suspect that her not having children is caused by witches.
Her own views:	Her aunts are talking nonsense, for she has been told by a gynaecologist that she has fibroids in her womb which prevent her from becoming pregnant. She has no problem in her job, except that some of her male counterparts want to be in her shoes.

Of the others, one is an eighty year old widow, a teacher and housewife, who has had five professionally successful children. She was accused of witchcraft by her husband's relatives, who said she used it to rule her husband and to educate her own children at the expense of the other nieces and nephews in the family. The attack became so severe that she had to leave her husband's house, where they had lived when he was alive, and move to a house built by her children. She herself is deeply hurt by the accusations. The other woman in this group is a fifty year old University lecturer, whose childlessness has been attributed to witchcraft, according to her in-laws.

Group 2: Those successful in business

This group of women consists of those who are successful in modern commercial businesses, and in all cases their success is attributed to a form of witchcraft, the acquisition of *sika aduro*. *Sika aduro* is the belief that certain medicine men can make people rich through supernatural means. The person acquiring *sika aduro* usually sacrifices a relative, or part of oneself, for the medicine.

Case 1

Age:	48 years.
Education:	Up to elementary school level.
Occupation:	Manufacturing of the local gin (*akpeteshi*). Business is very successful. She employs about twenty people and receives an income of ₵100,000 annually. (₵2.75 = $1.00 U.S.).
Marital status:	Married; husband a driver.
Children:	8 (2 graduates; others in secondary school).
Other views of her:	Husband's relatives and others, both male and female business counterparts who are not as successful as she, attribute her success to the use of witchcraft and the acquiring of *sika aduro*. She is accused of using her witchcraft to suppress her husband and to be richer than he is.
Her own views:	Accusations untrue. Her success depends upon her determination, hard work and the cooperation of her workers.

Case 2

Age:	52 years.
Education:	None..

Occupation:	Exporter and distributor of dress materials. Very successful and rich, with many customers and retailers. Annual income of about ₵200,000.
Marital status:	Divorced about four times.
Children:	None, but looks after nieces and nephews.
Other views of her:	Her success in business is due to the use of *sika aduro*, which is mainfest as a septic sore on her left foot. It is said the more septic the sore, the richer and more prosperous is the business.
Her own views:	She is a diabetic, hence the sore has taken a long time to heal. Her success depends upon her own business drive and the ability to form contacts with customers. She thinks she is being disturbed by witchcraft, however; hence, her barrenness and series of divorces. The witches of her maternal extended family want her to use her wealth for nieces and nephews, not for her own children.

The two other women in this category are also successful, one in the fish business and the other as a building contractor. Others attribute the success of the former to *sika aduro*, and of the latter to "bottom power," that is, sleeping with the men from whom she is awarded contracts.

Group 3: Small scale retailers and traders

These are women in more traditional occupations, in which great wealth is not accumulated and the charge of *sika aduro* is not made. These women may be accused of witchcraft in certain situations, but also may be seen as the victims of the witchcraft of others.

Case 1

Age:	25 years.
Education:	Up to elementary school level.
Occupation:	Buys and sells pepper, tomatoes and palm oil. Does not earn much profit in business, gets just enough to spend on her needs.
Marital status:	Married. Husband a driver. Has been married for over seven years.
Children:	None. Lives with husband's daughter.
Other views of her:	She is the only daughter of a mother, and her own mother and relations are not happy about her

childlessness. The wife of her husband's senior brother is accused of witchcraft and blamed for her childlessness. Her parents have been taking her to consult medicine men, and these agree that her brother-in-law's wife has used witchcraft to make her barren. One medicine man has asked her to stop trading in pepper, tomatoes and palm oil, since these attract witches.

Her own views: She agrees with the medicine man that the husband's brother's wife is the cause of her childlessness.

Case 2

Age: 45 years.

Education: No western education.

Marital status: Twice widowed. One husband died in his sleep, possibly of heart failure. The other died in a car accident.

Children: 6 (3 in secondary school).

Occupation: Sells cooked beans and *tatare*, a local dish prepared from mashed ripe plantain, mixed with flour and spices and fried in palm oil. She has been selling this for 15 years, helping her husbands financially with the upkeep of the children. Until the death of her second husband, she had a considerable amount of money in her savings.

Other views of her: After the death of the second husband, she was accused by the families of the husbands of killing the latter through witchcraft.

Her own views: She seems to accept the accusation and has decided not to remarry for fear of being a widow for the third time. She will use whatever money she has to go wherever the supposed witchcraft can be driven away from her. After the accusation of witchcraft, she lost her business because customers refused to buy from her. There was the normal suspicion that women who fry *tatare* use human blood in place of palm oil. Her case is worse, because she has been accused of being a witch. She now finds life very difficult because she has no way of earning money to look after her children and herself. She looks older and weaker than her age.

Another woman in this group is a cloth merchant, with children, who is accused of being a witch because she is always quarrelling with her husband's sisters. She, on the other hand, sees her sisters-in-law as the witches, who want to lord it over her in the household. Finally, there is a fish merchant, with ten children. She is accused of witchcraft because none of her three sisters has children, while she has ten. She is not bothered by the charge.

Group 4: Social failures

These women seem to be followed by tragedy and difficulty, which is attributed to witchcraft.

Case 1

Age:	60 years.
Education:	No western education.
Marital status:	Widowed twice. Divorced by the third husband when he discovered the first two had died.
Children:	4 (all married, with children. The two sons have become alcoholics).
Occupation:	Cultivates food crops such as plantain, cassava, and pepper. Even with farming and petty trading she cannot support herself and tends to lose money.
Other views of her:	She is a witch. Hence, she has been twice a widow and has two alcoholic sons. Hence, her failure in farming and trading.
Her own views:	She accepts the accusation that she is a witch, but she cannot control it. She has been attending a local spiritual church so that her witchcraft will be driven out of her.

Case 2

Age:	38 years.
Education:	Six years, but had to leave school because she always became ill during the examinations. She became a seamstress apprentice, but here too could not make any headway and left work.
Marital status:	Married a farmer at age 18.
Children:	After six years of marriage, she had a child which died at birth. Since then, she has been trying to have another but has been unsuccessful.

Other views of her:	She joined a spiritual church, where it was revealed to her that her childlessness was due to one of her in-laws, who is a witch. This relative has used witchcraft to make her barren so that her husband's responsibilities would be towards his maternal family.
Her own views:	She accepts that her unsuccessful educational career and her childlessness is due to witchcraft, from her own family and her husband's family.

Of the other women in this group, one has lost five children and was divorced by her husband, whose relations accused her of witchcraft. She became a prostitute to earn her living. The other is also divorced and childless, but her condition is attributed to the witchcraft of her aunt.

Breaking with Tradition, and Witchcraft Accusation

From these cases it is clear that there are various types of witchcraft accusation. There are those who use their supposed witchcraft to promote their own interests, in business or education; there are those who use it to promote others, such as their children or relatives; and there are those who are victims of the witchcraft of other women. The majority of those who accused women of being witches are women themselves—rivals, in-laws, business competitors. The implication of this is that women are the ones who have set the standards for women to follow, and those who break free of traditional roles will incur blame.

Conflict arises when women try to break out of traditional roles and leads often to witchcraft accusation. In marital and domestic affairs, such conflicts are associated with a woman's unwillingness to discharge her traditional duties as a wife or in-law. If, for example, a wife does not give in to the pressure and demands from her husband's relations, she is branded a witch. If, on the other hand, she gives in too much to them, her own family may see her as bewitched by the female relatives of the husband.

In trade and business, conflicts may arise between women competitors, or between women and men competitors. The success of women in business is attributed to their use of witchcraft. Women, it is believed, are not capable of achieving anything without the help of an external power or outside influence, such as witchcraft, *sika aduro*, or "bottom power". When women depart from tradition by owning fishing boats or employing men in their businesses, for example, witchcraft accusations against women increase. Belief in witchcraft, therefore, has been one of the traditional ways of expressing suspicion, anxiety, doubt and fear in the face of change.

In the context of the family, women may be accused of witchcraft if they have no children, or if they have too many children; if their children are unsuccessful, or if their children are too successful. Women may be seen as both perpetrators or victims of witchcraft.

The effects of witchcraft and witchcraft accusation on women vary depending upon the life situation in which a woman finds herself. Among the educated women in group one, the characteristic reaction to witchcraft accusation is that they care little for such social evaluations. These accusations do not prevent them from performing the new social roles in which they find themselves, in the University or elsewhere. They, therefore, stand the risk of greater and more accusations. However, it was discovered that even these women are not entirely free from using witchcraft as an explanation for misfortune or childlessness.

The successful businesswomen of group two may not have a high level of education, but have an outstanding business sense. They have organisational drive, and the ability to form and maintain contacts. They tend to be very fearless. They not only stand the risk of greater accusation of the use of witchcraft to succeed in business, but are also accused of *sika aduro* or of using "bottom power" to promote their business. Like the women in group one, these women do not allow witchcraft accusations to hinder their business. But they are also not free from using witchcraft as an explanation for personal or business misfortunes. When some were asked if they would like their children to go into business, they replied in the negative, because one in business so easily becomes the target of the evil eye from one's extended family.

Women in group three have maintained traditional roles as traders or hawkers. They are hard-working, sometimes outspoken, but generally traditional in their norms of household, motherhood, and the rearing of children. These women tend to be both victims and accusers of witchcraft. Sometimes they modify their ways of life to free themselves of its influence. For example, they may refuse to trade in certain items, such as pork, palm oil, etc. for fear of being victims of witchcraft accusation. They also tend to seek the protection of new spiritual churches and traditional shrines against witchcraft.

In group four are women who readily accept witchcraft accusations and also tend to accuse other women. They accuse relations, in-laws, or rivals for their failures in life. Sometimes they also blame themselves for using witchcraft, intentionally or unintentionally. They too seek the protection of the spiritual churches and traditional shrines.

Thus, one finds that among certain women rampant accusations of witchcraft, and the fear of being victims of witches, has an effect on ambitious women who want to break through the barrier of traditional occupations. These social accusations frustrate women, especially those who wish to appear decent in society. While among educated women, and those traders with foreign contacts, there is an increasingly indifferent attitude toward witchcraft accusations, there is still an undercurrent of traditional belief.

In general, women in high status positions are more likely to be accused of witchcraft, because they are often seen to be doing something against the grain of womanhood as construed in the traditional culture. On the other hand, even among more traditional women, social change and new forms of competition create a fertile ground for witchcraft accusation. Witchcraft is a way of dealing with women's power and its challenges, both within and without, and witchcraft accusation exposes the ambiguities and uncertainties created in the process of social change.

Femininity as Subversion: Reflections on the Muslim Concept of *Nushūz*

Fatima Mernissi

Nushūz is a Koranic concept; it means the rebellion of the wife against her Muslim husband's authority. The Koran only refers to *nushūz* in order to describe the punishment a husband must inflict upon the wife in case she rebels. Ghazali defines the *nashiz* (the woman who rebels, plural: *nawashiz* or *nashizat*) as a wife who confronts her husband either in act or word. He explains that the word *nashz* means "that which tries to elevate itself above ground".[1]

In this paper, I do not want to elaborate a theory of the concept of surrender in Islamic thought. Fatna Sabbah has convincingly done that in *The Woman in the Muslim Unconscious* (1984). She argues, and I agree with her, that "The ideal of female beauty in Islam is obedience, silence and immobility, that is inertia and passivity. These are far from being trivial characteristics, nor are they limited to women. In fact, these three attributes of female beauty are the three qualities of the believer vis-a-vis his God. The believer must dedicate his life to obeying and worshipping God and abiding by his will".[2] Fatna Sabah explains that the woman's obedience to the husband is not just a marginal device in Islam; she demonstrates that it is a central element and a key law for the viability of the system. "In the sacred universe," she states, after having analysed

[1] Ghazali, "The Revivification of Religious Sciences," Book of Marriage, Al Maktaba Al Tijariya, Al Kurba, Egypt.

[2] Fatna A. Sabbah, *Woman in the Muslim Unconscious*, Pergamon Press, 1984, p. 118.

the orthodox Sunni Islamic discourse, "the believer is fashioned in the image of woman, deprived of speech and will and committed to obedience to another (God). The female condition and the male condition are not different in the end to which they are directed, but in the pole around which they orbit. The lives of beings of the male sex revolve around the divine will. The lives of beings of the female sex revolve around the will of believers of the male sex. And in both cases the human element, in terms of multiple, unforeseeable potentialities, must be liquidated in order to bring about the triumph of the sacred, the triumph of the divine, the non-human."[3]

I want to suggest in this paper that women's disobedience is so feared in the Muslim world because its implications are enormous. They refer to the most dreaded danger to Islam as a group psychology: individualism. I want here to suggest that Muslim societies resist women's claim to changing their status, that they repress feminist trends which are actually evident all over the Muslim world, and that they condemn them as western imports, not simply because these societies fear women, but because they fear individualism.

Individualism, the person's claim to have legitimate interests, views and opinions different from those of the group, is an alien concept and fatal to heavily collectivist Islam. Islam, like any theocracy, is group-oriented, and individual wishes are put down as impious, whimsical, egotistical passions. I would suggest, however, that the woman, identified in the Muslim order as the embodiment of uncontrolled desires and undisciplined passions, is precisely the symbol of heavily suppressed individualistic trends. I believe that if the issues of the veil and of women's rights are so central to Muslim fundamentalist movements today, it is because these movements can be interpreted as strong visceral reactions against individualism. The primary issue being debated in the Muslim world today is democracy—the individual right to choose society's rulers. The right of each citizen to choose those who rule, through clear voting procedures, is a total reversal of the idea of personhood in Islam. It is the world upside-down. Democracy indicates clearly that it is the individual who is the sacred source of political authority, and not

[3] Fatna A. Sabbah, *op. cit.*, p. 118.

the group. Islam, like all theocracies, puts the emphasis on the *umma* as a mythically homogenous group, which is the legitimate source of authority. The objective of Muslim society is the survival of the *umma*, not the happiness of the individual. The latter is totally submissive to the religious law which binds his/her acts and thought in all spheres of human experience, from the most public to the most intimate.

In these few pages I want to indicate that we will not understand the resistance of Muslim societies to the change in women's status and rights if we do not take into account the symbolic function of women as the embodiment of dangerous individualism. It is this individualism that society has chosen to repress in order to safeguard a collective orientation. Therefore we will see, in the first part of this paper, the notion of *nushūz* (rebellion or subversion) as it is linked to one of the most individualistic concepts of Islam, the concept of *bid'a*, that is innovation; in the second part of the paper, we will see women's rebellion through the historical profiles of dissenting women; and in the final part, we will see the implications of women's dissent in the present situation, namely in the integral relatedness of three phenomena: women's claim to change, the disintegration of traditional society, and the invasion of western, capitalist, consumerist individualism. In this last part, I want to clarify why most feminists in the Muslim world are faced with the threat of being labelled as western agents, traitors or enemies of the community. The western hedonist and consumerist invasion of Muslim societies is, of course, seen as a disruption of the social fabric, and women who claim change—and therefore claim their own individuality—are viewed as agents of such disruption.

This paper will be impressionistic and suggestive in approach. I will not attempt, in this context, to prove each argument with precise scholarly elaboration. Since 1973, I have been working on a book which substantiates and elaborates this material. It is on the topic of femininity—submissiveness and passivity—a key symbol in any hierarchical ordering of the world, and will be entitled *Femininity, Aesthetics and Politics in Contemporary Islam*.

Individualism as a Crime against the Sacred Law: the Concept of *Bid'a* and Its Proximity to the Concept of *Nushūz*

Bid'a is "innovation". It is the capacity of the individual to change his or her fate, life and thoughts about people and things, and to act critically in accordance with one's own assessment of the situation. *Bid'a* is considered a deadly sin in Islamic orthodoxy. *Bid'a* is not only error, it is a crime, in that one steps out of the "right path" traced out and organised by the sacred law of the group. It is deviating from the straight path, the tariq al mustaqim, and is dangerous not only because innovators dissent from the community, but because in doing so they challenge the very existence of order based on consensus. In Islamic cosmogony, the sexes play an important role in symbolising obedience and authority. One sex can be the masters of women and the slaves of God, and that is the male sex; the other can be slaves only, and that is the female sex. In no way can women take the initiative. If they do, the whole order is in jeopardy, since their function and duty is to obey.

It is of real significance that Arabic has a special word for "women's rebellion"—*nushūz*. What happens, then, when *nushūz* occurs? What happens when women rebel and seize their own authority, refuse to obey the sacred laws in a theocracy? Did this ever happen? And if it did what was society's response? It was strong and immediate. Why? As we shall see, the resistance to women's rebellion does not concern women alone—it concerns men as well. If the women, the embodiment of duty, rebel, then what about the men who have the double role of master and slave? They are likely to be faced with the fact that their "slaves" rebel "better" than they do, and that their "slaves" exercise power and take the initiative. This, as one can imagine, undermines the whole hierarchical order.

I want to suggest through several examples that the notion of equality between men and women is profoundly threatening to the Muslim hierarchical order. The notion of a strong bond between a man and a woman, expressed in English by the word "couple," does not exist in Arabic. Arabic has fifty words for "love," but no word for "couple".[4] This linguistic lapse, far from being a random event, is as I see it, a crystal clear symbolic message in societies where rigid sex-role stereotyping is so fundamental to hierarchical order, that when women challenge the status quo they threaten not only patriarchal power (their relation to the husband), but the very existence of the entire system (and more specifically God's claim to obedience).

[4] See Fatima Mernissi, "L'Amour dans le pays Musulmans", *Jeune Afrique* Plus, Jan.–Feb. 1984, p. 23.

The inflation of words for love is, in my view, a mystification, an attempt to hide the absence of the couple in the Muslim family, which is made institutionally unstable by the practices of repudiation and polygamy.

In recent years, the threat of *nushūz*, women's rebellion, has been activated in Islam by the rise of women's consciousness regarding gender issues and by writings about women's liberation in the Muslim world. It is rooted, however, in the fears the *umma*, the Muslim community, has had for many centuries: the fear of dissent. The fear of the individual standing up to claim his or her private interests as a legitimate source of social organisation; the fear of change and innovation; the fear of division and dispersion within Islam; the fear of atomisation of the centuries old myth of group solidarity and collective spirit. The struggle of the Muslim community to maintain the myth of unity came from centuries of fighting heterogeneity and dissent, starting with the huge still unsolved problem of who should head that community. The authoritarian tradition of Islam came precisely from its expansion, its success in very different lands and cultures in Asia; Africa and Europe—all of which strengthened the authoritarian claim for unity. A claim which imperialistic interest nurtured precisely because dissent, from the start, was tearing that community apart.

In the 1980s, the fear within the *umma* is stronger than ever before, because there are threats to consensus not only from without (the West as a deadly enemy with an invading culture), but from within as well. The increasing access of the poor to education, the incredibly high social mobility, the polarisation of classes around economic issues, the emergence of women as salaried workers—all these pose a threat to the Muslim community as it traditionally viewed itself, a homogenous group.

Submission, in the Muslim tradition, has also come to include submission to God's interpreters here on earth: *khalīfs, imāms* and their empowered staff in private spheres, i.e. husbands. In the Islamic vision of human society based upon "submission" or "surrender" to God, authority flows from the top to the bottom. Every individual is integrated into a flawless order, with duties and rights clearly defined. A strong sense of belonging stems from integration into this pyramidal order, in which roles and ways of conduct are minutely defined according to age, sex and access to wealth and knowledge.

Access to knowledge is not a human right but a privilege bestowed by God upon believers. It is thus a key factor in the ordering of society. Islam is the religion of knowledge. Intelligence (*aql*) is an instrument of knowing God; with it one penetrates the meaning of the "signs" (*āyāt*) which only the elect can decode. In Islam there is no conflict between God and scientific enquiry, for the decoding of the "signs" of the universe expands our knowledge of God's might and his bewildering creation. But not all Muslims as individuals are equal in their ability to decode the signs of God, to know God, and to transcend sense and gross material involvement. Hence the necessity to rely on the group.

Submission, obedience to divine law, is for both sexes and is the duty of every Muslim who wants to strengthen the *umma*. Islam, submission, means to acknowledge the authority of the laws, not to make them. Making the law is the unique privilege of God. God makes his will known through his prophets and through signs available in our surroundings; the prophets' task is precisely to help make them accessible. There is no clergy in Islam as we are repeatedly told, but that does not mean that there is no male hierarchy controlling the understanding of the Koran's meaning. These are the elite male interpreters of the sacred laws, and when we are debating, let us say the veil issue, we are not debating how women feel about it, but what Abu hureira or Abu hanifa or Bukhari said, we are debating which male authority's opinion is the prevailing one. Not what women are feeling or desiring.

Feminists of the First Century of Islam: Sakina and Aisha

The ideal model of femininity upheld by orthodox Sunni Islam is that of an obedient woman, one who is physically modest. Such a woman does not challenge laws and orders. She veils her body and keeps it available for the husband only. Veiling goes together with a key attribute, modesty, and is the expression of the spatial confinement of women. Spatial confinement is the physical expression of women's exclusion from the public sphere, the sphere precisely of knowledge and power. This explains why Muslim conservative activists, manipulating Islam as a disciplinary framework for their claim to guide and decide for their supporters, will insist on women's modesty. Women's modesty has a wider symbolic function: it refers to the need for the believer to curb his initiative and critical judgement.

Muslim history, from the first century to the present, has had to struggle with women's refusal to conform to such models. Each century had to find a response to *nushūz* from the time of Sakina, a rebel of the 7th century (first Muslim century) to those women who presently rebel, such as those in Egypt, Algeria, Morocco and elsewhere. Women always struggled against the passive models of femininity but they never were as threatening as they are now, because women's dissent expresses itself through writing. Before, women's resistance to patriarchy was not recorded, it was oral, it confined itself to tales, proverbs or acts. A look at several instances of *nushūz* across the centuries will give us a sense of the continuing threat women rebels pose to the public realm.

Sakina's Rebellion: The First Century

Starting with the first century, *qādis* and *imāms* seem to have faced the refusal of some women to accept the Muslim laws related to veiling, seclusion, polygamy and obedience to the husband. These women refused to veil, and insisted on the right to go about freely without asking the husband's permission. They insisted on keeping the right to entertain relations with men other than their husbands, often poets with whom they could engage in intellectual exchange outside the house.

These women also refused the basic principle of Muslim marriage: the husband's authority over the wife and his right to polygamy and repudiation. They insisted on putting conditions which preserved their freedom in the marriage act, and deprived the husband of the right to change residence at will, to have many wives, or to divorce by repudiation. They therefore secured for themselves the right Islam denies a woman: the right to leave her husband when she pleases.

Muslim theologians could not prevent this first wave of women "feminists" from subverting the law because they had three assets which gave them incredible power over the *qādis* and *khalifs* in charge of enforcing law and order. The three assets were beauty, intelligence and aristocracy. This combination was enough to justify a woman's claim to *nushūz*—rebellion against the prevailing models of femininity.

The conditions Sakina put in her marriage act with one of her husbands, Zayd, made of her a celebrity and a *nashiz*, a rebellious wife. She stipulated that he would have no right to another wife, that he could never prevent her from acting according to her own will, that he would let her elect to live near her woman friend, Ummu Manshuz, and that he would never try to go against her desires. (*Aġānī* XIV, pp. 168, 169. Mada'īnī, *Kitāb al Murādafāt*, p. 66.) When the husband once decided to go against Sakina's will and went one weekend to his concubines, she took him to court, and in front of the Medina judge she shouted at him, "Look as much as you can at me today, because you will never see me again!" (*Aġāni* XVI, p. 155.)

Sakina was described by al-Zubairi, a historian who, like many others, was full of admiration for her, in these words: "She radiates like an ardent fire. Sakina was a delicate beauty, never veiled, who attended the Quraish Nobility Council. Poets gathered in her house. She was refined (*zarīfa*) and playful."

Sakina, extravagantly elegant, set the tone of fashion in the then economically thriving Hijāz, Arabia felix, where happiness and the good life were possible thanks to Islam's conquering power. The power of the Muslim empire had shifted by then from Mecca to the North, to Syria and Iraq. Rich Quraish families whose wealth had been enhanced by the triumph of Islam, lived lavishly and peacefully in the increasingly politically marginal Arabia. One example of this lavish, relaxed and hedonistic Arabian life is that not only did women copy Sakina's hairdo, but men did too! The pious Khalif 'Umar ibn'Abd al- 'Aziz felt, in time, the need to intervene and ordered his "police" to punish and shave the heads of those men who insisted on adopting Sakina's hairstyle.

Another *nashiz* of this century was 'A'isha bint Talha, the daughter of Khalif Abu Bakr through her mother. She refused to veil, and when asked why said, "God the mighty distinguished me by my beauty. I want people to see that, and acknowledge my superiority over them. I will not veil. No one can force me to do something." (*Aġāni* XI, p. 176.)

These *nashiz* who defied openly the Muslim model of female modesty and obedience were, because of their social rank, very prominent women and were, therefore, a threat to the pattern of religious authority. The theologians decided to fight back and to put a stop to *nushūz*. In law, *nushūz* is addressed as a social problem. For example, al-Muwatta (II, p. 6) states that a man has the right to take his wife where he wishes, regardless of what *nashiz* women put in their marriage contracts. Another example in al-Muwatta (II, p. 14) tries to discourage *nushūz* by stating that the husband is not bound by marriage contract conditions depriving him of his right to polygamy.

Feminism as an Internal Threat to Muslim Order: Implications of Women's *Nushūz*

Although women have had access to education only in the last few decades, they have gained an incredibly high visibility in the public sphere. In most Arab countries for example, one fourth of the university teachers are women. Although women are barred from important political posts, they have gained substantial access to middle level positions in national administrations and do strive to get a more and more important share of the salaries distributed in both private and public sectors.

Moreover, they have now started to use writing to express their desire for changing their status and the society around them. Nineteen eighty-three witnessed the appearance in Arabic of a feminist magazine in Morocco, *The Eighth of March*, which started selling 20,000 copies within the first few months. Nineteen eighty-five witnessed the publication of another "popular" magazine in Tunisia called *Nissa* (women). These examples are perceived as extremely dangerous by many conservatives, since they do not try to proselytize among elites or in university settings, but try to recruit followers from among lay persons. Feminism is no more limited to a few women's salon-like discussions; it has become identified by many women as the ground for voicing economic and political discontent which is impossible to push through trade unions and political parties. Let me simply cite three instances of women's rebellion in the present century, primarily to give a sense of the ways in which *nushūz* continues to be a threat in the Muslim world.

The first was in Algeria during the Revolution. The renowned historian Harbi, an important political figure of revolutionary Algeria, in exile since 1973, gave an interview in *Revoltes logiques* called "Women in the Algerian Revolution". It is perhaps the most discrediting documented statement on the ambiguities and hesitations of the Algerian revolution when it comes to the issue of women in relation to equality and democracy. Harbi explains that the revolutionary "brothers" were totally traditional in their contacts and encounters with women in the Maquis, the guerilla camps. They did everything they could to prevent women from escaping traditional roles, they used women for both traditional needs, such as sex and cooking, and modern needs, such as logistics and carrying arms.

This I mention in order to explain that one of the most important modern revolutions the twentieth century has witnessed, the Algerian revolution, showed that Arab society, even as it was forced to make many sacrifices and to adopt radical change, resisted violently the idea of sacrificing sexual inequality. Algerian revolutionaries hoped to keep women in their proper place, even as they fought for radical change in almost everything else.

A second example is from Tunisia. In March of 1983, the monthly journal for "democracy and socialism," *L'Avenir*, one of the voices of opposition to Bourgiba, published an interview with a Muslim feminist entitled, "I am a Rebel". Only those who knew the story behind that title could appreciate the challenge it posed.

The Muslim woman about whom the article was written was Nawal el Saadawi, the Egyptian writer, doctor and feminist. President Bourgiba who listened to the interview on television, was furious when he realized that she never mentioned his name when talking about liberation movements among Arab women. Bourgiba then gave orders to dismiss the person responsible in Tunisian television, since he had let an Arab woman talk about liberation without mentioning Bourgiba, the "Great Warrior" (al-Mujāhid al-Akbar).

For Bourgiba, a man who is one of the most advanced on the women's question, women's liberation is a man's affair. And it is true that, until the last two decades, the liberation of women was a man's prerogative. The Arab woman, according to modern Muslim thought, is a simple instrument: she will obey, when told to liberate herself according to orders. Now, for *L'Avenir* to repeat that Nawal proclaims herself a rebel is to tell Bourgiba that women rebel, sometimes even without being told to do so!

The third example is from March 1983 in Rabat. In the crowded room of the Human Rights Association, Rue Soussa, which is also the Headquarters of the Moroccan Branch of the Arab Writer's Federation, two hundred people gathered. The group became sharply divided when a number of women, most of them wives of political prisoners, started to talk about their experiences as women in an authoritarian state. They began to analyse their own daily struggle with their husbands, with the prison administration, and with the justice ministry. But all said that these latter struggles were minor compared to those with their own "revolutionary" husbands: the struggle to get their own men to rise higher than the prerogatives of husbands and the privileges of patriarchy to become real persons in relation to their militant wives. To be a political militant, they said, does not automatically liberate a man from oppressive attitudes and actions toward his wife.

The reaction in the room was very strong. Male "militants" screamed that the women were serving a conservative state and police apparatus, which tried to degrade and find fault with revolutionaries. And now women, the very wives of political prisoners, were becoming critics, enemies of the revolution!

These women decided that, for them, there is no difference between men unless that difference is materialised in action, in conduct. A leftist militant is different from a feudal lord not when he says so, but when he actually treats women differently. A woman's experience of a revolutionary man, in his intimate behaviour, is a determining criterion and guarantee of the truthfulness of his claim to be a true revolutionary. The private sphere of a political man has not only to be integrated in practice, but has to be considered one of the key determinants of his revolutionary life.

When this was said, chaos set in. The session continued for five hours, with interruptions and insults. Dialogue finally became impossible.

Conclusion: the Umma and the Challenge of Individualism(s)

Let me return, now, to the initial question: What happens when a woman disobeys her husband, who is the representative and embodiment of sacred authority, and of the Islamic hierarchy? A danger bell rings in the mind, for when one element of the whole structure of polarities is threatened, the entire system is threatened. A woman who rebels against her husband, for instance, is also rebelling against the *umma*, against reason, order and, indeed, God. The rebellion of a woman is linked to individualism, not community (*umma*); passion, not reason; disorder, not order; lawlessness (*fitna*), not law.

The battle between men and women is an aspect of the battle between good and evil, which is a fundamental form of cosmological conceptualisation not only in Islam, but in the Jewish and Christian traditions as well. The world is not only the scene of competition, but of polarisation between two great competitors. And the polarisation implies a hierarchy. One side of the hierarchy—that aligned with God—is destined to win over the devil and his allies.

The Good	*The Evil*
God	Devil (*Iblis, Satan*)
Men, Husband	Women, Wife, Desire (*as-sahwa*)
Reason	Passion (*al-hawa*)
Order	Disorder
Law	Lawlessness (*fitna*)
Obedience, Consensus	Rebellion (*nushūz*), Dissent
Pre-defined Sacred, Eternal Plan	Innovation, Freedom
The Collective Interest (*umma*)	Individualism

Recent studies have supported this dualistic way of thinking in Sunni Islam. On the parallels to the Devil, Iblis in Muslim thought, Galal al Adm's *Critique of Religious Thought (Dār al-Tālia Beyrouth* (1980) is a concise analysis of the reason-desire dualism. Fatna Ait Sabbah's *The Woman in the Muslim Unconscious* is probably one of the most recent restatements of that analogy.

Sensual involvement with the gross, material world of earthly pleasures is in the private sphere. It takes place in the domestic realm, in the women's world. In this world, access to knowledge is limited. The private sphere is at the bottom of the pyramidal hierarchy. To be a woman is to be excluded from authority (al-Sultah) and knowledge ('ilm), both being God's attributes. This is precisely what womanhood is about: to be excluded from the sphere of sacred ritualised and collective knowledge, the sphere in which decisions are made according to the divine code, orders formulated, laws promulgated. And yet the authority and knowledge of the masculine would be inconceivable without the obedience and submission of the feminine, of women.

In principle, one might say that everything in the public sphere is male. The public sphere of prophets, *imāms* and *khalifs* is monosex and homogeneous. The private sphere of women is duosex and heterogeneous; its heterogeneity comes from the existence of women. The public sphere is characterised by orders and laws; the private sphere is under the control of the representative of the public sphere, the husband. He embodies the interests of the Divine and of the law. In relation to women, the man is not in the posture of "submission," but in command.

To be a man, then, is to be *both* an obedient submitter, in the public realm, to God and his earthly surrogates, who are all males, *and* a master to whom submission is made, in the private realm, where men master women. This is the pyramidal structure of the hierarchy. And it is in this structure that *nushūz*, innovation or women's rebellion, is a threat. Innovation alters the laws, the sacred order, the privilege and hierarchy—all of which are eternal. The believer can only reinterpret; he cannot create for creation is the monopoly of God.

Thus, women's rebellion raises the entire complex of questions relating to individualism. Individual freedom, which women's rebellion represents, challenges the entire notion of community as primary. However, it is also because individualism is encroaching from another quarter that it poses such a threat when expressed by women as well. That other quarter is capitalism, which is based upon the profitability of individualistic innovation. Capitalism is seen as ferociously aggressive and fiercely individualistic. Arab countries have also become dumping grounds for capitalistic goods: western arms, films and consumer goods constitute a virtual invasion. Innovation—the freedom to doubt—is precisely what makes scientific enquiry and the western ideology of capitalism so strong and successful! And innovation is what makes women's rebellion so subversive from within.

In the struggle for survival in the Muslim world today, the Muslim community finds itself squeezed between individualistic, innovative western capitalism on the one hand, and individualistic, rebellious political oppositions within, among which the most symbolically "loaded" is that of rebellious women. The common denominator between capitalism and new models of femininity is individualism and self-affirmation. Initiative is power. Women are claiming power—corroding and ultimately destroying the foundation of Muslim hierarchy; whence the violence of the reaction and the rigidity of the response. Femininity as a symbol of surrender has to be resisted violently if women intend to change its meaning into energy, initiative and creative criticism.

The Image Inside: Women and Profession in a Socialist Country

Elisabeth Adler

The three key words of this collection—women, religion and social change—have particular relevance in the country where I come from. In the German Democratic Republic, a socialist country, the social change which has happened was radical change. For women, this meant full equality. Religion, however, is seen and functions, for the most part, as a hindrance to radical change.

Where I come from: The German Democratic Republic

In the context of the North/South division of the world, the developed and developing countries, I would like to draw attention to the fact that I come from Eastern Europe, for the difference and division between East and West is no less real. Look at the arms race! I do not come from the First or Third World, but from the Second World, although we do not call it by this name. I come from the socialist block of Eastern Europe, more precisely from the GDR. I am from Berlin, and people in the USA often ask me about living "behind the wall," referring to the wall which divides Berlin. From my perspective, of course, I live "in front of the wall," not behind. It depends, always, on one's point of view.

The GDR is a small country, less than one third of the former Germany, with 17 million inhabitants, more than half of whom are women. In a nuclear war, even in a so-called limited nuclear war, we would certainly be extinguished. The border between the two social and economic systems, the capitalist and the socialist, was established by the decision of the Allied Forces in 1945. This was an understandable and deserved consequence of the fascist Second World War, which cost the lives of twenty million Russians, five million

Poles, and six million Jews.

The Fascist period from 1933–45 was the darkest time in German history. But Hitler was not a terrible accident in our history; unfortunately the majority of the people were really for him. I cannot go into the historical reasons for this. I shall only mention one: people were looking for a strong man. For centuries, education had been geared to obedience toward fathers, patrons, or generals, and authoritarianism was the result. In the first movement for women's emancipation, even before the time of the First World War, women had spoken against war and militarism. If there was a progressive line in our recent history, I think it was upheld primarily by women. But during the Fascist period, there was a regression. The ideal woman was the mother, the mother being only at home, educating brave boys to become warriors and good girls to become mothers again.

From May 8, 1945 onward, the day of liberation from Fascism, different developments took place in West and East Germany. In the West, reconstruction and restoration took place with the help of the USA, while in the East social change took place, with the aim of establishing socialism and, finally, communism. Social change meant the breaking down of class structures and the attempt to bring about social justice and equality for all—women included. Equal opportunity, equal pay, equal rights—these were not only on paper, but put into practice. This was one of the very positive examples of social change that took place in our society.

In the GDR, I work for the church as Director of a Christian Academy, for lay women and men. Nominal membership in the churches embraces about half of the population, but in fact only one tenth of those participate in the life of the church. Only on Christmas Eve are the churches too small. The majority of Christians are Protestants, mostly of the Lutheran tradition; the minority, Roman Catholics. The churches are relics of the past, which will die out according to Marxist teaching. But church and state have found a *modus vivendi*. The 500th anniversary of Luther's birth has even caused state celebrations!

"My Profession is/is not My Life"—Women about Themselves

In the Evangelische Akademie Berlin-Brandenburg, the church institution for which I am responsible, we organise weekend conferences and evening seminars for women and men, on different subjects of current interest. Last year we offered a seminar on the theme, "My Profession is/is not My Life—Women about Themselves." The invitation described the issue this way:

> Professional work and equal status within profession are rightly regarded as important signs of women's emancipation. However it seems as if professional occupation does not have the same importance in the life of a woman as in the life of a man. Who among women would say, My profession is my life? One who has a top position? One who is single? One who has got her 'dream-profession'?

There were also quotations from Maxie Wander's famous interviews with GDR women on the invitation:

"In my professional work I regained my self-confidence."

"In my job I am absolutely equal with the men. But it is also true that this is not enough."

"How can I function well in my professional life, if my private life is not in good shape?"

The seminar was open to both men and women. About 50 women and 15 men attended the three evening sessions. Each session was introduced by two women talking about themselves. Then there were discussions in groups and in plenary. A woman psychologist reflected and commented on what was said.

Some Facts about the Women's Situation

As a background to this seminar, I would like to say something more about women's situation in the GDR. The constitution and laws provide for the equality of women. There is equal opportunity for education, equal chances for government employment and a professional career. Ninety-nine per cent of women get professional training after finishing school; 87 per cent of women between ages 16 and 60 work, or are training to work; 48 per cent of all students are women; 44 per cent of industrial workers are women; 43 per cent of agricultural workers are women; 73 per cent of education professionals, 49 per cent of medical doctors, and 33 per cent of parliament members are women.

The high percentage of working professional women is possible because the state provides for child care. Therefore 60 per cent of the children are in creches, or daycare; 89 per cent of the children are in kindergartens. Women can stay home and are paid six weeks before and twenty weeks after their first child is born. They can continue this leave from work for 26 weeks more, without being paid but keeping their jobs. Before and after the birth of the second child, they can get paid leave for one year.

The divorce rate is high. Women, being economically independent, can afford to ask for a divorce. Single mothers, divorced or unmarried, are treated as equals, and even receive special support by the state.

Thus, the problems of women in the GDR do not exist so much in the realm of rights and opportunities, but rather in the realm of self-identity and relationships. Customary roles do not change as quickly as laws. In 1975, an inquiry among 100 children was published; one of the questions put to them was, What do you see mother and father doing? They responded along rather traditional lines.

	Mother	*Father*	*Both*
Cooking meals	86	6	8
Reading books	12	76	12
Doing the laundry	95	1	4
Drinking beer	3	78	5

Of course, the division of labour changes quickly. Today, with washing machines in most households, very often the father does the laundry, in part because the realm of machines is that of men. However, women are still responsible for about two-thirds of the housework and two-thirds of children's education, according to a recent publication.

How Women Feel about Their Professional Life: Three Accounts

In the following, I present three summaries of the presentations which women gave in the seminar, "My Profession is/is not My Life," when asked to talk about themselves.

(1) **Ruth**. (Studied theology, now a social worker, married. Three children.)

"I studied theology, did my examinations, and then got married. I did some part-time work in a local congregation. Later, I worked for a doctoral thesis, which was not accepted because it did not fit into existing patterns. When I was pregnant with my first child, this meant a revolution in my self-understanding. I was no longer an individual, but a social being. I always felt that the life of the children depended upon my life. I like to be present all day at home with my children, but I also had an inferiority complex toward my intellectual friends. I read many books while the children were at school or asleep. After 13 years, I started to work again. Theology was no longer an option for me. I trained as a social worker. It was hard work to take and pass the examinations with much younger students. Now I am through, and I like my work because it is work with people. In the family we now live together as five grown-up persons."

(2) **Angelika.** (Teacher, single.)
"My profession is not my life, but I like it. I have chosen to become a teacher, although I always wanted to be a librarian. But I was afraid that I would live with my books in a "library ghetto," and lose touch with people. I am single, not really by choice. But I did not want marriage without deep love, and without full conviction of its necessity. To be single is quite normal here, and a big change in our time. In former times, I would have had to go to a monastery, or marry someone according to the will of my parents. To be single does not mean to have no personal contacts. My profession gives me both: work in my special field of literature and history, and dealings with people—pupils, colleagues and parents. My so-called private life—books, theatre, friends, and their children—is not too much separated from my professional life. My life is not split.

(3) **Kamilla.** (Medical doctor, divorced. Two children.)
"My professional work is my contribution to the life of the community. I am a medical doctor in a large clinic. I like my profession, but it is not the 'dream-profession' that some would believe. Do you remember a painting of a woman doctor after work, recently shown in an exhibition of contemporary GDR paintings? She was sitting in a chair, but not relaxed; rather dead, tired, worn out. In her face you read, "I have done what I could, but it was not sufficient." For me, my profession is my own life. In marriage, I had to give up too much of my own life, and this I could not do anymore. I feel real

tensions between my attempts to be a good medical doctor, and a responsible and loving mother. Women feel the tensions between different responsibilities more than men do. My ideal would be professional work, which is manageable without bad conscience, but which is not identical with the whole of my real life.

Points of Discussion

The discussion that emerged from these and other experiences of professional life centred around two major concerns. First, the issue of *bad conscience*. In spite of chances and opportunities for women in the GDR, we still have a "bad conscience" toward the family, toward the profession, or both. Women have to play a double role. They often feel torn apart. Is part-time work the solution? Should women refrain from accepting leadership positions? Should women sacrifice their careers?

Theoretically, most women said, no. In practice, this is often the price they pay, and bad conscience is a perpetual problem. New roles are not fully internalized. Ruth said, "I always used to have a bad conscience when I read a book." A male participant said, "I always have a bad conscience when I don't read my scientific journals."

The female writer Christa Wolf puts it this way: "Women pay for their independence with a heavier load of work and responsibility, and with bad conscience towards husband, children, household, profession, state (as superman!). Only if we overcome guilt feelings can we help the men to recognize their own imprisonment in structures of achievement and subordination."

A second recurring concern in the discussion was *self-realization*. In the seminar, few women were present who had leadership positions. Those who had, expressed their reluctance and dislike of giving orders and fitting into hierarchical structures. Women felt that men are more ambitious than they, and move more easily in the professional world, which is of their own design. Women felt that they would like to introduce different values into the professional world. Only then would self-realization be possible professionally.

Again, Christa Wolf writes: "The chances our society gave to women to do what men do, led the women to ask, 'After all, what is it that men do?' and, 'Do we want to do this?' Women don't want to specialize. More and more they want, rather, wholeness. They don't want to function in male structures. They don't want to dominate and to subdue, but to cooperate and trust. They no longer ask for equality, but look for new styles of life." ("Berohrung," Essay, 1978).

This case study of the seminar at the Evangelische Akademie is useful for our understanding of women in the GDR, for the seminar revealed both the problems and the hopes we have as women. Women accept and use the equality which our society guarantees. They are now seen and heard as never before, especially through their professional work. Women seek their own identity in work, and in personal relations, striving for wholeness. Women question the man-made professional world with its orientation toward material gains and success, and they try to introduce new values—cooperation, trust, relationship, and community. And women try to cooperate with men in changing attitudes, values and lifestyles, knowing that only together will they succeed.

PART THREE

CHANGING LEADERSHIP ROLES: RELIGIOUS INSTITUTIONS AND WOMEN'S CHALLENGE

Introduction

Not every religious tradition has an ordained or consecrated leadership, but in those that do the question of who is ordained to fill leadership roles is an important one for women. It is a question that must not be minimized, for the image of women is shaped not only by the myths of the past, but by the roles which women claim, and transform, in the present. And indeed, as women claim leadership roles they do transform those roles and challenge the prevailing image of woman and the prevailing notions and styles of leadership. These presentations explore the issue of women's access to and leadership in central religious roles.

For the most part, religious authority has long been the domain of men. Rabbis, priests, imams, brahmins and monks have been vested with the ritual roles, the interpretive authority, and the leadership of the traditions, whether by calling or by birth. This is not the entire story, of course. India has had its women saints and gurus, and there are countless local leaders of women's own systematic tradition of rites and rituals. In many parts of Africa, women did indeed have priestly roles in traditional religions. With the intrusion of a Christian tradition which held women in low esteem, this began to change. Now the twentieth century move for women's ordination in many African Protestant churches has meant arguing again for a level of authority women once had! Finally, in virtually every culture the heart of the religious tradition, at the local level and in the home, is performed, maintained and transmitted by women. Here again, one confronts an old and pervasive disjunction: the indomitable presence and influence of women at the domestic and grass-roots level, and the virtual absence of women at the public level.

In the Christian and Jewish traditions, the question of women's ordination to the priesthood or rabbinate has been central for at least two decades. It is, of course, inextricably related to other questions: the transformation of sexist and patriarchal ritual and theological language, and the reinterpretation of scriptural traditions from the perspective of women.

Since both the Christian and Jewish traditions are pluralistic, change has not occurred evenly in either tradition. In the Jewish tradition, for instance, the Reformed and Reconstructionist traditions have now had women rabbis for about ten years. The Conservative tradition voted in 1983 to admit women to its rabbinical schools in preparation for ordination. The Orthodox tradition, however, is still closed to the possibility of women rabbis.

Constance Parvey was the fifth woman to be ordained in the Lutheran Church in America. That was in 1972. She reminds us that the first conference on the ordination of women was held in Boston in 1882, and some denominations, such as those which formed the United Church of Christ, have ordained women since the late 19th century. However, most Protestant denominations did not move to ordain women to the ministry until the middle of the 20th century; the United Methodist Church began ordaining women in 1956, for example. In 1974, the famous "irregular ordination" of eleven women to the Episcopal priesthood took place, an ordination performed by bishops supportive of women's vocation to the priesthood. Not until 1978 did the Episcopal church vote positively to receive these women's ordination. At the time of the Harvard conference in 1983, the Church of England was still resistent to the ordination of women, but in 1984 it finally voted to move in principle towards it, by referring the issue to each diocese. The Roman Catholic Church however, issued a Declaration Against the Ordination of Women in 1976, and the churches of the Orthodox tradition still do not ordain women and maintain that it is not an issue in their tradition as priests.

In this chapter, **Judith Plaskow**, a Jewish feminist theologian, carries forward some of the themes and questions we have explored in the previous chapter, especially the question, Who defines women? Women and women's roles have often been defined by the religious tradition; now Jewish women must take up the task of their own self-definition. Judith's presentation is not focussed on the rabbinate, but on the related and much broader issues of the definition of woman in the Jewish legal system. It is not enough to be included in structures that remain the same, she argues. It is not enough for women to be counted in a minyon, a quorum for prayer; women must also write the prayers that are said. The work of Judith Plaskow, a Professor of Religion at Manhattan College, has made a major contribution to the religious critique of androcentrism. Her book *Womanspirit Rising*, edited with Carol Christ, is a landmark in feminist thought.

Sandra Wilson is an Episcopal priest. She is the rector, or priest in charge, of St. Mark's Episcopal Church in Bridgeport, Connecticut. She is the first woman rector in the diocese of Connecticut and the first Black woman ordained to the priesthood in the churches of the Anglican communion in the world. As an economist, Sandra worked for a time in New York City. After her studies at Union Theological Seminary, she worked in suburban and rural parishes, before being called to Bridgeport. Here Sandra examines her own experience in the hierarchy of the Episcopal Church and sees parallels with the dilemmas and experiences of women and Blacks in hierarchies everywhere. She also describes the resistance of some members of her parish to the new style of leadership which she brought to her work.

Daphne Hampson comes with quite a different experience, that of having worked very hard to gain the right for women to be ordained in the Anglican Churches in Britain. She herself had felt called to the priesthood, but was blocked by the position of the Anglican Communion regarding women's ordination. She earned a doctorate in History at Oxford, followed by a doctorate in Theology at Harvard Divinity School. Daphne is now a Lecturer in Systematic Theology at the University of St. Andrews in Scotland. She expresses here both the pain and the insight of the many women who have struggled unsuccessfully to participate more fully in the Christian community. Daphne argues that it is not simply the priesthood that is patriarchal and sexist, but the whole of the tradition, with its ideological underpinnings in a dominant, patriarchal God. Having left this tradition behind, Daphne continues nonetheless to work as a theologian—struggling with questions of religion, community and God from outside the confines of a patriarchal Christian tradition.

All three of these papers raise in various ways *the* question of religious feminists: Can the tradition be changed, reformed and reformulated from within? Or are the structure and the presuppositions of the tradition so fundamentally awry that women must find new life outside the tradition, in exodus?

The struggle for legitimacy and recognition is one in which women in Buddhist countries have also been engaged. The Buddhist tradition, like Christianity, is an historical tradition which catalyzed around the life of an individual, in both cases a man. In both cases there developed monastic as well as lay traditions. Christian monasticism was open to both monks and nuns. The vocation to a life of chastity and service to God was, in fact, considered honourable for women. To be a nun or woman religious was not, however, to have any priestly role. Male priests would come to the convents to administer the sacraments. In the Buddhist tradition, there was an early controversy about whether or not women could be admitted to the *samgha*, the community of ascetic seekers who have taken up the way of the Buddha. After some deliberation and with reservation, it is said, the Buddha finally decided to accept nuns (*bhikkunīs*) as well as monks (*bhikkhus*) into the *samgha*. Aside from the *samgha* there is no Buddhist "priesthood" quite comparable to the rabbinate or Christian priesthood, although in Japan monks who serve temples are often called "priests". In a sense, one might say that the issue of women's access to central roles in the tradition was "solved" in the time of the Buddha, but the order of the nuns has not been consistently strong through the ages. In places the order has disappeared, and where it exists, the status of nuns in relation to monks has been highly problematic.

In her presentation, **Chatsumarn Kabilsingh**, Assistant Dean of the Faculty of Liberal Arts at Thammasat University in Thailand, reviews the history of the Bhikkhuni Samgha, which died out in South Asia after about the 11th century. She examines the low status within Thailand of a category of partially ordained women called *ji* or *mae chi*, and sets out the prospects for the revival of the Bhikkhuni Samgha in Thailand. The pioneer in that revival is Chatsumarn's mother, the Venerable Voramai Kabilsingh, who obtained full ordination from the order of Buddhist nuns in Taiwan and has returned to Thailand to generate an order there. In the past year, Chatsumarn had started the *Newsletter on International Buddhist Women's Activities*, to link Buddhist women throughout the world by providing information on Buddhist women's activities and on the current worldwide status of the Bhikkhunī Samgha.

Kumiko Uchino is a Japanese scholar, with a doctorate in Sociology from Keio University in Japan, who looks at the history of Buddhist nuns of the Soto Zen sect in the Japanese context. She discusses the low status of nuns and their subjugation to monks during the Meiji era in the late 19th century, and then the emergence of a new era of self-consciousness with the establishment of the Soto Nuns' Organization in the early 20th century. The repeated proposals and petitions of the Nuns' Organization to the Soto Assembly, and the gradual accumulation of gains and achievements is a story which women of many religious traditions and cultures will recognize. With its full documentation of the Soto Nuns' Organization, this paper makes a unique contribution to understanding the goals and strategies of one particular women's movement within the Buddhist tradition.

The Wife/Sister Stories: Dilemmas of the Jewish Feminist

Judith Plaskow

Speaking as a *Jew* from the *Jewish* feminist perspective, I want to explore the complex situation in which the Jewish feminist finds herself, and the particular dilemma of one who seeks to forge a Jewish identity for herself in the midst of a culture that cannot imagine why she would bother.

My jumping off point is a Biblical passage or, actually, a series of passages which, to my mind, are paradigms of the Jewish woman's situation. Three times in the Biblical book of Genesis, twice with reference to Abraham and once with reference to Isaac, we are told that one of the patriarchs, spurred by famine in the land of Canaan, journeyed to a strange land with his wife in search of food. Afraid that the people of the land would kill him in order to be able to marry his beautiful wife, the patriarch asked her to say she was his sister in order that he might be treated well on her account. In the narratives concerning Abraham, the king then takes Sarah into his house on the assumption she is Abraham's sister, only to be punished or threatened with punishment by God for taking another man's wife. The king, realizing what has happened, indignantly confronts Abraham with his deception.

Three years ago, I was teaching a course in feminist theology at a Jewish conference at which there was also a course on the Jew as a stranger. A few days into the conference, one woman defected from the stranger course to mine.[1] The teacher of this course had begun by using his wife/sister stories to illustrate the relation of the Jew to Gentile culture. Abraham, the first Jew, afraid of rejection by what

[1] The defector was Martha Ackelsberg who first spurred me to think about these stories.

he perceived as a hostile society set up a situation in which he was bound to be rejected. "That's very interesting and useful," my woman friend said, "but what about what Abraham does to Sarah?" "Oh," the class groaned, "not the women's issue again; that's not what we're talking about here."

My class, of course, was more than happy to talk about the issue, and ever since, these stories have fascinated me. They seem to me to capture perfectly the position of the Jewish woman as the "other's other". In these stories, the male Jew, perceiving himself—however rightly or wrongly—as "other" in a Gentile culture uses the woman as a buffer between himself and that culture, doubling her otherness. Thus Abraham recapitulates in relation to Sarah his own relation to the wider culture. The male Jew as other in turn defines as other the woman who shares his otherness with him. And Sarah's capacity, the Jewish woman's capacity to demur from this situation is hampered by the fact that there may be real danger out there. Perhaps the Egyptians or Abimelech *would* have killed Abraham, and thus how could Sarah refuse to go along with his ruse?

This is one way of looking at the Jewish feminist dilemma. In addition to illustrating women's situation as other, it helps us understand part of the reason why Jewish feminists have been less radical in our criticism of tradition than our Christian sisters: we are afraid of being without allies. But I don't want to focus on the precariousness of the Jewish woman's situation because in fact Jewish feminists *are* refusing our otherness both in the tradition and in the wider culture. Like other women, we are taking upon ourselves the right to define ourselves rather than having our place and our being defined for us. Judaism, like all other traditions, is a patriarchal tradition we are trying to transform.

It has become clear, however, that while we may share a common commitment to change, the specific content and texture of our situations is very different. What does it mean to be "other" in the Jewish tradition, and what does it mean to move beyond that otherness? The central category of Jewish religious life from the first century to the end of the 18th century was *halachah* or law. Deprived of the Temple and its sacrificial cult by the Roman destruction of Jerusalem, the Jews developed a portable religiosity based on prayer and the study and elaboration of Biblical texts. While this textual elaboration, or *midrash* as it is called, was partly narrative and theological, legal *midrash*, the application of legal texts to everyday situations, has had a certain priority in Jewish life. Women's situation has been defined, then, not so much by a set of ideas or concepts but by a legal system which seeks to realize the reality of God in every detail of human existence. Statements or opinions about women help us to understand the context of the law, but women are defined, first of all, by what they can and cannot and must *do*.

This does not mean, however, that we can generate from the law a comprehensive statement of women's position. The many laws pertaining to women in Jewish sources do not add up and are not intended to add up to an overarching statement of her position and status, and the search for such a statement leads to contradiction.[2] Analysis of patterns of women's "exclusion and participation"[3] as they appear in Jewish law makes clear that there are areas of obligation men and women share, areas from which women are excluded, and areas in which the law provides female oriented rituals. Thus feminists can focus on aspects of Jewish texts which assume women's subordination, and apologists on those aspects which seem to support "equality in difference," but only because both are imposing a foreign category on the literature.

These considerations, however, while cautionary, do not prevent us from making certain generalizations. First, whatever the legal sources have to say about women, good or bad, there is a sense in which women's real concerns are not represented. As Jacob Neusner has pointed out, women become important or are taken notice of in the law precisely when they ruffle the smooth ordering of things.[4] When a woman is about to leave a marriage or leave her father's house to enter into one, or when she has taken a vow or is suspected of having committed adultery, the law then becomes interested in her. When her sexuality rears its head in a potentially threatening way, or she is about to be at the centre of an important property transfer, the law must step in to regularize her irregularity and ensure her return to the normal state of daughter/wife/motherhood. But if we want to know how women functioned daily as mothers,

[2] Jonathan Webber, "Between Law and Custom: Women's Experience of Judaism," *Women's Religious Experience*, Pat Holden, ed. (1983).

[3] The term is Rita Gross's, a feminist scholar and co-editor with Nancy A. Falk of *Unspoken Worlds: Women's Religious Lives in Non-Western Cultures*.

[4] Jacob Neusner, "Mishnah on Women: Thematic or Systemic Description," *Marxist Perspectives* (Spring 1980).

wives and workers—let alone what they themselves felt about these roles—the texts tell us next to nothing. In fact, Neusner says he cannot think of a single sentence in the *Mishnah*, an important code of law, dealing with women as mothers.

Second, insofar as women's concerns are not represented by the legal texts, we do not really get from them a picture of women as moral agents. The question has been raised of how moral roles and models for women in Judaism are different from those for men. Insofar as the legal sources address only specific male concerns about regularizing women, the texts give us women not as actors but as persons acted upon. Here, I think the wife/sister stories, although narrative texts, are again instructive because they indicate that once women are defined relationally, we get to see their decision making only as circumscribed by particular sets of relations. Sarah can, in a variety of ways, make the best of a bad situation, but we do not get to see her formulating her moral choices from her own perspective.

Third—and for me, this is the most important point—the invisibility of women cannot be remedied within the legal structure. In fact, the Jewish feminist movement of the last ten years has focused largely on *halachah* and the rectification of certain problems it raises for women. For example, according to Jewish law, women are not required to put on a prayer shawl or phylacteries or say the *she'ma* three times daily. But since in Jewish law, one who is not obligated to perform a commandment has a lower status in its performance than one who is obligated, women cannot form part of the minyon or quorum for prayer made up of those obligated to pray. Divorce is another important feminist issue. According to Jewish law, only a man can write and deliver the *get* or divorce decree which ends a Jewish marriage. This means that in a case in which a man cannot or will not give his wife a *get*, she is forever prevented from remarrying.

These concerns can and have been addressed within a halachic framework, and adjustments have been made. In fact, the tradition has been trying for hundreds of years to remedy the inequity of the divorce laws by finding ways to get a recalcitrant husband to give his wife a *get*. But these only partially successful efforts reveal very clearly that the desire to render justice to women is secondary to the preservation of the halachic system. For really the only way to solve the problem of divorce is to give women equal agency, to allow them to write a *get*. But this is precisely what has not been and cannot be done within the traditional framework, because it would entail a recognition of women's situation as women, which goes beyond the system. It is to just such a recognition, however, that we as feminists are committed. Once we begin to see women as a class, and gender as a central category for the analysis of any culture or tradition, we are bound to break out of a system which renders women's status invisible. At this stage, in any case, a feminist Judaism must insist upon the importance of women's experience and, thus, on shaking up the categories and processes of Jewish life and thought.

I must add that, although I have been speaking about traditional Judaism, these last comments apply equally to liberalism. Over the past 150 years, the various forms of liberal Judaism—Reform, Conservative, Reconstructionist—have to different degrees rejected the binding authority of the law and with it the place assigned to women. Gradually, women have gained access to Jewish education, to the right to participate in synagogue ritual and—in the last ten years—even to the rabbinate. Women are now ordained as Reform and Reconstructionist rabbis and will soon be admitted to the Conservative seminary. While I do not want to underestimate the importance of these changes and the possibilities they have opened to women, since they are what enable me to question the tradition today, it remains the case that these changes have come out of a liberal commitment to equality which entirely fails to recognize that *real* equality of women is not the same as integrating women into male institutions and systems. Reform Judaism in particular, which is the oldest of these movements, assumed that if it abolished women's traditional legal status, women would simply become equal without there being any need to attend to the nature of or barriers to their equality. Thus, Reform has had no vocabulary for understanding why it took 140 years for the first woman to be ordained or what these ordinations yet portend. In other words, a thoroughgoing feminist analysis is as important to liberal Judaism as it is to Orthodox Judaism, although liberalism provides more space in which this analysis can be performed.

Let me reiterate, however, that insistence on feminist criticism is made more difficult by Jewish feminist awareness that feminist criticism of Judaism provides fuel for anti-Semites. According to the new feminist form of anti-Semitism, Christianity can perhaps be redeemed from sexism, but for some strange reason, Judaism cannot. Actually, I think this is a problem Jews share with Muslim women:

sexism becomes an excuse for dismissing a tradition which may be oppressive differently, but is really no more or less oppressive than the tradition of those doing the dismissing.

Let me also address the other side of the Jewish feminist situation: the theological and material resources for change which the Jewish tradition provides. Sometimes the situation of the Jewish women feels to me like Wittgenstein's duck/rabbit: a simple figure that from one perspective appears to be a duck, from another a rabbit, but one that is hard to see as both at the same time. I use this image to express my sense of the duality of the Jewish woman's situation. Sometimes I perceive the Jewish tradition as the oppressor of women, systematically negating and excluding our experience, making us the "other's other". Obviously this is the perspective from which I have spoken thus far. But at other times, I look at the strength of Jewish women and see this perception as absurd. I know that we as Jewish women have not necessarily experienced ourselves as oppressed, and that the experience of non-oppression is not simply a matter of false consciousness—although I do not deny the reality of false consciousness—but comes out of a real history of integrity and power.

First, we American feminists, for the last fifteen years, have been trying to create womanspaces in which we could come together out of our fathers' and husbands' houses and share our experiences and visions as women. But in traditional Judaism, with its sharp sex role division, women have always had and still have that womanspace. Whether it was in the market or the ritual bath, or whether it was in the form-creating idle chatter of the women's side of the synagogue, women shared a common life that we deeply desire and yet lost when liberal Judaism gave us the precious right sometimes to act as men. What women did with this common life is now our task to discover. For example, what have the rituals surrounding menstruation meant to women? Anthropological evidence suggests that blood taboos which appear very oppressive to women can and have been used by women to their own ends. Was this true in the Jewish tradition, and how? Or Rosh Hodesh, the celebration of the new moon, which was traditionally a women's holiday and which contemporary Jewish feminists are recovering and developing—what did it mean to women and how did it affect their lives? What can it mean to us?

Second, the Jewish male ideal is the scholar spending his time in uninterrupted study. This fact, combined with the precariousness of the Jewish economic situation in many times and places, gave women an important and sometimes crucial role in economic life. In the middle ages, for example, Jewish women were involved in a variety of occupations some of which involved travel away from their families for extended periods of time. While the economic importance of women necessitated certain changes in Jewish civil law—so that women would be responsible for their own debts, for instance—it is unclear whether it had any impact on their religious status. Bernadette Brooten has demonstrated, through examination of inscriptional evidence, that in a very early period of Jewish history, women seem to have played some leadership role in the synagogue.[5] Whether this correlated with some particular economic role in the community or whether there were other periods of female religious leadership is still being explored. But even if we find no correlation between significant economic roles for women and improvement of their religious status, we cannot ignore the impact of economic role on women's sense of self. Thus, if the duck is exclusion of women from public religious life, the rabbit is a role acknowledged by the whole community as vital and one which must have provided women with a sense of energy and worth.

I do not mean to suggest for one minute that either of these points obviates the need for change. It is clear that womanspaces, like halachic tinkering, can help preserve an unjust system by rendering it bearable and providing shared self-validation which does not threaten the status-quo. The challenge is to use those spaces in a way which is transforming, knowing that we have not invented them, that we have a heritage of power to draw on.

Being the "other's other," we can use this power to articulate our claim to justice in a tradition which already partially knows our situation. I began by suggesting that Sarah shares with Abraham a sense of strangerhood which is recapitulated in her own relation to him. "Our ancestors were strangers in the land of Egypt"—this is where the Jewish story begins. As one Jewish feminist has pointed out, however, this shared experience can provide the basis for a new *halachah* and a new ethic which demands of the Jewish male the

[5] Bernadette Brooten, *Women Leaders in the Ancient Synagogue*, California: Scholar's Press, 1982.

same decency he demands of the community at large.[6] A decent Gentile should not join a golf club which excludes Jews; a decent Jew should not join a synagogue which excludes women. A decent Gentile should not attend a medical school which does not admit Jews; a decent Jew should not study at a Yeshivah which closes Talmud study to women. These are the injunctions to which liberal Judaism has already responded, but they are not enough.

We are not stopping here. We are also using our power to reclaim our heritage in an ongoing *midrash* which places Sarah at the centre. I mentioned earlier that Jewish religiosity is based on the elaboration of Biblical texts. The wife/sister motif is no exception: the tradition plays with it in a variety of ways. Abraham committed a great sin in risking Sarah's honour, says one commentator. He failed to trust in God, says another, for God would have delivered him from famine in Canaan. The second time Abraham passed off Sarah as his sister, the *midrash* tell us, he did not ask her permission, for he knew she would refuse. The commentators know there's a problem. They circle round; they circle round. They're still concerned with Sarah's beauty, the immorality of the Egyptians, Sarah's honour defined in terms of her availability to only one man. But the process does not stop there. It is also in our hands. Judaism is open. We think we know something of what Sarah felt, and much more will we uncover and come to know. We are telling and retelling our own stories. We are speaking as Jewish feminists, taking self-definition into our own hands.

[6] Esther Ticktin, "A Modest Beginning," *Response* (Summer, 1973).

“Which me will survive all these liberations...” On Being a Black Woman Episcopal Priest

Sandra Wilson

At this point in history every woman’s story is an intensely personal story. I hope to show in the particularity of my struggle, some of the universality of the struggle of many women in hierarchies. I speak as a Black, American, Woman, Priest in the Episcopal Anglican Church in the USA. The Episcopal Church is known here as a white, male, elitist, hierarchical church, and the priest is too often considered the “little god” of the parish.

I have been a part of the Episcopal Church all of my life, as has my family for the five generations before me. Many people ask how on earth I wandered into the Episcopal Church. Surely I must have been a Baptist originally. I was not. However, as a young person, I began to learn the rules of being in the Episcopal Church as a Black. I learned, as I moved out of the soft cocoon of my childhood parish, that Black people in the Episcopal Church were merely tolerated, and that there was much information that was not being passed our way. As I grew up a little more, I began to understand that lack of access to information for Blacks in the Episcopal Church meant that we would obviously stay in our assigned places: those tolerated people who help others to feel that the church is somehow integrated, although there need be no interaction.

As our role in the church became clearer to me, I decided to become a student of history and I discovered that Blacks too have a history in the Episcopal Church in the United States. Through many articles and books, the white roots of the Episcopal Church, dating back to the settlement of Jamestown, Virginia, are common knowledge, as are the achievements, the power and the glory of its elitist members. But Black history in the Episcopal Church also dates back to Jamestown, for the people who came to Jamestown did not come by themselves to do their own work. The Black people who were brought to serve as servants, as slaves, took on the religion of their masters. So we Blacks have a stake and a claim in this church, even though it considers us marginalized people. It is a stake and claim with which we must today force the church to deal.

I use the church as my case study, but what I have to say is, I believe, applicable to Black women in institutions in all of society. The model of hierarchy here is this: At the top of the ladder is the "WASP," White Anglo-Saxon Protestant, male. Next is the WASP female, followed by the non-WASP male, the non-WASP female, the Black male and, of course, at the bottom of the ladder, the Black female. Now, there is also a hierarchical structure in the Episcopal Church. Among the ordained clergy there are three orders. The lowest order is that of the deacons; the next order is that of the priests; and the third and highest order, that of the bishops. Within any particular local church one might be, again in order from the bottom, a deacon in training; a curate or assistant in the parish; an associate rector; or a rector, the one who has been duly elected and given responsibility as the chief pastor of the parish. One can also be a bishop. However, as we know, that office is not yet open to women.

Women have been ordained in the Episcopal Church in the United States since January 1, 1977. There are, at last count, 630 women ordained. Of that number, eight are Black women; 32 are rectors of parishes; and of those 32, there is but one Black female rector. Looking again at the history of the church, one can see that Black men have been priests in the Episcopal Church since the 17th century. And yet, after 300 years there are 380 Black men as priests in the church. And after less than a decade, there are 630 women priests in the church. That makes my position rather difficult , as I find myself standing on the margins as both a Black person and a woman.

What is it to be a rector? I was elected by a parish, after it had adamantly insisted that it would not even interview a woman. It is a radically conservative parish. However, our bishop has affirmative action policies. He provides the parish with a list of candidates, on every list there is a woman, and they are bound by the bishop to interview her. My committee has since told me that, on the night of my interview, they called all around trying to get every person on the committee to have a different illness, so that they would not show up! But they arrived, and I arrived. And somehow, in the movement of the Holy Spirit, they were able to envision, after they had laid eyes on a woman priest for the first time in their lives, the possibility of a woman as their pastoral leader and spiritual guide. After the election took place, I took my place, as the bishop said in the letter of institution, as a "full member, ready to take my share in the councils of the Church," and as a fully tenured person. This election is for "life," and as we are fond of being reminded, the priest gets to determine how long "life" will be.

What happens, then, to the Black woman and to others on the hierarchical ladder, when the Black woman, through election, moves out of the assigned spot on the bottom and ascends to meet the WASP male in a position of responsibility and authority in the hierarchy? It is then that those who feel that they are more deserving, and who feel that the hierarchy exists to provide orderly ascent, begin to rebel and work for the destruction of the one who has got out of line. It is then we understand that racism is not simply a male prerogative. It is then that we begin to see the next person down the ladder from the WASP man, pulling her sister down.

This long-standing model finds the white male profitting, as usual, from the ensuing fight. In any institution run by white males there is a need for coalition building among all on the lower rungs. We need to understand our interconnectedness and interrelatedness as members of the fractured family of God, and to understand that the movement forward of the Black woman is *our* movement forward. We need to understand that the destruction of the Black woman is, as well, a destruction of ourselves. Simply removing the Black woman does not guarantee that any of those in the other positions on the ladder will get her position. What it generally guarantees is that we will have left yet another spot clear for the white male.

In this context, the ethical questions are: How do we join forces collectively? How does this transformation from ladder hierarchy to group begin to take place? Can the ascent of the Black woman ever be meaningful to anyone, other than her? On whose terms will she be successful? I do not think that any of this can happen until some kind of a supportive community emerges. We must begin with a commitment to the transformation of our sisters, so that we can somehow envision and work for a structure that is much less like this ladder and much more like a circle. For it is only then that all those on this ladder who feel that they have been stepped upon by the one who was "ascended" from the bottom, will be able in some way to share in the transformation of community that represents.

The institutional church in the Black community has been an integral cultural and social force in our lives, throughout our history in the United States. During the time of slavery, it was the one institution in which words of hope were spoken, were sung and, most importantly, were believed. Ministers have always been the leaders in the Black community. They have been more influential than any others in organizing and mobilizing masses of people. The church was an integral part of my life from the earliest stages of childhood. My little Episcopal Church was Black. It was a community. It was love. This church, together with my family, instilled in me a sense of the need to serve humanity, and also a sense of the necessity for fighting. The times in which we now live are no less difficult than the times in which the church first had its rise. And we are finding in the Black community that people are coming back to the institutional church, more and more of them, to find a word of hope to be spoken, to be prayed, to be sung, and to be believed.

I believe that the Black Church is trying to take seriously its responsibility to all who are in the midst of poverty. It must minister to those in material poverty, and must also minister to those who are deeply in the midst of spiritual poverty. It must nourish them with things spiritual, that they might not only look around themselves, but also reach out and reach back, and enable other folks to have life. Somehow the Black Church, as it deals with the pain and frustration of everyday life, needs, more than ever before, to reach each ache.

But the Episcopal Church is not the Black Church, with its sense of community. And in order to survive in the Episcopal Church, one needs support. The community model is hierarchical. What one finds in this hierarchical community are often subtle attempts at the annihilation of the Black woman. There are three steps. The first step is isolation. We leave you alone. We isolate you from all support systems, and we have begun the process of annihilation. The second step is rejection. If, after the isolation, we can reject all that you stand for, and convince others to reject you, then the battle is won. The third step is accomplished: annihilation. But we must understand that to annihilate the Black woman is to annihilate ourselves.

I dreamed as a young child of being a priest. I was a great embarrassment to my family because, at about age eight or nine, when the priest would bless the church at the end of the service, I would sit in church and bless him back. My parents said, "You can't do that!" So, I would go home after church and set up the piano stool, and get the oil and vinegar cruettes from the dinner table, and a piece of white bread, and a cookie cutter, and I would celebrate the communion. Needless to say, my parents had serious problems with this. I dreamed, however, not of being a little man priest, but of being a full woman priest.

Some fifteen years ago, as this call to the priesthood manifested itself, I came to understand that getting through the hierarchy of the church is not a matter of just doing the right things. One cannot simply dream of becoming a priest, and have it happen. One must begin to know the system, and to find supporters within the system, and to work with others, enabling one another to stand up and to fight. One has to be willing to fight, so that one can enable others to follow, so that one can reach around and enable others to dream their dreams.

In my priesthood and that of my sisters we are trying very hard to bring people to the presence of God—a presence that is both female and male. On my first Sunday as rector in my parish in Bridgeport, people piled into the church, and there were chairs in the aisles and they were waiting to see what this new person was going to say. So I explained to them what I like to call my "sheep-dog theology". Very often at ordinations, we read from the Gospel of St. John, "I am the Good Shepherd. The Good Shepherd knows his sheep, and the sheep know Me." Then someone ascends into the pulpit and explains to the new ordinand, "You are about to become the shepherd. Care for your flock well." The ordinand sits there on that first day, nodding. I believe strongly, however, that priesthood finds itself in a different analogy, that of the sheep-dog: an animal, just like the sheep, working in the midst of the fold, who sometimes gets dirty or mangy, who sometimes loses the way, but whose primary responsibility it is to round up the sheep, and to move them toward the Shepherd, whom we both serve.

I explained this, and it was rejected by many people, for they did not want a sheep-dog. They wanted a shepherd. They wanted a "little god," to deify, to put up on a pedestal. I have been dealing with that rejection and we continue to go back and forth between shepherd and sheep-dog. I do not feel ordained to be a "little god," for I do not understand priesthood in that way.

This experience gives an example of the kinds of rejection we will all face as we try to spin out new patterns, as we try to look at new ways of expressing who it is that we are. We must not be deterred by the rejection. We must not be deterred from spinning out new patterns. The power is there. We just need the strength to follow out what we know.

As a young girl growing up in the South, I learned the privileges of being white and male quite early. But I had these remarkable parents who insisted, "You can do anything you want to do, as long as you are willing to work hard enough to do it. And we will support you. We may not always have the money to support you, but we will support you spiritually and emotionally." The challenge to me was to turn insult into opportunity and to learn how to use the very system of hierarchy that was used against me, to rise—and to help others to rise. Let me give you some examples of what I encountered along the way.

When I was a freshman in college, I arrived in my intensive German class and encountered a member of the American Nazi party. He was a delightful man, but he did not want me in his class. So he called me out and said, "You lack the ability to learn German, because Black people cannot learn foreign languages. But I am going to give you a choice. You may stay in this class and expect to fail at the end of the year. Or you may withdraw now, and pass." I had never failed at anything before and was devastated that he would make a suggestion like this. But, after consultation with many people, I decided to get out. I went on with my work in college, determined to prove him a liar one day. And that day did come. I applied to intensive German studies programmes, spent five months in Germany at the Goethe Institute studying, and went on to the University of Vienna to study theology and economics—all in German. And I did well, and came back, and tried to have a conversation with a friend outside his office, and he got up and slammed his door. That was a kind of victory. I could have carried his condemnation around for the rest of my life.

In my first parish, the rector and I would stand at the altar rail on Sunday mornings. He would be handing out communion, and I would be handing out communion, and people would stand in line down the aisle on his side of the communion rail as my side was empty. We talked about this, and I suggested the parishioners were upset because I was a woman. He said they were probably more upset because I was Black. In that same parish, I experienced women's rebellion against a woman's ordination. For example, my vestments hung in the closet next to the rector's vestments, week after week, and I concluded that mine were not being washed, while his were. I spoke to the Altar Guild and got the response, "You're a woman. You can wash your own clothes!"

Last year, while teaching at a college and working as a University chaplain, several white women made an appointment to see me. They said, "We realize that you are probably very qualified to be here, but we want you to know that we will not be coming to see you this year because we do not feel that there is anything that a Black woman could possibly have to tell us." One final example: this year I was appointed to the Commission on Ministry of our Diocese, which examines candidates for priesthood. Not along ago, one of my colleagues, a white woman priest, asked, "What committees are you on in this Diocese?" When I told her, her response was, "Well, what did you have to do, with whom, to get that position!?"

Somehow we need to begin to understand that the destruction of the Black woman is, indeed, our own destruction. Black women in our churches today have a heritage of strength and faith, and we must continue to be strong in character and in faith. We must reach other brothers and sisters with a sense of the commonality of our struggles, on behalf of Black people and on behalf of all humanity. We must continue to work within the walls of the church, challenging theological pace-setters and challenging church bureaucrats. We also must continue to push outward the church walls, so that it may truly serve the community. We must ever be aware of our infinite worth, of our Godliness in the midst of our creatureliness, and of our ultimate liberation from the barriers of sex, of race, and even of the church, into a community of believers. I conclude with a poem from Audre Lorde, "Who Said It Was Simple":

There are so many roots to the trees of anger
that sometimes the branches shatter
before they bear.
Sitting in Nedicks

the women rally before they march
discussing the problematic girls
they hire to make them free.
An almost white counterman passes
a waiting brother to serve them first
and the ladies neither notice nor reject
the slighter pleasures of their slavery.
But I who am bound by my mirror
as well as my bed
see causes in colour
as well as sex.

and sit here wondering
which me will survive
all these liberations.

Women, Ordination and the Christian Church

Daphne Hampson

At the time I left the church in 1981, I had for twenty years wanted to be ordained. I had, during the previous three years, given all my strength and energies to trying to get women ordained in the Anglican Churches in Britain. I was the chairperson of the Group for the Ministry of Women in the Scottish Episcopal Church, which I with others had founded. This was the first movement within an Anglican Church in Britain to embrace a broad spectrum of opinion in the church and to be actively engaged in campaigning on every level. We were highly organised. (The English movement for the Ordination of Women was later founded.) I also took a major part in the English campaign. I was the person who wrote the theological statement circulated to all members of the General Synod of the Church of England before the unsuccessful vote on women's ordination in 1978.

I want to speak, firstly, about what it felt like in the campaign; secondly, to discuss the nature of that campaign and the issues which have been raised; and thirdly, to reflect briefly on the future for women in their thinking about God. In recent years I have been keen that people not confuse "religious" with "Christian". Leaving the church was, I am sure, made easier in my case by the fact that my allegiance to basic Christian doctrines—Trinity and Incarnation—had always been weak and was fast disappearing. They were a thought structure I had tried to take on board while a member of the church. Where else, after all, was I to express my love of God, my desire to serve, my wish to preach? I think that before I reached the confidence of my late thirties I should not have had the nerve to say that I was not a Christian. Now I have reverted to something in many ways much closer to what my mother taught me. That was religion. Christian doctrine was a relatively superficial layer; religion goes much deeper.

The Campaign for Women's Ordination

To work for women's ordination in Britain between 1977 and 1980 was lonely and discouraging. Few women were interested, and those who were, were disorganised. I was immensely frustrated at the simple things that were not done, while the opposition, highly organised, and at times unscrupulous, got away with murder. I took on the campaign on all fronts: writing theological material, keeping a disparate group together, sticking stamps on envelopes, and making long distance telephone calls. I felt worn out by "our side," quite as much as by anything the opposition did. Indeed it had crossed my mind to muse what bliss, by comparison, it would be to work for the opposition: what use they would have made of one! When the first women were allowed to put on clerical collars in Britain, at the time women in Wales were ordained deacons, I was the only woman to come from the wider movement, although it took me nearly ten hours to travel from central Scotland. There were no coachloads, no photographs taken for *The Church Times*. There was no organisation. One could multiply the examples.

The movement in the church in Britain pressing for women's ordination was many years behind that in the United States in getting organised. I was out of step. And desperate to do something. A battle had to be fought, in an organised and quiet manner, and won. It was not only just that I had by this time spent several years in the States; as a child of 12 to 14 in the 1950s, I had been furious, in the church which I compulsorily attended while at boarding school, that all the people "up front doing things" were male. As a doctoral student in Oxford in the 1960s, confused and hurt, I refused to ask for confirmation, for I did not think that a church which discriminated against women could be counted as fully Christian. I was working at that time on the subject of the Confessing Church in the Third Reich, and thought that Bonhoeffer's stand was right: that the refusal of the national church in Germany to ordain Jews made it less than Christian. So it was not that the issue of the ordination of women suddenly dawned on me in the 1970s.

Thus it is not actually appropriate in my case when people say, "You should have stayed inside the church and fought." I did. I left in the end because I was sick. It was on the way back from the hospital in Cambridge, Massachusetts, with Britain at a distance, having been told that I must have an operation on my throat, that I decided that there had to be some basic changes in my life. First of all, and I knew this with great clarity, I had to leave the church. It was not insignificant, I have since thought, that it was my throat that was wrong. Everything was bottled up there. I had never openly expressed rage or anger. I had argued with sweet reasonableness, persuasion, and academic know-how. Alone, I had cried at lot. Since I have left the church, my body has largely healed. There has been no operation. The real pain is the undoing which happens internally. I had let other people get at me. The grounds on which I had been forced to argue, as I shall later show, were themselves destructive of me. I had, at the worst, lain awake at night, feeling my body and crying out what was wrong with it, such that because of it I could not be ordained. I was a theologian by profession, an able preacher I must admit, and no one had suggested, pastorally unsuitable. Yet every young student of mine who was a man could offer to be ordained, and I not. I think many people have not understood what *a priori* discrimination—discrimination because of one's body, or how God has made one—does to one in terms of self-destruction. Black people perhaps have. It was Bishop Desmond Tutu who, alone of all the Bishops who spoke at the debate on the ordination of women at the Lambeth Conference of Anglican Bishops in 1978, struck a chord with the women waiting to get news that evening. He said, comparing the situation of women in the church with that of Blacks in South Africa, "a child of God subjected to that kind of treatment, actually gets to doubt that he is, or she is, a child of God". One of the good things that has happened since I left the church is that I have come to feel good again about my body, and about having been born a woman. I have healed both spiritually and physically.

The fact that I could not offer for ordination, while my friends and even younger people could, came as all the more of a shock because I had never known discrimination before. Growing up in Britain after the war, I had acquired an education, and no one had ever said, "No, because you are a woman." It was not an issue. It was the church, and the church alone, the place where I most wanted to be accepted, that drew attention to my sex. It is, then, a different situation from the past, when women could not be ordained, but neither could they be lawyers, members of parliament, or university lecturers. The church is completely out of step with British society. We can, apparently without difficulty, have a woman in the highest office of state as Prime Minister. Yet women in England and Scotland are not admitted to the lowest order of the church, that of deacon.

Some of the things I experienced profoundly affected me. I had to learn that one is not only affected by ideas in books, but by what one experiences—a revelation for me. I had been a student throughout the 1960s, but I had never demonstrated. I was not the sort. The church drove me to that. It was because of the church that I was shoved behind a police barrier, so that the 400 Bishops of the Lambeth Conference might be protected from me and a few others who had assembled wearing T-shirts proclaiming, "Ordain Women Now". It had been forbidden to carry banners. It was shattering that afternoon in Westminster Abbey to watch the procession into choral evensong of four hundred Bishops and their advisors, all men, among them my friends, and to know that I was divided from them, irrevocably, by the fact that I was a woman. I felt entirely left on the sidelines—automatically, by definition. It is out of experiences such as these that one finally gets up and leaves—to preserve one's human dignity.

Women's Ordination: The Issues and Arguments

I want now to turn to the nature of the arguments about "women's ordination," as it is always misnamed. The issue is the ordination of persons without respect to sex. I wrote a pamhlet while involved in the campaign. It is called, "Let Us Think About Women," and it shows on the front cover a puzzled bishop confronted with the idea of women. That is what one was up against: it symbolizes the situation exactly. We had to convince a male world. The issue of power relations here is important. Once, while in the thick of the campaign, I was, at a meeting, asked to express myself on paper, a task with which I always have the utmost difficulty in complying! But on that occasion I drew, with verve, a picture of a lot of people, almost all men, walking through two lobbies to vote, while women watched from the gallery. That was what it felt like. While I was inside the Church, I thought that logic and emotion lay with the movement to ordain women. Now I am not so sure. I see the ways in which the opposition's arguments are consistent with Christian doctrine. But therefore I have left Christianity, not simply the church.

In the Anglican Church, a "symbolic" church in which the priest in the eucharist is held to be by many in some sense a "representative" of Christ, the argument has in the first place centred around the issue of Christ's maleness. Now to say that a woman cannot be a priest because Christ was male is a distortion of Christology. For classical Christology did not say that a single human being, Jesus of Nazareth, was "God," but that, in Christ, God took on "humanity," in which we are all included. We are all "in Christ". A man baptised into Christ bears no special relation to Christ through his maleness, though he bears a greater resemblance to Jesus. Now, the priest in the eucharist represents Christ. The eucharist is not a play about Jesus of Nazareth, in which case the actor would have to be Jewish, male, etc. If God is not in God's self male (and that no one has suggested), and the second person of the Trinity is like the first in all respects save in their mutual relation, then it cannot be said that Jesus "as the Christ," as the second person of the Trinity, is male, although the incarnation may have been in male form. Baptism is into Christ, not into Jesus of Nazareth. And if baptism overcomes the differences of race, class and sex, for all are one in Christ, it is inconsistent to introduce these divisions again at the level of ordination.

However those opposed to women's ordination may say that symbols are profound. It is not insignificant that God became incarnate as a man, or that "he" has revealed that we should call him "Father." For the male represents the active, out-going force, and the female the passive, receptive pole. Thus God's relation to the Church is like that of male to female. The church is "female" in relation to Christ. It is the "bride" of Christ, and is represented by a human person who is female, Mary. One must not confuse symbols, for they operate at the deepest level. Thus it was first C.S. Lewis, to my knowledge, arguing against the ordination of women, who commented that a Mother-daughter religion would be wholly different from the Father-son religion which is Christianity. I am inclined now to agree that a male view of God is instrinsic to Christianity and cannot be separated from it.

This leads to the second main area of discussion: Biblical "revelation". The issue is both the terms used for God in the Bible, and the respective roles given to men and women. It is clear that the

Biblical language for God is overwhelmingly male. He is Father, King, Lord, Judge. Women have unearthed a few passages, notably in the Old Testament, where God is described using female metaphors. (And duly elevated them to a canon within the canon!) But women are quite clearly, in the Biblical world, subordinate to men, from the creation story forwards. In the New Testament there is talk of male "headship". The question then arises as to whether this should be for all time, or whether there can be a legitimate "development". Women can also argue, in particular from Galatians 3.28, which states that "there is no more male and female," for all are one in Christ, that a new principle of equality in Christ has been annunciated.

But women who argue in this way put themselves in a trap. For they tend to reinforce the idea that the criterion as to what should happen in the church now is what happened in the early church. They are implicitly agreeing that *that* is what counts. Thus women may argue, as they frequently have, that the Bible also has female metaphors for God, that Jesus's attitude toward women was exemplary, and that St. Paul intended that there should be equality in the order of salvation. But the *terms* of the debate have been granted. An opponent of the ordination of women may then point out that Biblical imagery for God is overwhelmingly male, that the disciples were male, and that the New Testament teaches a subordination of wife to husband. One needs first to debate the relevance of the Bible.

It is, however, very difficult for women to make a radical move here, and to argue from an *a priori* equality of women. For Christianity, like Islam and Judaism, is an historically based religion. It is based on certain texts from the past, which are held to be normative, and the events of which they tell. It is not an a-historical religion which simply starts from human experience of God, giving as much validity to each and every experience in different times and places. Nor does it start from reason. There is always an historical referent. Thus people arguing for the ordination of women seem to have implicitly agreed that it has got to be supported by arguments from the Bible. The most that one can do is to extrapolate from likely texts, or to argue that this is the "meaning" of the texts given in a different age. That the Bible might actually be sexist, and therefore dismissed at least when it comes to speak of the relations of women and men, seems to be too radical a move to make.

Thus, I have myself spent hours arguing, when writing a paper with others justifying the ordination of women at least to the diaconate, that Phoebe of Romans 16 was indeed a deacon. We conducted historical research (and we had some very fine scholars in our group in Scotland) as to the difference or equality between men deacons and women deacons (or were they deaconnesses?) in the second century. The question has thus become: can one argue for what one wants, within the terms in which the debate has been set? Maybe one can. I am not saying it is impossible. However I found it extremely undermining to have to argue in these terms. It was astonishing to a woman like me, who had a good job, and a house loan, to be faced with the issue of it mattering what women did or did not do in the second century. It seems that in this debate there has often been a failure to understand that a woman like me simply feels nothing in common with women of the second century.

I have found that this credibility gap opens up in particular in relation to the Virgin Mary. She is frequently exalted by opponents of women's ordination as being the true model for women; she is the highest to which humanity has attained. And not a few feminists seem to want to make common cause with her as a counterweight to the male Christ. I find myself incredulous. In the first place anyone who knows anything about Biblical scholarship is going to find this quite bizarre: we know almost nothing about the mother of Jesus. But, quite apart from this, what is her place in the story? She only enters it because she is humble and obedient, and produces a male child. I have far more in common with the men in the Biblical story: in terms of initiative, independence and ability to have control over my life. I feel little if anything in common with women of earlier generations. This struck me when looking at paintings in Italy with a mixed group of people. The men in our party had "ancestors" in the men depicted in a 15th century frescoe. I felt no association with the women.

Moreover the fact that texts from the past are normative tends to undermine any fragile equality gained in the present. If I hear the parable of the prodigal son, on one level I hear that the Father, to whom God is compared, welcomes back his prodigal son who has squandered his wealth, and I compare myself to the elder son who fails to rejoice at his brother's return. On another level, which operates all the more powerfully through being subconscious, I hear that God is to be compared to a good Father, not a Mother, who divides his property between two sons, not daughters. Thus the long arm of the past stretches forward into the present, influencing people's expectations. This is not trivial. The medium is the message. And the Bible is read not just as any book, but as one which conveys what is normative for human relations and for how we should think about God.

I have come to conclude that a real equality for women cannot be gained within the Christian framework. I do not think that the revolution which women want to accomplish is possible simply as a revision, for which Christianity itself allows. For Christianity is an historical religion and draws on past events, seeing them as normative. In particular a man, Jesus, by definition is central to the religion. When I was teaching in North Carolina in 1970, I went to a meeting in a Black church hall, where they had a very striking picture of a Black man on the cross. It was simply called "Black Christ." I realised that I had never before really thought about the problems which Black people face, and I saw in a new way their need to have God identified with them. I have often since wondered what it means that it is not possible to put a woman on the cross. For I think you cannot. She would not be recognised in the same way as "the Christ". It would just be a woman on a cross. This may mean that there is no place, ultimately, for women within the Christian tradition. For I agree with those opposed to women's ordination: symbols go deep.

The Christian tradition may, then, in feminism, have come up against something which it cannot handle. It has no way of taking on board a real equality for women without crumbling in the process. It comes out of a world which was patriarchal and is tied to that world. It has no neutral framework which can absorb human equality. Feminism, in this respect, is different from other liberation movements which Christianity has espoused or been persuaded to espouse. One could, in their case, appeal to Christianity itself in their defence. Feminism challenges the maleness of the whole tradition. But this is to say something of the utmost importance for human affairs. For in the past Christianity has always been not too far out of step with new human ethical insights. Perhaps Christianity cannot, by definition, really let this one challenge it to the core, and can only imperfectly absorb it. There may be a deep incompatibility.

The ordination of women may, then, tend to mask what is at stake. I suppose that had I stayed in the United States I should have become a deacon, and then a priest. I should not have seen the issues so clearly as I now do, having been in a situation where this has not been possible. The very fact that women can be ordained in the United States muddles the issue. It seems that all is possible. The wider confrontation is surely yet to come. The fact of women's ordination does not necessarily help women. It may mean that, through a longing to be ordained, they are prepared to play second fiddle in a male tradition. Certainly the grounds on which one was forced to argue for women's ordination were, through their presuppositions, deeply painful. What did it mean to have to argue for equality within one's own church, within one's own home, to which one found one did not fully belong on account of one's sex?

The Future for Women?

The transition from being Christian to post-Christian is a huge one to make. As going to the eucharist, then reading one's Bible, fall away, one wonders what will remain. Will prayer remain? To stop conceiving of God as "Father" and to move to other conceptions is very difficult indeed. For in the case of God, it is not as though we have "God" there for inspection, so that we can draw a symbol for God in the way in which we might symbolise other things. In the case of God, the symbol, or the word we use, or the image which comes to our mind *is* our God. The symbol reaches into the very nature of the thing. To lose the symbol, if one is not careful, is to lose the reality. And to change the symbol is deeply to change the reality.

I think women are then at a very creative point. We have the possibility of creating something new and, one would hope, much more relevant to our present society than the old image. I think that many women are indeed beginning to conceive God very differently. Increasingly God comes to be seen as spirit: as one who moves among us, between us, and is within us. It is a much less authoritarian notion of God. God is no longer a "thing," "out there," a sort of "super-person". I think this can only be for the good.

Women are beginning to think of God as one who is supportive of us, through whom we come into being, rather than as dominant and over-against us. I find women working with all kinds of fascinating imagery, which sees God as encompassing us, surrounding us. I am reminded of the woman who came up to Ronald Higgins who, in British society, has spoken powerfully of the catastrophes about to overtake humankind. She said to him, "You have given us the cross, but where is the encompassing circle?" The women at Greenham Common speak likewise of "embracing" the base—a deeply religious concept, inviting change to take place. I think then that we are in a position to think out essentially new imagery for God, imagery which may be very helpful for our world. We need to dare to develop our gifts as women.

The Future of the Bhikkhunī Samgha in Thailand

Chatsumarn Kabilsingh

I attempt in this paper to study the possibility of forming a Bhikkhunī Samgha, a Community of Buddhist Nuns, in Thailand. In doing so, there are three areas to be considered. First, the nature of the Bhikkhunī Samgha in the Ancient Period; second, the religious position of the Thai women called *ji* or *mae chi*; and finally, the ordination of the first Thai *bhikkhunī* and the possibility of a Bhikkhunī Samgha.

The Bhikkhunī Samgha in the Ancient Period

While it is not possible to review the entire history of the Bhikkhunī Samgha in this context, several points should be noted to enable us to understand the present situation in Thailand, especially the controversial points which affect the status of the *bhikkhunīs*.[1]

First, one might ask, is it true that the Buddha did not want to accept women to the monastic Order, the Samgha? It is said that the Buddha hesitated, and allowed women to join his Order only after his disciple Ananda's third appeal. This fact has often been used to argue against the acceptance of the Bhikkhunī Samgha. On closer study, however, it seems that the Buddha's hesitation seems not to be based on his objection to women joining the Order as such, but on other social problems which would stem from this.

First, it was said that his mother, Queen Mahāpajāpatī herself, was the first candidate. Since she was not accustomed to hardship, it

[1] For a fuller treatment of women and Buddhism, see, for example, I.B. Horner, *Women Under Primitive Buddhism*, (London: Routledge and Kegan Paul, 1930) and Nancy Falk, "The Case of the Vanishing Nuns," in Falk and Rita Gross, eds., *Unspoken Worlds*, New York: Harper & Row, (1980).

was almost unimaginable that she should go from house to house as a *bhikkhunī* begging for meals. Perhaps it was from pity or compassion that the Buddha refused her request to join the Order. But he must also have observed her earnestness, for she had followed him to Vésāli along with 500 royal women, and she had already donned the yellow robe and shaved off her hair. Indeed, she had already, by her determination, become a *paribbājikā*, a female wanderer. Had the Buddha not accepted her she still would have been a wanderer, leading her followers. Thus, it would have been improper for the Buddha not to give her protection and spiritual instruction, and the strong determination and sincerity of Mahāpajāpatī played a vital role in bringing about the admission of women to the Buddhist Samgha.

There were other problems as well. For example, it was a strictly observed custom of the Śākyas to marry within the clan. But the 500 royal women, leaving their domestic obligations, posed the problem of the shortage of female members in the Śākya clan. This objection was removed when it came to light that their husbands had joined the Order as well.[2] The issue of separate residential arrangements must also have occupied the mind of the Buddha. In addition, the Buddha perhaps thought about the issue of suitable teachers to impart religious training to the women. Finally, for women the life of homelessness was hazardous, and so it would require a great many precautions and protections.

These are a few of the possible reasons for the Buddha's reluctance, but had he thought these obstacles could not be overcome, he would never have given permission. He was reluctant, but he gave his consent. His reluctance should not be thought of as a negative thing. After all, we have read in the *Mahāvagga* that he was also reluctant to preach the Dhamma after his enlightenment.

With the acceptance of women into the Order, eight rules or *gurudhammas*, were laid down for them. At first glance these rules appear to degrade women and place them in submissive roles in the Order. But in order to understand them, it is necessary to take into account the general social background of the period of the rise of Buddhism. The position of women in India was limited, and women were subject to their male counterparts.

[2] R.S. Hardy, *A Manual of Buddhism* (London: Williams and Norgate, 1880), pp. 283, 307 ff.

Rule One, for example, states: "A nun who has been ordained (even) for a century must greet respectfully, rise up from her seat, salute with joined palms, do proper homage to a monk ordained but that day."[3] This must be seen in the context of the general social setting of the subjugation of women to men. *Bhikkhunīs* are supposed to greet monks respectfully, provided they are well behaved. But the rule is automatically lifted if the monks misbehave.

Rule Two states: "A nun must not spend the rains in a residence where there is no monk." This must be seen as an answer to the Buddha's concern about the security of *bhikkhunīs*. The rule restricts them to spending the rain-retreat where there are *bhikkhus* from whom they would receive protection. Again, there is a tone of traditional influence: that a woman is always to be protected, and when she joins the Order the duty of protection falls on the *bhikkhus*.

Similarly, Rules Seven and Eight enjoin nuns not to abuse, revile or admonish monks. Here again, it is made clear that the Order of *bhikkhus* is to give protection and exhortation to the *bhikkhunīs*. Therefore, it is not proper that *bhikkhunīs* should admonish the monks. The total value of the *gurudhamma* rules is their concern for the well-being of the *bhikkhunīs* and for the long-lasting unity of the two Samghas. They are not against women, as such, but it was clear that the Bhikkhunī Samgha was to be submissive to and dependent upon the Bhikkhu Samgha.

Let us turn now to the relationship between the two Samghas. It was true, as the Buddha might have expected, that not all of his male followers were happy with his decision to accept women. One can imagine that this was true especially among monks who were previously of high castes and never allowed women any status of their own. The dislike which some of the monks had for the Bhikkhunī Samgha was expressed clearly after the death of the Buddha at the First Council, where Ananda was blamed for being the chief cause of the Bhikkhunī Samgha.

There is some evidence that the *bhikkhunīs* may have been ill-treated by the monks, as one can glimpse in a study of both the *bhikkhu* and *bhikkhunī pātimokkha* rules. The *bhikkhunīs* were supposed to render services to the monks, such as washing and drying robes and sitting mats, cleaning the hall, etc. Such services were so time consuming that the Buddha had to set rules forbidding

[3] I.B. Horner, tr. CV. X, *Sacred Books of the Buddhists*, p. 354 ff.

such practices (*Bhikkhus' Pacittiya* 4, 7; *Thai Tripitaka.*) It was the Buddha's idea that the *bhikkhunīs* should be submissive, but only as younger sisters are submissive to elder brothers. Both *bhikkhus* and *bhikkhunīs* alike should be treated as children of the Buddha. But many evidences tell us that the monks still tended to treat the *bhikkhunīs* as they might have treated women in the Brahminical tradition. They often treated them more like servants than younger sisters or counterparts. Yet, throughout the remaining years of the Buddha's life, he seems to have tried to change the negative attitudes of the monks, with rules laid down to protect the *bhikkhunīs*. After his death, however, there was no supreme power to see to their well-being.

It is important to mention the role of Ānanda in connection with the Bhikkhunī Samgha, for he was one of the few monks who played a vital role in its establishment. He was a popular and successful preacher among the *bhikkhunīs*. As both cousin and personal attendant of the Buddha, he was a key figure not only for the Bhikkhunī Samgha, but for the growth and establishment of Buddhism.

To review the status of *bhikkhunīs* during the Buddha's lifetime, we should say that many of these women attained spiritual enlightenment and were highly praised by the Buddha. The *Therigatha*, "Psalms of the Sisters," mentions and reveres Mahāpajāpatī, as founder. Dhammadinna was said to be foremost in wisdom and had a great ability to preach. Patācarā was foremost in Vinaya and brought a great number of women into the Order. Bhadda Kapilāni was foremost in remembering past lives, and Bhadda Kundalakesā was foremost in intuition. The *bhikkunīs* studied and preached Dhamma, gained disciples among ministers and people of high social standing, and proved that they were as capable as the monks as propagators of the new faith.

The Religious Status of Thai Women Today: The "Jī's"

The ordination of *bhikkhunīs* as discussed above has never taken place in Thailand, but there are Buddhist women ordained in Thailand as *jī* or *māē chī* (female ascetic, or nun). Such a Buddhist woman has a shaven head, wears white, and observes five of the eight precepts. She may live in a *wat* (Buddhist temple) or may prefer to stay at home. According to Buddhist classification, they are really only lay women, for they observe the same number of rules as lay women, even though they are ordained. *Bhikkhunīs*, on the other hand, would observe 311 rules in the Theravada tradition.

There is no historical record of the beginning of the ordination of the *jīs*, due to lack of central organization, lack of concern on the part of *jīs* themselves, and lack of concern on the part of the monks. There were several cases in the past when female members of the royal family became *jīs*. In other countries, the status of *jīs* would have been much improved with the grace of royal participation, but regretfully this was not the case in Thailand. The few royal *jīs* were primarily interested in the practical matters of their own spiritual growth and, thus, had no influence either in academic or administrative fields.

According to a survey and study of the "*Māējī*" done in 1981 by Mrs. N. Panjapan in a long-range programme for the development of women in Thailand, there are not more than 20,000 *jīs* in Thailand. For the most part, they are poorly educated. Only 40 per cent of them have completed grade seven; only seven per cent have completed secondary school. Most *jīs* are either single, divorced, or separated. Like the monks, more than half were previously farmers. They became *jīs* primarily out of the wish to cut themselves off from the ties of worldly lives. Only 20 per cent expressed the idea of wanting to help the community.

As *jīs*, these women usually have to support themselves financially, which costs from 100 to 1000 *bahts* per month. This financial assistance is provided usually by relatives. For those who do not have such means, their lives as *jīs* could become miserable.

The present status of the *jīs* is still difficult. They have no social recognition; they are not welcome in some *wats*, where the head monks would think them to be a nuisance. The Department of Religious Affairs has paid no attention to them, since the *jīs* find no place in any existing religious structure and do not quite fit any of the religious categories. They are neither considered "ordained" in the full sense of the term, nor "propagators" of the Dhamma. At best, they are "residents" of the *wats*. Yet many *jīs* do not themselves understand their position and the injustices done to them.

Recently there has been a new movement among the *jīs*. Under the patronage of some learned monks at Wat Bovornnives, a "Thai *Jīs* Institution" has been formed. Although the organization is still in its formative stages, there is some improvement. The *jīs* are being encouraged and supported for further study, both in the Dhamma and the Vinaya.

In general, however, the status of the *jīs* is still very low, especially when compared to that of the monks. Let me summarize again the reasons for this. First, *jīs* are more lower class than middle class. They are primarily from families of farmers, with very low educational background. They are not able to look beyond their own sphere of existence and are generally not aware of their own problems. They are religiously conservative, understanding *nirvāna*, for example, as personal spiritual salvation. Therefore they tend to sever themselves from any work which might be considered worldly. *Jīs* are generally looked down upon by society, and by the monks. They do not have a proper religious status and are accepted by neither the monks nor the laity. Becoming a *jī* is often seen as the resort of those who have failed in worldly lives. More degrading is the fact that some elderly *jīs* who have no financial support have to beg for their living in public.

For all these reasons, becoming a *jī* is still not a satisfactory Buddhist institution in which a respectable Thai woman might pursue a religious life. The objections are so critical that some, myself included, have come to suggest a revival of the Bhikkhunī Samgha in Thailand.

The Possibility of a Bhikkhunī Samgha in Thailand

For the past 700 years, the Bhikkhunī Samgha has not existed in Thailand; therefore the concept of the *bhikkhunī* is remote and foreign to ordinary Thai perception. There is also the prevailing belief that the Bhikkhunī Samgha died out in the time of King Aśoka in the fourth century B.C. Some educated Thai people are aware that *bhikkhunīs* still exist in Mahāyāna countries, such as Taiwan and Japan. But Thailand is a Theravāda country, and Thai people would generally think the Mahāyāna to be inferior in its authenticity. But the belief that the Bhikkhunī Samgha is a Mahāyāna innovation has no academic support, as this study has shown.

There is much historical evidence to prove that there were *bhikkhunīs* in India, even at a late period. For example, there is a list of names on the wall in the cave at Ganheri, stating the names of *bhikkhunīs* who were students of *bhikkhunī* teachers named Mitasiri, Kata, and Patumanikā.[4] There are at least eight places in the edicts from Amaravati which mention *bhikkhunīs*, besides the numerous records from cave-temples in western India which refer to *bhikkhunīs* and their activities. In the ninth and tenth centuries, the number of *bhikkhunīs* was greatly reduced. With the destructive invasion of the Turkish Muslims in the 11th century, the Bhikkhunī Samgha disappeared, not before but along with the Bhikkhu Samgha.

In the third century, Anulā, a Ceylonese princess, received *bhikkhunī* ordination from Indian *bhikkhunīs*, along with a great number of Ceylonese women, and Ceylon became a strong nucleus of the Bhikkhunī Samgha. With regular and continuous royal support, the *bhikkhunīs* in Ceylon seemed to enjoy a better status than their sisters in India. Their activities were reported as late as the tenth century when a hospital was built in front of a *bhikkhunī* temple, according to an edict at Gugurumahantāmana, mentioned in the *Cullavamsa* (42:68). Unfortunately, there are at present no *bhikkhunīs* in Sri Lanka, and the reason for their disappearance there has still to be explained.

Buddhism spread to China during the Sui Dynasty and became prosperous during the T'ang Dynasty. Chinese women who had taken faith in Buddhism expressed their desire to receive *bhikkhunī* ordination. This desire was fulfilled in A.D. 433 when a group of Ceylonese *bhikkhunīs* arrived by invitation and gave ordination to 300 Chinese women at Southern Forest Monastery in Nan King.[5]

As far as Vinaya is concerned, Mahāyāna does not differ greatly from Theravāda. The Vinaya rules as observed by Chinese *bhikkhunīs* were mainly those of Dharmagupta, which is in fact a sub-branch of Theravāda. It is apparent that the *bhikkhunī* ordination in China was a direct lineage from the Buddha's time.

At present the Bhikkhunī Samgha holds a strong base in Taiwan. According to the author's personal observation in 1970, there were at least 4,200 *bhikkhunīs* spread throughout the island of Taiwan. They have their own monasteries, enjoy social acceptance and prestige, and receive sufficient financial support from the public. They lead active lives and some of them are highly educated, including among them professors of philosophy and Buddhism at the National University.

[4] *Annual Report on Indian Epigraphy*, (1949–50), p. 33, no. 22.

[5] E. Conze, *Buddhist Texts Through the Ages* (1964), p. 223.

If Thai women should wish to form a Bhikkhunī Saṃgha in Thailand, then it is possible for them to gain authentic ordination and the lineage of the Buddha by receiving direct ordination from the Bhikkhunī Saṃgha in Taiwan.

The attitude of Thai women is a serious and sensitive factor which must be taken into account in considering the possibility of a Bhikkhunī Saṃgha in Thailand. Thai society has always been a paternal society, with male members heading the families and in charge of their welfare. During the Ayudhya period, with the influence of Indian Brahmanism, the status of women was further degraded. It was only in and after the reign of King Rāma IV of the present royal dynasty (1851–68) that Thai ceremonies were freed from the heavy conservative hand of Brahmanism. And along with this change, Thai women began to enjoy rights and freedom.

Since Thailand never had *bhikkhunīs* all religious activities have been performed by the monks. It is the monks who uphold the teaching of the Buddha. Buddhist monastic rules prevent close relationship between the monks and women, and this results in the alienation of women from monks and from Buddhism altogether. As a group, women do usually come in contact with the monks when they gather to listen to sermons. The approved relationship, therefore, has always been one-way—with women playing the passive role of supporters and listeners. It is, therefore, hard to imagine that Thai women would know and seek their right to a religious life, as it has been given to them by the Buddha.

In Thailand there is a wide range of prejudice about women's inferiority and a resistance to the entry of women into the profession on an equal basis.[6] This prejudice extends to religion, and Thai women who are equipped socially and educationally find no room for their activities in it. Religion, that is the Buddhist tradition, is always taken to be the sphere of men. Therefore, Thai women are generally not interested in Buddhism, a fact which widens the gap between it and women. The more Thai women remove themselves from an interest in and study of Buddhism, the less possibility is left for them to grasp and appreciate their religious heritage and rights. In addition, of course, the status of *jīs* is considered socially degrading. Thus, Thai women feel safer seeking to develop themselves in other spheres of interest.

[6] This has been pointed out by Prof. S. Dhammasakdi, a former prime minister of Thailand in *The Status of Women in Thailand*, (Bangkok, 1972).

The development of a Bhikkhunī Samgha depends also upon the acceptance of the monks. As Thailand never had *bhikkhunīs*, the Thai monks have very scanty knowledge of them. Their knowledge regarding *bhikkhunīs* is limited only to those rules concerning *bhikkhunīs* which they have studied and recited but have never actually observed, since *bhikkhunīs* do not exist in Thailand. It is the monks themselves who are partially responsible for the mistaken idea that there were *bhikkhunīs* only up to the time of Aśoka in the 4th century B.C. Thai monks have little interest in learning of the *bhikkhunīs*' existence or of their fruitful activities outside Thailand. They are simply satisfied with the idea that, at present, there are no *bhikkhunīs*, in Thailand or anywhere else. Their understanding is both partial and non-academic.

There is, however, some change among the younger generation of educated monks. Most of the senior monks with administrative positions in the Elders Assembly have well-educated younger monks acting as their secretaries. Their world-view is more liberal than that of their predecessors, they are more open-minded and have respect for the opinions of one another. Most important, they are aware that Buddhism is not only the monks' responsibility, but that of *bhikkhunīs* and lay people as well.

It is inevitable that these secretaries will be of some influence upon the Elders themselves. In the years to come, with a group of better educated and more liberal Elders, the acceptance of the Bhikkhunī Samgha is foreseeable. The Elders Assembly passes on its decisions to the Government through the Department of Religious Affairs. Hence, the acceptance of the Bhikkhunī Samgha depends primarily upon the decision of the Elders Assembly.

The interpretation of *nirvāna* as a private spiritual goal also needs to change in order to bring about the Bhikkhunī Samgha. Is *nirvāna* achieved privately, or in the process of social involvement with others? Generally, Thais tend to strive toward this goal privately, and social involvement is considered a hindrance to the achievement of this goal. But this is too narrow and limited. It projects a negative meaning to the people and it renders *nirvāna* something remote and meaningless to the masses. As a result, those few women who are interested in Buddhism might well find the forming of a Bhikkhunī Samgha unnecessary to their private spiritual goals.

It is women themselves who must seek their religious right to become *bhikkhunīs*. In Thailand, the majority of women are still unaware of this right, but some women who are interested in religious lives have been trying to find a solution to their problem.

There is in Thailand today one Thai *bhikkhunī*, the Venerable Voramai Kabilsingh. Taking note of her ordination and work is a fitting conclusion to our discussion of religion and social change and a hopeful sign of the future.

Kabilsingh first began to move toward ordination when, as a married woman, she became deeply concerned with the plight of the poor, especially children. She became increasingly interested in the study of Buddhism, thinking that a religious organisation such as the Samgha should be an active agent in helping those children. In 1956, Kabilsingh received ordination into the order of the *jīs* from the abbot of Wat Bovornnives in Bangkok.

Kabilsingh was not content with the status of the *jīs*, however. In the monastery she put on a light-yellow robe, to distinguish herself both from the white-robed *jīs* and the saffron-robed monks. In 1971, after learning of the authentic ordination lineage of the *bhikkhunīs* in Taiwan, she went to Taiwan and received the full ordination of a *bhikkhunī*.

The centre of her work and activities is at a new temple south of Bangkok called Wat Songdhamma-kalyani—"Women who uphold Dhamma." Whether or not her personal success as a *bhikkhunī* in modern Thailand will prove sufficient to launch a new movement of Buddhist women, it is clear that an important step has been taken in her full ordination to the *bhikkhunī* order and an important link with the ancient heritage of the Buddhist *bhikkhunī* tradition, been re-established.

The Status Elevation Process of Sōtō Sect Nuns in Modern Japan

Kumiko Uchino

Introduction

In the Buddhist tradition, women are regarded as impure, having a more sinful *karma* than men, and unable to attain Buddhahood. Many Buddhist scriptures describe women as filled with evil desires and as harmful obstacles to men, who are striving to attain enlightenment. One scripture says that if one sees a woman, one will lose virtue in one's eyes; seeing a snake is far better than seeing women.

Even nuns, who shunned all worldly attachments, were segregated from and had heavier precepts than monks. Two hundred and fifty precepts were imposed on monks while the figure for nuns was five hundred. In addition to these precepts, there were eight laws, called the *Hakkeikai*, which were written especially for nuns and placed them under the control of monastic orders. According to the law, no matter how long a nun had been in service, she was required to obey and worship even those monks who had taken the tonsure only the day before. Nuns were not permitted to hold the special long meditation (*ango*) without the presence of monks; they were forced to ask a monastic order to send them a preacher twice a month; they were not allowed to speak of a monk's sin or mistake, but monks could condemn those of nuns. Nuns who violated the precepts had to repent and be confined for fifteen days, a period twice as long as that required for monks.

The status of nuns was determined not only by Buddhist dogma, but also by general views of women in society. In addition to the discriminatory attitude toward women in the scriptures, none of the sacred places and mountains in Japan allowed women entry until 1873.

Here I will describe the elevation of the status of nuns and the modern Japanese equality movements for nuns of the Sōtō sect, which has been the largest Zen Buddhist sect in Japan. Focusing on the changes in Sōtō law, I will analyze the relationship these have to the waves of feminism and modernization that have swept through Japanese society.

Nuns in the Meiji Era (1868–1912)

The Sōtō Zen sect, which currently has two head temples and 15,000 branch temples, was founded by the Zen Master Dōgen in the 13th century. Dōgen was exceptionally understanding of women and affirmed the possibility of Buddhahood for them. In his best known work, the *Shōbō genzō* ("The Eye of the True Law"), he criticized the negative attitudes toward women held by the many monks who would prevent them from gaining access to them or to sacred places. He also emphasized the equality of men and women in attaining Buddhahood.

But these ideas and beliefs were not transmitted to his pupils. Dōgen's view on women disappeared during the expansion of the Sōtō school, and the head temples on the mountain refused admission to women until the Meiji era. This discriminatory policy of Zen Buddhism was strengthened and institutionalized under the religious control of the Tokugawa Shogunate in the 17th century.

During the three hundred years of feudalism in the Tokugawa era, a period when the status of women was at its lowest point in all of Japanese history, nuns were located at the bottom of the religious system. As was the case in other sects, the nuns of the Sōtō sect were allowed to live only in hermitages, even though the temple in their area might have been uninhabited and the people in need of a priest. Nuns were neither permitted to hold the Zen retreat (*ango*), regarded by the Sōtō sect as its most important religious activity, by themselves nor allowed to attend retreats held by monks at the temple.

Nuns did not have the right to perform the initiation ceremony to the Buddhist priesthood for young nuns, which meant that they could not become formal Zen masters. No matter how long they might have trained their successors, they still had to ask a priest from the temple to perform the ceremony, and he became the novice's nominal teacher. Nor were nuns allowed to inherit the unbroken line of teacher-pupil tradition from Dōgen, as true Zen Buddhists.

In those days only priests at *hōchi* temples (the middle of three ranks of Sōtō temples) were qualified to perform funeral services, which prevented nuns from having access to a major source of income. Thus, they did not have the opportunity to achieve economic stability. They had to support themselves by assisting priests at funerals and memorials, by chanting *sūtras* as an accompaniment, or by washing dishes and clothes for priests.

The colour of monks' clothing was changed when a higher rank was attained, but nuns' clothes remained black, which was the colour of the novice throughout their lives.[1] This second class citizenship held by nuns during the feudal period remained unchanged through the modern Meiji age, in spite of the fact that the government instituted many radical policies in the world of religion.

Since the Meiji Restoration in 1868, Japan has greatly modernized and industrialized; many reformations have taken place in the field of religion. In 1872, the Meiji government issued a law allowing priests to eat meat, get married, and have free choice of tonsure, and in 1873 the same policies were adopted for nuns. This law shocked Buddhist society, and many sect leaders announced their disagreement, demanding its revocation. The government's answer was that the issue could not be judged as a matter of national law but as religious law, in which the government should not interfere. The Meiji government left the decision with individual Buddhist sects. At the same time, the prohibition of women from sacred places was abolished.[2]

The issue of matrimony had a different impact on the lives of priests and nuns. Matrimony was prohibited in the Meiji era by the Sōtō law, but many priests married anyway (although most of them were unregistered), and by the end of the 19th century about half of the priests were married. On the other hand, there are neither records nor examples of nuns marrying, a fact which shows that married nuns with unshaven heads would not have been defined as nuns by the society at large, and that their marriage meant a return to the secular world. Solving the issue of matrimony made the priesthood one of the social professions, a fact which enabled priests to combine their religious and daily lives with a wife and

[1] Sōtō Sect Complication Committee, ed., *Sōtō shū nisō shi* [The History of Sōtō Sect Nuns] (1955), pp. 315–326.

[2] Yoshihiko Umeda, *Nihon shūkyō seido shi*. [A History of Religious Institutions in Japan] (1971).

children. But nunhood was considered by more traditional standards, and nuns have maintained their ascetic lifestyles until the present.

According to Japanese government statistics from the Meiji era, 10 per cent of all Buddhist clergy were nuns, and this ratio is reflected in the make up of the Sōtō sect. In 1891 about 2,000 nuns were registered in the Sōtō sect, and in 1935 the number of nuns increased to 2,382, while the number of priests was 28,093—the same ratio as in the Meiji era.[3]

The status of nuns in the Sōtō sect did not change in the Meiji era. An important reason for this low status was that nuns lacked an educational background, both within the religious body and in the society in general. Zen Buddhist schools were open only to monks, and society was indifferent to women's education. There were many illterate nuns who learned to chant *sūtras* by ear.

The compulsory education policy of the Meiji government, which made elementary education obligatory for all children, gradually improved the position of women. Changes in the world of nuns took place first in the field of education. In 1902 the first new provision for nuns since the Meiji Restoration passed the Sōtō sect's assembly. This act established three schools in which nuns could study both basic Sōtō dogma and general areas such as history, geography, mathematics, etiquette and sewing.[4] While this provision aimed at giving nuns a general cultural education and cultivation, the level of the school was far below that for monks, who had both a university and special monasteries for meditation.

After the provision was issued, schools for nuns were established in Aichi, Toyama and Niigata prefectures between 1903 and 1907. This quick response was the result of the concentrated activities of nuns who had worked for higher education. Among the nuns who studied at these schools were some who were very active and later became leaders in the equality movement, working to organize other nuns.

Nuns from 1912 to 1944

During the Taishō era (1912–1925) nuns lived in a society which was swept by waves of democracy and liberal theories. Awakened by

[3] *Bukkyō nenkan*, [Buddhist Almanac] (1935).
[4] *Sōtō shū nisō shi*, pp. 402–412.

social trends such as feminism and the suffrage movement, the nuns developed a higher level of "feminist" consciousness, and several equality movements were launched. In 1925, the first Sōtō sect Nun's Conference ever was held at Sōjiji Temple on the six hundredth anniversary of Sōtō founder Dōgen. The 300 nuns who assembled at that time submitted a petition containing the following statements to the Sōtō administration:

1. Nuns have a duty to cultivate their own self-belief and enlighten the people.
2. Nuns have a right to a convent for Zen meditation.
3. Nuns deserve suffrage in the Sōtō sect.
4. Nuns have a right to perform initiation ceremonies for nun pupils.
5. Nuns have a right to serve as missionaries.[5]

In 1930 a second Nuns' Meeting was held at Eiheiji. This conference, which seems to have been influenced by the prevailing "Taishō democracy," issued new demands for equality. Its manifesto pointed out the prevailing liberalism in society and appealed for a new awareness of nuns, who continued to be suppressed by the world of Buddhism. Three new points were added to the five made by the first meeting:

1. The right to transfer the orthodox line from teacher to pupil.
2. The opening of a special seminar on Sōtō doctrine for nuns.
3. The right of nuns to become priests at *hōchi* level temples.

In 1937 a third meeting was held, after which a petition was sent to the Sōtō administration every year; the nuns' demands became more concrete as time passed.[6] But these movements were not strong enough to make the Nuns' Organisation an effective pressure group.

The majority opinion concerning nuns held by the priests of the Sōtō sect was the "division of labour" theory, according to which monks should learn the scriptures and preach, while nuns should take care of women and children like benevolent mothers. A typical opinion is that found in the preface of the 1915 issue of *Jōrin*, a

[5] *Sōtō shū nisō shi*, pp. 402–412.

[6] *Sōtō shū nisō shi*, pp. 440–441.

journal published once a year at the Kansai Nuns' School.[7] The author, a priest named Kondō, who was the principal of the school, pointed out three morals that innately belonged to women: obedience, patience and precision. He said the mission of nuns was to go back to their temple after school and to guide women, to teach them sewing, the tea ceremony and flower arrangement, and to educate them to become good wives and wise mothers. He emphasised these three morals and criticized the "new women" who were the topics of much of the journalism during the Taishō era.

The most negative opinion toward nuns denied their existence altogether, holding that the most healthy and favourable life for women was one of marriage and bearing children. People who held this opinion regarded the celibacy of nuns as a consequence of some unexpected choice of life.[8] The opinion reflected a contemporary view that the woman's place was at home, and her role was to procreate and serve her family. In the Buddhist world the status of nuns was considered secondary, and they were not accepted as independent priests.

The priest Den, a teacher at the Kansai Nuns' School, pointed out five problems in the nuns' world:

1. A general women's problem: The Sōtō sect should elevate the status of nuns and change the attitudes of the priests.
2. A humanitarian problem: Reconsider the nuns' extreme asceticism.
3. A social problem: Eliminate nuns' alienation from society and from women's roles such as home-making and infant rearing.
4. An education problem: Raise the educational standards of nuns by increasing their financial support. (The Sōtō sect spent 600 yen per nun and 180,000 yen per priest, at pre-war currency values.)
5. A religious problem: Reconsider the bachelorhood of nuns, as had been done for priests.[9]

[7] Soken Kondō, *Kansai Nigakuin seito ni shimesu*, [A Speech for the Pupils of the Kansai Nuns' School] (1915), pp. 1–2.

[8] Kakugo Furukawa, *Sōryo saitai ron* [*The Theory of Matrimony for Priests*] (1938), p. 69–77.

[9] Taikan Den, "Nisō kyōiku mondai" ["The Question of Educating Nuns"] in *Jōrin* 2:6–8 (1913).

Den finally emphasised the necessity of understanding on the part of priests and society for the resolution of nuns' problems. His sympathetic opinion was a minority in the Sōtō sect, however, as the majority of the priests saw nothing wrong in the miserable situation of nuns.

In *Jōrin* 5, the nun Kuga Kanshū criticized the indifferent attitude of the Soto administration, which belittled nuns, giving them no education opportunities. She indicated that nuns were handicapped by the fact that they had to support themselves without any stable financial source, as compared with priests at *hōchi* level temples who had regular parishioners. She also criticized the general attitude toward women in society, and the conservative priests who thought nuns with a higher education would become conceited and depraved in terms of traditional moral attitudes such as obedience and modesty.[10]

In 1923 the first independent article of nuns appeared in Sōtō law. This bestowed the titles of Shūso and Oshō upon nuns. But it did not mention any rights that these titles would carry, although the monks with the rank of Oshō were allowed to run *hōchi* level temples. In 1929, a new article was issued which defined "nun teachers". The Sōtō sect gave the title of "nun teacher" (*Ama Kyōshi*) to those who had graduated from nuns school, and "*Ama Kyōshi-ho*," a higher level, to those with fifteen years experience as a nun, but these were titles only, and carried no practical guarantees within the Sōtō sect.

As educational standards went up, the academic field in the Sōtō sect was gradually opened to nuns, and in 1925, Komazawa University, a Sōtō university, permitted nuns to enter as auditors. Five nuns, including Kojima Kendō, a pioneer in the nun liberation movements, attended lectures.

Apart from the inconsistent nuns' meetings and several gains in education, nuns realized but few advances during the "liberal" period in modern Japanese history. Soon after the Taishō era, society became militarized and freedom of activity and gathering was restricted. There was also a gap in consciousness between nuns in the countryside and their younger and better educated sisters in the cities. Nuns had to wait until three conditions necessary for equality were realized: organisation (the Sōtō Nuns' Organisation); a devoted leader (Nun Kojima Kendō), and favourable social

[10] Kanshū Kuga, *Atte tsumarazu* [No Meaning to Exist] *Jōrin* 5:18–19, (1916).

conditions (the democratization of society brought about by defeat in World War II).

Equality after World War II (1945–1979)

World War II contributed to the establishment of an organisation of nuns. In 1943, a special seminar for training nuns was held in Tokyo by the Sōtō sect administration. Its goal was to elevate the patriotism of nuns, so they would cooperate with the war. About thirty representative nuns assembled from all over Japan; they were informed that 3,000 nuns were registered in the Sōtō sect, and this fact motivated them to create an organisation. At the end of a three day seminar they presented a petition for an organisation of nuns.

In 1944, they assembled again to found the organisation, but their activities were directed towards the war and they did not attempt any movement for equality. The organisation was called "The Nuns' Organisation for Protecting the Nation," and was not connected to the nuns' meetings of the Taishō era in terms of leaders or consciousness. It was primarily concerned with nursing children evacuated from the cities, and lasted until the end of the war in August, 1945.[11]

When the war came to an end the organisation lost its *raison d'être* and was at the point of dissolution. The nun Kojima Kendō, a teacher at the Kansai Nuns' School, devoted herself to transforming the organisation into a status elevation movement. After the 1943 seminar, Kojima came back to the Kansai Nuns' School and organised a group of nuns for the war effort; they were assigned by the government to work at a gunpowder factory. Kojima Kendō planned to hold a five day seminar for the group in August of 1945, just before the war ended. In spite of the chaotic situation brought about by defeat, she decided to hold the seminar as a memorial to those killed in the war.

At the seminar, Kojima Kendō proposed that the organisation continue to exist, even though the war was over. The Sōtō sect president who attended the memorial, agreed with Kojima's proposal and the bureau was set up in the Tokyo Sōtō office in 1946. Kojima became the first director of the organisation and started a campaign for enlightening nuns, visiting nunneries all over Japan. She also

[11] *Sōtō shū nisō shi*, p. 416.

held meetings at each nuns' school to present four new proposals to improve the status of nuns. These were:

1. Permission for nuns who had graduated from the nuns' schools to enter Komazawa University as formal students.
2. The appointment of nuns as principals of nuns' schools.
3. The abolition of discrimination in matters of ceremonies, in temples, in suffrage, and in the qualifications of teachers.
4. The establishment of a special convent for nuns to practice Zen meditation.

The points were presented to the Sōtō sect Assembly in 1946. Some were accepted and incorporated in the new Sōtō Constitution (Kojima, interview). This new constitution apparently continued the progress toward equality, but was not accompanied by any substantial reforms. The nuns' organisation had to work for twenty years for real equality. However, in the new 1946 constitution, nuns made some substantial gains:

1. Nuns gained equality in the qualifications of teachers, and the integration of name and title for both monks and nuns.
2. The existence of certain female Zen masters, who had been neglected for a long time, was acknowledged, and it was made compulsory to record their names in the nuns' career list.
3. Nuns were allowed to hold Zen meditation by themselves.
4. Nuns who were qualified teachers gained voting rights.
5. Nuns were allowed to become orthodox pupils in the Zen priest transmission lines.[12]

The constitution did not, however, grant nuns the right to perform initiation ceremonies, the right to receive the line from a nun teacher, the right to manage temples of the *hōchi* level, or the right to run in elections. Although nun Zen masters were recognized, it was only nominally, in a document; they were not allowed to have their own pupils. The same was true for their rights as teachers. Nuns did not have proper monasteries or facilities to train themselves to attain higher status. They could not send representatives to the Sōtō Assembly, and very few priests in the Assembly were sympathetic to the idea of nuns' rights.

In 1948, the organisation presented a new petition to the Sōtō

[12] *Sōtō shū nisō shi*, pp. 446–448.

Assembly, criticizing it for making only nominal reformations in the status of nuns and not institutionalizing any actual improvements. The Assembly approved the right of nuns to stand for election, and Kojima did so, to demand equality. Although she was defeated as an alternate candidate in the election, she became an Assembly member in 1951 due to the death of the member from her district.

In the Assembly, according to Assembly records, Kojima spoke out against the continuing unequal situation of nuns, pointing out the imperfections in the new constitution that allowed them to receive the line of dogma from male Zen masters but refused to allow them to transmit it. She asked the members to reconsider the unequal doctrine, holding that prohibiting nuns to transmit Zen teachings was a violation of the Buddhist precept against killing, in that it severed the line of Zen priests. It was also against the spirit of Buddha, who admitted nuns to Buddhism, to restrict the right of succession of the line only to priests. In October of 1951, nuns acquired the right to perform the initiation ceremony and to transmit the teachings of Zen masters; these enabled them to have their own formal nun pupils and nun Zen masters.

After solving these substantial and fundamental problems, nuns continued their campaign for genuine equality, in which they would be regarded not as secondary or exceptional cases, but as fully equal to monks. In 1957, the Sōtō council abolished the custom of making the Sōtō president the head of the nuns' organisation, and Kojima was inaugurated as its head. The organisation then became independent.

Under Kojima's leadership, the nuns' organisation continued to promote its work for perfect equality. In 1970, at the 28th Sōtō Assembly, equality was achieved by reforming the law. Nuns were granted the opportunity to become priests of *hōchi* level temples and to hold the long Kessei Ango meditation service by themselves.

Actual equality in education took almost the same length of time. In 1947, three nuns attended the Sōtō education council to request the repletion of facilities for nuns. In 1949, Komazawa University became coeducational and four nuns entered as formal students. In the same year nuns were allowed to attend the special seminar to become missionaries, and several nuns received training in preaching, which had been regarded as the role of monks. In 1950, four schools for nuns were allowed to function as Zen monasteries for nun teachers at a higher level. Other special seminars and training courses were also gradually opened to nuns, but they had to wait until 1968 for permission to build a special monastery and to obtain the title of missionary at the highest level. This special monastery was a substitute for that of the head temples, which nuns could not attend. It was the result of a continuous effort of the nuns' organisation, which had sent a petition every year since 1953. With this special monastery, full equality was achieved in the educational field, and four nuns, including Kojima, were appointed as missionaries.

After achieving its first target, the nuns' organisation extended its activities to the reform of the Sōtō sect system, criticizing the current system of the sect and the lives of priests. The 1968 meeting of nuns decided to present a petition for the reformation of the sect's election system, focusing on the political conflicts between the two head temples. In 1974, the nuns made election problems one of their five important issues, and declared that nuns would hold a neutral position, outside the whirlpool of political strife.

As women's status in society was improved after World War II, the nuns' organisation was forced to confront another women's problem: the rise of the power of priests' wives; this touched the most fundamental points of priesthood and definitions of Buddhism.

The Wives of Priests

In Buddhist doctrine, matrimony has traditionally been prohibited. In Japan it was also prohibited by civil law until the Meiji era. Evidence that temple priests did, however, marry can be found in the Yōrei codes of the 7th century, which allowed priests' families to inherit any private fortune. [13] During the Edo period, from the 17th century to the 19th century, matrimony was severely punished. Priests found to be married were exiled to an island. Informally, however, many priests lived with women in their temples, and regulations forbidding women to stay at temples were frequently issued by the Tokugawa shogunate.

The freedom of matrimony granted by the Meiji government was quickly accepted by priests. In spite of the formally negative attitude in the Buddhist world, more and more priests married, and by 1912,

[13] Kenji Eguchi, *Shūkyō dantai hōron* [The Law of the Religious Body] (1941), pp. 263, 276.

the end of the Meiji period, half of them had married. Some 80 per cent of the priests in the Sōtō sect had married by 1935.[14] But the status of their wives was very low. Matrimony was prohibited in Sōtō law and most of the marriages were unregistered. Their children were counted as pupils rather than children in the census. Social condemnation of these temple wives was severe, and because the marriages were unregistered, very few intelligent women with higher education became priests' wives. For those who did, their actual lives were not far from those of maids or slaves. It frequently happened that after the death of a priest his family would be dismissed by the new priest of the temple. In the Taishō Era, the protection of priests' families became a topic of discussion in many Buddhist sects. But the family protection law focused mainly on the protection of the successor of the temple and neglected the rights of the wives. In 1901, Sōtō law prohibited women from staying at temples, but in 1923 it permitted priests to register their own successors if the successor could take the priest's place within five years of his death. The priest who acted as a substitute priest at the temple until that time was obligated to bring up or to educate the successor.[15] There was no mention of wives, but the Sōtō administration had to admit their existence and ask for their cooperation during the war to manage temples in the absence of priests who were drafted and sent to war.

In 1943, at the same time of the special nuns' seminar in Tokyo, a seminar for priests' wives was held at Eiheji, one of the two head temples of the sect. About 120 representatives attended from all over Japan. They received lectures on Sōtō doctrine for three days, the priesthood initiation ceremony, and a Zen Buddhist surplice. In 1944, the Sōtō administration issued a rule on families which allowed wives to enter the priesthood and gave them the title of nun. Wives whose husbands entered military service could receive the lowest nun title, "*Ama joza*," and could work as assistants if they attended a seminar. Wives who shaved their heads and attended a seminar more than three times were regarded as nuns and ranked as nun teachers on the elementary level. The definition of "wives" *included those whose marriages were unregistered*, which shows us that quite a few common law wives lived in the temples.[16] This proclamation

[14] *Sōtō Sect Manual*, 1935.

[15] Bureau of Religion, Ministry of Education, *Shūkyō gyōsei* (1933).

[16] *Sōtō shūho* [Soto Sect Bulletin], 123.

formally guaranteed the lives of the wives, so long as they would consent to run the temple and to educate their children as successors.

The rights of wives, granted for convenience sake during the war, were carried into the new Sōtō constitution of the post war period, where it was written that they should be the product of legal marriages. The change, defining wives as married women only, was a reflection of the society, in which equality of men and women became the ruling ideology under the occupation of the United States. Following this new proclamation, most wives married.

Under the influence of the democratic reformation that was taking place in society at large, the Sōtō sect adopted a positive policy to educate wives and protect their rights. One of these was determined to be the right of the wife to veto any possible successor to the temple after the death of her husband. In 1950, the Sōtō sect decided to recommend life insurance for its priests, for the sake of their families and parishioners.[17] Then, in 1954, a duty was imposed on temples to protect the priest's family should he die.

Any successor was required to win the agreement of the former priest's family in order to be appointed. In 1977 a new set of regulations was issued concerning the wives of priests, which granted them the privileges of a sub-teacher if they successfully completed a correspondance course and a seminar. Thus, priests' wives have gradually become an important force in the enlightenment of parishioners.

As the power of the *jizoku*, the priests' wives, grew, these wives soon came into confrontation with the nuns. The nuns' organisation submitted a petition in 1968 critical of the Sōtō administration for qualifying the wives as teachers too easily, and demanding that the wives undergo more severe training. The nuns' 1974 meeting took up as one of its topics for discussion the question of *jizoku*, and proposed that wives should undergo a certain period of compulsory religious practice at the convent. At the 1976 conference of Sōtō monasteries, the Aichi Convent brought up the *jizoku* problem and proposed that the sect should give wives a different title, one that would not be accompanied by the taking of the tonsure or undergoing the practice of long meditation.[18]

One of the most serious problems at the convents was that nuns,

[17] *Sōtō shūho*, 204.

[18] *Otayori* 68, [Newsletter of the Sōtō Nuns' Organisation] (1976).

unlike priests, were unable to pass their temples on to their children, which made the choosing of a successor difficult. The nuns were discouraged by the lax attitude of the Sōtō administration toward the *jizoku*: they themselves underwent much more severe practices and continued to maintain the Buddhist lifestyle that had been traditional since the religion was introduced to Japan, but priests' wives were granted many of the same privileges without having undergone the same hardships.

The sect administration, from the perspective of the nuns, avoided any definite answer to the nuns, replying only that the *jizoku* were not permitted to perform the role of priests at funeral or memorial services.[19] At present, wives must remain as assistants, and are not allowed to perform priestly functions, but it is possible that their roles will expand as their educational standards improve. It is possible that wives will become nuns and run temples along with their sons after the deaths of their husbands. They would not be nuns under the old definition, which is a reflection of a society in which the lives of women have become diversified by a greater number of choices.

Conclusion

One of the striking features of Japan's modernisation has been the increase of women's activities in society. In the case of the Sōtō nuns, however, this has led to an unexpected antagonism between the celibate nuns and traditional housewives.

The power of women has, in fact, been realized in two contradictory ways: the appearance of nuns who are widows with children and the expansion of the roles of the wives of priests—both have worked to confuse the traditional category of single nuns living apart from the secular world.

The current status of nuns gives us two points from which to reconsider present society. The first of these is religious. The maintenance by the nuns of the traditional ascetic Buddhist life constitutes a silent criticism of the lives of priests, who live in the midst of both secular and religious activities. It also prompts us to reconsider the activities of Buddhism itself, which in Japan has become what might be called funeral Buddhism, one to which families turn only for death rites.

[19] *Ibid.*

At the same time, however, the nuns have had to confront the problem of a lack of successors. Until the end of the war, young girls became nuns during childhood and were brought up in convents. A decrease in the number of children per household, a general decline in religious beliefs, and an elevation of the standards of living, however, have all worked together to decrease the number of women who wish to become nuns. This problem with successors has become a distressing one for the nuns' organisation, and raises yet another point, the feminist aspect.

The less well defined nature of nuns in Sōtō Buddhism, as expressed above, prompts us to reconsider attitudes toward men and women, the lives of women, and the nature of home, marriage and profession throughout the entire society. The tonsure, for example, is the symbol to the priesthood, and the shaven head of the nun once proclaimed a renouncement of the secular world and devotion to her profession. For these nuns there were but two choices—whether to live a religious life or give it up and return to the secular world.

Now, however, the dilemma is whether to accept different types of nuns, such as widows with children or nuns who have not shaved their heads; this reflects the widening of choices for women who wish to lead "religious" lives. The many uncertain aspects in the world of nuns is but a reflection of the changing status of women in the present society.

PART FOUR

ORGANISING FOR SOCIAL CHANGE

Introduction

Change requires organisation. As we have seen, the seemingly intractable opposition to women's ordination and women's leadership within religious traditions did not begin to move by force of nature, but only as the result of relentless work by women, who formed strong organisational networks, like that of the Sōtō nuns in Japan or the Anglican women in Britain and the United States. However, women have organised not only to achieve ends within religious institutions; they have also organised along religious and ideological lines to work for social change in the wider community. In this section we wil look at the work of four women's organisations that are enlivened and motivated by religious or ethical commitments. These are not simply goal or power-oriented organisations, like political parties or interest/action groups; they are primarily *value-motivated* organisations.

We are reminded by women throughout the world that injustice and violence are not simply the excesses and extremes of militaristic or totalitarian regimes; they are built right into the foundations of major cultures and civilizations and into the foundations of global interaction and interrelations—political, cultural and economic. Therefore change means not only skilful and powerful organisation, it means *re*-organisation, at the level of the foundation.

An issue that inevitably arises in a women's organisation working for fundamental change is that of structure. If cultural patterns of dominance and hierarchy have kept women "in place," then it is not enough simply to move some women up in the hierarchy, even where it is possible. Someone will be in the old "place," and things will be fundamentally as they were before. Women can work to get a bill passed in a patriarchal and hierarchical legislative body by organising in a matriarchal and hierarchical way, if we choose to do so. However, if women organise together to address and to change the fundamental presuppositions of social structures such as patriarchy and hierarchy, we cannot organise in a patriarchal and hierarchical way. If we do so, we create among ourselves the very structures we seek to change. Here the medium is the message; the means is the end. The process of change does not simply lead to a desired future goal, but begins the construction of that goal. The Gandhian vision of social change, in particular, emphasises this "constructive" aspect of reorganising fundamental structures of society, including the family, from the ground up.

All of the groups about which women speak in this section are what might be called "grassroots" organisations. They are local, and it is in local communities that their effectiveness lies. And yet they are all part of wider networks. They are "knotted-in" to other local groups of the same organisation or of the same ideological commitment. The fact that they are grassroots organisations is not incidental to their being women's organisations. First of all, for better or worse, it is at the grassroots that women live. Second, and all for the better, it is at the grassroots that those fundamental changes that affect peoples' lives either will or will not take place, the most important of such changes being peoples' own sense of empowerment to change.

The issues about which these organisations are concerned are not what are sometimes thought of as "women's issues". They are indeed women's issues, for they affect women critically. But they are wider social issues which women have organised to address: untouchability, ecology, health, drug abuse, family planning, poverty, and nuclear weapons. Along with the organisations discussed here there are many others—from the powerful womens' associations of the Black churches in South Africa to the pan-Arab Association of Solidarity between Women in the Arab world, to socially and politically active groups such as Church Women United in the U.S.

Radha Bhatt has worked since 1952 in Lakshmi Ashram, a Gandhian ashram for girls and women in Kausani, in the Almora district of the Kumaon Hills, in the foothills of the Himalayas. For the past ten years, Radha has been the leader of this ashram community. Lakshmi Ashram is a residential school for young village girls of the Kumaon Hills, who learn the basics of education. It is also a training centre for older girls, who learn the skills of spinning and weaving *khadi*, handloom cotton or wool, for cottage industries. With the Gandhian ideals of self-reliance and bread-labour, Lakshmi Ashram is also a subsistence farm, on which all members of the community work daily in the gardens and dairy sheds. And, as Radha tells us in her presentation, it is also the base for wider community action projects in the villages of the Himalayan foothills region of Kumaon. Through its Gandhian basis, Lakshmi Ashram is also linked with other Gandhian institutions, including Gandhian women's projects, throughout India. The All-India Gandhian women's workshop, mentioned by Devaki Jain, held its 1982 meeting at Lakshmi Ashram.

In the Netherlands, **José Höhne-Sparborth** is involved in another kind of grassroots movement for social change, loosely called the "basic community movement" or the "grassroots movement". For twenty years, José has been a member of a Catholic congregation of religious women, the Sisters of Providence. For the past seven years she has lived in a Dominican community of women and men, called "Giordano Bruno," after the Dominican who was executed for alleged "heresy" in 1600. This basic community is one of many in Holland which José describes as the "other" tradition of Christianity—the revolutionary tradition, dedicated to a witness among the poor and the marginalized, and committed to social change. In the Netherlands, one of the major commitments of Giordano Bruno and other grassroots communities is halting the spread of nuclear weapons, and educating people as to the connections between the arms race and the conditions of poverty and injustice in the Third World.

The National Council of Jewish Women, a United States organisation, is a more established women's organisation, launched in the late 19th century. Today the NCJW has a national organisation and local sections throughout the country, and for the most part has a traditional hierarchical structure. **Judith Aronson** presents a portrait of one of these local sections, that of Los Angeles, in a time of transition. The transition she describes is an important one for women and women's organisations: from a volunteer service orientation toward problems "out there," to a recognition that some of the problems are right here, in our own lives, our own families, and our own communities. The transition was from being a service organisation of volunteers that "delivered" charity and help to the needy and sent clothing to the poor abroad, to a women's organisation that continues these projects, but also recognizes the neediness of some of its own members. Judith presents a vivid picture of NCJW's Council House in Los Angeles.

Finally, **Baroroh Baried**, a Professor at Gadjah Mada University in Yogyakarta, examines the history and the work of the Indonesian Muslim Women's Organisation, of which she is now the President. The organisation is called Aisyiyah, after the wife of the Prophet Muhammad. Its parallel men's organisation is the Muhammadiya. Both began in a period of Islamic reform in the early 20th century. Here Baroroh Baried describes the background of this movement in Indonesia, which has the world's largest Muslim population. She goes on to tell of the activities of the many local Aisyiyah groups throughout Indonesia—in kindergartens, in health education, and above all, in family planning. Especially effective has been Aisyiyah's use of its network of women's Koran study groups to raise consciousness on family planning, and on other matters crucial to women and to the welfare of their families.

Lakshmi Ashram: A Gandhian Perspective in the Himalayan Foothills

Radha Bhatt

I come from one of the villages in the far interior of the Middle Himalayas, an area remote from so-called modern development. Yet I doubt if these villages are really "backward," if judged by human values. The area is rich in humanity, although there are problems that need social change to bring solutions. My organisation, Lakshmi Ashram, is helping the people of this area to bring about such change, along the lines of Gandhian ideals.

I would like to present some of my experience of work in this field, gained over the past 32 years. To my mind the most important factor in bringing about change in society is fearless thinking among the people, and Gandhi's contribution to the world was his generation of this power of fearlessness, particularly in the hearts of the downtrodden and poor. Thereafter they were able to stand up and say, "We won't tolerate this injustice." This fearlessness is a basic factor in bringing about long-lasting social change.

The exploited and weak people and classes are so because they have lost the courage to stand up against injustice and exploitation. After a while, a sense of fatalism becomes fixed in the minds of these people, and they lose any confidence they once had in themselves. When this happens, people cannot even understand or recognise the nature of the injustice or exploitation to which they are subjected.

It is very difficult to generate the capacity of fearlessness in them, but Gandhi was able to do so. He was able to regenerate their ability

---

Reprinted by permission of *The Modern Churchman*, New Series, Vol. XXVI, no. 3 (1984).

to analyse justice and injustice, and to fight for justice; to understand equality and inequality, and to resist inequality. The fearlessness of the common people was a great strength which he discovered and brought out into the struggle for political liberation in India. And Gandhi gave it a right sense of direction in the revolution of social values. It was of great significance that this revolution, political and social, was carried out by the farmers, the women, and the other down-trodden people of India.

When I think of the farming women of these Kumaon hills, an example of their fearless action comes immediately to mind. I was not lucky enough to experience first hand the movements of women and men led by Gandhi, but I saw the fearless power of which he spoke among the farming women of Kumaon in 1967. At that time, Lakshmi Ashram was campaigning alongside the village people against the liquor shops. The women of the Garud area had stood firmly against the government liquor shop in their village, and every day hundreds of women were picketing in front of it because they wholeheartedly believed it was a dangerous threat to their families and their economic well-being. Over a period of six months, the campaign was taken up by some hundred villages, but still the district authorities continued simply to wait and watch. It was finally decided that a few women should go and talk with the District Magistrate. Four women were selected who were absolutely committed to liquor prohibition. These illiterate women needed someone with them to make all the arrangements for their 60 kilometre journey by bus to the district headquarters. I was deputed to accompany them, for I doubted if they had the courage to speak face to face with the District Magistrate. They could not even speak in Hindi, only in their local Kumaoni language.

Yet the next day in front of the District Magistrate they spoke so fearlessly and perfectly that I was astonished. They started arguing with him, and the talk began to get quite heated.

"If I don't agree, how can you stop the liquor shop?" shouted the District Magistrate.

"We can set fire to the shop," the women spoke firmly and calmly.

"That is an offence. Do that and you will find yourselves in handcuffs," he said.

"Then come with ten thousand handcuffs. We are not just one or two. Thousands of us are picketing the liquor shop. We have no fear of jail or even death, for our lives are completely destroyed by this drinking. We can face every danger."

The District Magistrate looked into the eyes of these illiterate village women and found them ablaze with determination.

No, not with handcuffs, but I will come myself to see these fearless women like yourselves, he thought to himself.

Needless to say, the District Magistrate was so overwhelmed by the atmosphere that he ordered the shop to be closed down, and said, "This is the miracle of Gandhi, whose spirit is working in these women."

In the eight districts of the middle Himalayas where I have been working these last 32 years, the people are exploited in many ways. They have had no equal chances of development. In such an exploited and underdeveloped society the women find themselves in an even worse position, for they are considered as secondary persons within their own society. Till today they do not get even five per cent of the opportunities for development, education and freedom. So they have come to accept this as their fixed due with a spirit of fatalism.

These women, however, are not weak in any way. Working hard in the midst of nature in the fields and forests, by the rivers, and in the mountains, they have become very persevering and tolerant. They are wise and practical, bearing the responsibilities of their families without the help of their men. But social injustice had killed their self-confidence to such an extent that they could not contemplate any thought of change or self-discovery in their lives. They used to say, "We are just like cows in the *goth*," the *goth* being the cowshed on the ground floor of their homes. And thus were they considered by society.

To gain their active participation and give them the confidence to act together fearlessly for social change is not very easy, yet if it can be achieved it is very effective. This was the experience we in the ashram had gained, but still I had my doubts as to whether the village women themselves would be able to lead such revolutions. The women of Khirakot village changed this apprehension of mine by their action. They shed new light on my whole way of thinking.

Khirakot is a village in the Someshwar valley, having a population of 150 families. It lies just above the Kosi River on the lower slopes of the hillside. Above the village is their own village forest, while higher up lies the government reserve forest. Most of the men of this village are away in employment. Out of some 500 men only 25 or 30 remain in the village. Therefore, the responsibilities of daily life within the family are borne by the women.

The pine trees of the village forest of Khirakot were lopped to such an extent that only the lower stems were left on the land. These branches were lopped off and used for fuel, but this in turn caused a complete lack of the pine needles that are used as bedding in their cattle sheds.

One morning the women coming down from the distant government reserve forest with heavy headloads of dry pine needles felt it was just too much for them to walk so far every day, leaving their children and cattle alone at home for hours at a time, and finally reaching home so tired that the rest of the day's work was impossible to finish.

They discussed the matter among themselves, and decided that they should protect their village forest against the lopping of branches for fuel by their own and neighbouring village women. If the pine trees grew bigger, then their needles would be available close to their homes. And if the forest were managed properly, then fuel wood would also be obtainable from these trees without destroying the whole tree. They spread their ideas among the other women of the village, and they all became convinced, not by holding any formal meeting, but at the water places or along the village paths where they met one another.

Thus, after four years of continuous efforts by the collective leadership of these women, a fine pine forest can been seen above Khirakot village. The forest has already begun to provide dry pine needles for their cowsheds. This leadership is not tired, but rather increasingly enthusiastic about ideas. In the first month of 1983 they involved the menfolk in their endeavours. Every family of the village agreed to pay a rupee a month as salary to a forest guard, a young man from their village. The women's group collected the money and helped the young man guard the forest.

This is a rare example of collective enterprise in the present day atmosphere of the welfare state that is India, where people have lost their initiative for such collective action and have instead grown accustomed to asking for grants from the state, even for a very small work project.

The method that can succeed in such leadership is completely non-violent, with no aggression, no hatred, no competition. In Hindu philosophy, non-violence is one of the main principles of the religion, and Gandhi, who in his life tried to act in a non-violent manner, both as an individual and collectively, had his family roots in the Hindu Vaishnava tradition. There, in his daily family life, he gained a deep inner consciousness of truth and non-violence. In his life, truth was his aim, and non-violence was the means to attain it. Truth was his God, and non-violence was his religion. Once when someone asked him to which religion he belonged, he replied, "Previously I used to say I believed in God, but now I say I believe in Truth. I was saying that God was Truth, but now I am saying that Truth is God. There are people who disagree with the existence of God, but there is none who differs as to the existence of truth. Even an atheist believes in truth."

This sense of non-violence also permeates the consciousness of the women among whom I have been working all these years. Yes, this awareness is more alive, stronger and clearer in the women than among the men. The following example will make this clear.

This incident goes back to 1957 when India was moved by the revolutionary action of Bhoodan, the land-gift movement. Our organisation, Lakshmi Ashram, was spreading this idea in the far flung villages and valleys of Kumaon. I went from village to village and door to door, along with other girls of my ashram. We walked along the high and narrow paths, our rucksacks on our backs, conveying the message that the big landowners should be able to spare and donate a part of their land to the landless people of their village. In the Himalayan region, however, there are few true landlords, and the majority are small farmers with holdings roughly similar in size. Even so, one can find a poor landless man or widow in every village.

That day we had walked a distance of some 30 kilometres, and had conducted four small meetings in villages along the way. It was getting dark, evening was closing in, and we had finished the last meeting of that day. We had found accommodation for the night in the house of a typical farmer of that village. While he was preparing food in his kitchen for us, we were sitting under the low roof of his house around an open fire in the middle of the room, which was full of smoke. He had been joined by some men and children from the neighbouring houses.

Then a figure appeared out of the thick cloud of smoke and sat herself down beside me. Her clothes were torn. She said calmly, "I want to donate one *nali* (1/20 of an acre) of my land as Bhoodan."

"But how much land have you got in all?"

"I have some, by the grace of God," she said.

"She has only three *nalis* of unirrigated land," said one of the village men.

She kept quiet.

"Why do you want to donate something when you have such a little piece of land?"

She spoke after a short pause, "I have two sons. If God had offered me three, wouldn't I have distributed the same land among them?"

Needless to say, we were all impressed, and words were not necessary.

"Do you have any landless person in your village to whom you want to give it?" I asked again.

"Yes, one widow who has a son."

"Is she somehow related to you?"

"No, she is a Harijan. But she is a human being, and she also has a child. Just like me. Please don't try to stop me. This is my religion. I am illiterate, but still I know that our religion preaches that we should share our meal. Lord Krishna has said, 'The one who cooks only for himself is a sinner, therefore eat, only after distributing among others.' " (Bhagavad Gita 2. 13).

These hill women have such a sense of religion, not in their minds alone, but in their hearts, and in their souls. It is this that gives them the strength for non-violent action, be it in development work, revolutionary social change, or in opposing injustice and exploitation.

Gandhi has declared many times that non-violence is the tool of the brave, and that there is no place in non-violence for cowardliness. This kind of brave action had been taken by these hill women when they fought against the timber contractors in Chamoli District, hugged the trees, and flung their bodies before the axes. Their action gave birth to the famous non-violent ecological movement known in India and throughout the world as "Chipko". Similar action was taken by the women of Khirakot when they fought against the businessman and the government who had started a soapstone quarry on their village land, which had spoiled their village forest, their cultivated land, their drinking water, and the footpaths to their fields. They were bold enough to struggle for two and a half years against these two big powers in India. They were so powerful that they could motivate the men of their own families and villages for this cause. They were able to proclaim strongly, "This is our forest, our land, and our paths, and the businessman is exploiting us. We will not tolerate it."

The women of the villages in Kumaon have met with success in such non-violent actions. I would say that they succeeded because their actions were non-violent, for non-violence is the only tool for such common people. And where are the roots of this non-violence? I believe they are rooted deep in the culture and religion of our people.

The Grassroots Movement in the Netherlands: The Community Called "Giordano Bruno"

José Höhne-Sparborth

The Context of the Netherlands

There are 500,000 officially unemployed in the Netherlands. Our multinational corporations find cheaper workers in El Salvador, South Africa, Pakistan and other countries; the rest is done by computers. It is said that twenty families are the owners of the whole of Holland—its industries and great projects. Nobody knows exactly who they are, for there is no other country in the world where the privacy of great owners is protected and kept secret as perfectly as in Holland.

Our actual government, a Christian Democratic and Liberal coalition, is very interested in showing itself to be cooperative with the Reagan administration. I am afraid that we will continue to get our missiles, although 55 per cent of the population is absolutely against further armament. Our government has also cut back state aid to those most in need. And for years, it has spent millions of guilders for improvements in industry, without any substantial spending for improvements for workers. We are a democracy, so we have the right to protest against these policies. And we have been doing so already for years. We are also a democracy in the economic sense. Anyone with energy and a good idea may open up his/her shop. We have always been traders, and everyone is welcomed by us—as long as we can use them.

The Netherlands had what some call a "Golden Century" during its colonial period. Proportionally, we sent the most missionaries all over the world to convert the "pagans" to Christianity. Now we have lost the colonies, and many people from our former colonies are living with us. In their own countries, they learned Dutch ways. They learned our history, and not their own. And now, in Holland, they are foreigners. They come from such places as Surinam and Indonesia, and they include Hindus, Muslims, Christians and others. Finally, I have to say: we exported our way of trading, our way of believing, our morality; and I am far from optimistic about our "contribution" towards "developing" others.

In 1581 we became our own nation after 80 years of continuous war between Dutch Calvinists and Spanish Roman Catholics. The Catholic church is now the largest church in Holland, and within the Catholic Church there are 105 religious orders for women, 40 for priests and 10 for brothers. Of the Netherlands it is said, "One Dutchman is a theologian, two Dutchmen make a church, three Dutchmen make a schism." Next to the Catholic Church, there are the Reformed Church and the Calvinist Church, both large churches, and then 77 other Christian churches, followed by a number of sectarian groups. Since 1960, many foreign workers have come, with their families, from Turkey and Morocco, and Islam is now the second religion in our country.

In the Netherlands there are about 20 national peace organisations, beginning as early as 1924. In politics there are about 20 parties, three large and the rest smaller. There are many women's organisations, and several feminist organisations. Beside these organised groups, there are, in every place and in every parish, women's groups that gather to talk and to study their own situation and common problems. In Holland there are also about 120 grassroots communities, 60 of them now organised in a national grassroots movement, or "Basic Movement" for Christians.

The Context of Europe

In addition to being Dutch, I am also a European woman. Within Europe, we live with the north-south conflict. Italian, Portuguese and Spanish people have come with their families to Holland for ten or fifteen years, to make enough money to buy a small field in their own countries. Their return poses a great social problem. Their countries of origin are generally poor and the poorest people are the ones who have come to us. Now they have to go; we don't need them any longer. In the meantime we have become a nation very mixed ethnically, and discrimination is growing. It is strongest in the lower classes, because the dominants play the game of "divide and rule". Dutch workers are played off against foreign workers by big industry, by our liberal party, and by some local churches, afraid of the influence of other religious ideas. Most of the inhabitants of the Netherlands belong to one or another minority group, but the majority is dominant.

Within Europe, we also live with the west-east conflict. From my town, 400 km to the east, is the border of the socialist countries. Most of our people do not know what is going on there, but they all have a great bias, directed by politics and newspapers. We are more afraid of the "atheistic" Russians than of the godless nuclear armaments. For this reason we are completely oriented toward the United States, across the great ocean. The American people are somehow nearer to us than our neighbours, the people of East Germany. We have lost our own culture and taken over the American, because the Americans were our liberators in the Second World War. Hardly anyone knows that the Russians lost twenty million people in the same war. Yet we, as Dutch people, are still oriented across the ocean, because of economic and ideological interests.

When refugees come from eastern Europe, they are immediately given asylum. Refugees from Latin America, however, often need years before they are, and they have to prove that they are in danger. A few months ago, five Kurdish people were sent back to Iraq: they have since been killed.

Ours is a kind of "NATO Christianity". The pact between the North Atlantic culture and the Christian religion is complete. This dominant tradition keeps its dominance by a mixture of rationalism and sentimentalism. A rationalism that, like technology and industry, is so overdeveloped that ordinary people cannot understand it anymore. On the other hand the churches with their moralism, liturgies and badly used symbols make such an appeal to the sentiments, that these same ordinary people stay attached to their churches.

The same churches teach the workers the so-called Christian values: humility, modesty, simplicity. Whoever wants to reach the top of the tree has to develop such qualities as self-sufficiency, security, perseverance. Obedience is also important. Calvinists are very obedient to the government. Dutch Catholics are very obedient to the Fope. But now, in the best sense, we are frustrated by this obedience.

Basic Communities

I live in a Dominican community, with two women and two men. There are many people who are part of our community and who work in our house. We have named ourselves "Giordano Bruno," after a Dominican who was burned in 1600 because he was accused of being a heretic. We have chosen this name because we believe in that *other* tradition of Christianity—the non-dominant tradition that always is murdered and burned, but that is also the tradition of sustained revolution. It started with the exodus of Moses, it continued with the prophets and with Jesus, with the religious orders of earlier times, with the heretical movements often led by women, with the missionaries who opposed slave-trade and proselytising and now with the grassroots movements, the peace movement and the feminist movement. We as a community are engaged in all these three—grassroots activism, the peace movement and feminism. I will try to elaborate my hopes for the Christian tradition, helped by these movements.

In the 1960s, the churches began to learn that Christianity needs political engagement. Our missionaries had come back from the colonies, now liberated, and they told us what happened there. They spoke of poverty, violations of human rights, and torture. Most of the grassroots communities rose up in response to Third World issues. In a short time, however, they learned something about the relation of these to the First World. When in 1977, 60 basic community groups formed themselves into a national grassroots movement they could say of themselves: "Most of us belong to the middle class of our society, a middle class which at decisive moments in history has chosen loyalty to the existing order in preference to solidarity with the underdog, a middle class which has refused to think in terms of conflicting interests. Now things must change. We know that our economic system basically answers to the description of a capitalist system."

These grassroots groups have chosen to undertake a new reading of the Bible. There they have discovered again the great stories as revolutionary stories that moved people against slavery. Rather than forcing "Christian values" upon the shoulders of people struggling for human rights and dignity, it is important to realize that the law of Moses was given to his people only *after* they had freed themselves from slavery. It was given as law to liberated people.

The grassroots groups in Holland will not build another new church. We are all still members of our own churches, often very active in them. But as a movement at the *base* of the churches we try to help Christian churches find a way back to their own tradition of liberation, and find a way out of their pact with imperialistic culture. For the past two years, we of the grassroots movement have had observer status in the Council of Churches of the Netherlands. This gives us the possibility of intervention with difficult issues: civil disobedience, refusing to pay the part of taxes used for armaments, the economic boycott of South Africa, legislation about many Islamic and Christian Turkish people, and equality for gay people.

As we made our first steps, we learned a great deal in one particular struggle alongside illegal alien workers in danger of being expelled by our government. For ten months they took refuge in a number of churches, and in the end were helped only by grassroots communities and a few parishes. During this struggle these groups learned what solidarity means that one cannot dictate conditions for the help one offers. Our groups learned that they could not make the decisions, but that the illegal alien workers themselves would have to decide how to act and how to fight. Although it was our money and time, it was their risk. The misery of the most powerless had to determine *our* act: that is what we learned again about the Gospel.

It seems to me that the radical ideas in these base groups are still too often intellectual, and that there is a danger of simply importing liberation theology from Latin America. The groups try to "read the Bible with the eyes of the poor". I think this is a mistake, we have to try to read with *our* eyes in fact—the eyes of dominant people who are intensely aware of the poor and of our relationship to them. When we do not learn this, we get caught in the trap of criticizing others, without changing ourselves, in spite of all our structural analyses. I think that the women within the grassroots movement help everyone to understand this; and a real struggle has started between men and women about just this problem.

The Grassroots Movement and the Peace Movement

The peace movement is old in the Netherlands. But the most important and internationally well known is the Interkerkelijk Vredesberaad (IKV), The Interchurch Peace Council. It was established by several churches in 1967 to educate the churches on issues of war and peace. By 1977 the IKV launched a focussed campaign with the slogan: "Help rid the world of nuclear weapons, beginning in the Netherlands." In a very short time, in all parishes all over the country, peace groups have sprung up. Each year in September they organise a peace-week. During this week, in schools, churches, and many other common places there is information about the arms race, and about the relation of the arms race to the problems of the Third World. We find from such information that what would be needed on a yearly basis to help eliminate hunger, illiteracy, illness and homelessness is spent for armaments in merely two weeks! In the Netherlands, this church-based peace movement has helped to stimulate a growing awareness about the danger of the nuclear arms race.

One problem is that the leaders of this peace movement have not taken much more than first steps. They have aimed at gaining a majority, and in this they have succeeded. But the local peace groups need more. They have asked for a better political, economic and social analysis of the whole society in which this armament is going on. Some older, more radical peace groups and the grassroots movement have helped these local peace groups.

For the past year the peace movement has been in a critical period. The top leadership of the IKV suddenly started speaking against the governments of the socialist countries. They saw all anti-government movements in the socialist countries to be their allies, without looking at the real nature of these movements. They simply interpreted them as emancipation movements. And they declared existing peace movements in Eastern Europe not to be real peace movements. They took the dangerous path of dictating to other countries what it means to act as a peace movement. By this policy the IKV peace movement has come into conflict with the governments of Eastern Europe and has endangered many contacts, carefully built up over long years. The grassroots movement has begun an important discussion with the IKV on this issue, and now, after a year, there seems to be some change.

There is also a growing Women's Peace Movement in Holland, with 200 groups and about 10,000 members, and these women will go to Prague. They have set their own conditions: to make a contribution just as women. I think that the Women's Peace Movement is more realistic, more genuinely interested in contacts, and not as biased and arrogant as the others. Some of the special issues this Women's Peace movement would like to study are: the participation of women in fascism and in war; the possibility of developing contacts with the wives of workers in military industries; and the specifics of aggression in the world. Since 1945, for example, about 140 wars have been suffered by countries in the Third World. In about ten cases the Warsaw Pact countries have intervened, while in about 60 cases the NATO-countries have intervened. The Women's Peace Movement is also interested in studying the roots of western anti-communist biases.

In the 1960s many emancipation movements arose, but the only one which has really carried through is the feminist movement. Over the last ten years, increasingly one finds feminist groups in local church parishes. Until now, the Christian feminist movement has been primarily inspired by that in the United States, but now we are beginning to become truly Dutch, with numerous local women's groups as well as academic groups. The accent is on a movement within the churches, although in the religious orders there has until now been generally less interest in the feminist movement. Our Catholic sisters are for the most part content with their position—to be led by priests.

The feminist movement and the grassroots movement are united in their wish to stay within the churches. Both are looking for a better, truer tradition within Christianity. Both have learned that much of the Bible and much of the older tradition was annexed by a dominant, white, rich, West European minority. We have to regain our revolutionary stories and tell them again on behalf of the powerless.

We women in the First World belong to the dominant group. Being women, however, we have an unequal position as compared to men. In this double position we are in particular danger. Fighting against this inequality could easily lead us into an equally dominant position ourselves, and this would by no means be liberating to society as a whole. In my opinion the "doubleness" in the Christian church, with its dominant and its revolutionary strands, and the "doubleness" in the position of Dutch women as both dominant and unequal, are clearly related. It is for just this reason that women, far better than others, can liberate Christianity from its dominance. Women cannot export their struggle, as some in the peace movement try to do, by blaming aggression on the socialists, for example. By the same token, women cannot import liberation, as some in the basic movement try to do, by adopting the struggles and the liberation theologies of Latin America. Women have their struggle right here: in their own homes, in their own families, in their own bodies.

In our struggle, we learn that women's values, just like Christian virtues, may keep us in slavery. For this reason, we must always ask: Patience, of course, but with whom? Will we be patient with the rich, as long as there are so many poor? Humility, yes, it is good. But is humility good with someone who profits by my ignorance? In our doubleness we must learn that we live in a web of power. We have to ask, again and again, in whose interest we are acting. The real test of our struggle for social change will be if we can free ourselves from our powerless position, without attaining the kind of power which enslaves others.

I think that the doubleness in Christian faith could be an important instrument in the liberation of women, and of men. And staying in the liberation tradition of this religion, we can be protected from taking over the dominant position in society ourselves. On account of our own struggle for freedom we can make the Christian communities listen again to the best part of their tradition. Having experienced the dominance of this religion, we can point out the dangerous aspects of it. It must be possible for us to free Christianity from its own poverty.

In fact, the Christian feminists in Holland are in danger of stopping their reflections about equality at their own front door. In Holland everyone may open his/her own shop, including women's groups. Women have gained real ground. At worst, in crisis, we may give back some of the ground we have gained. But, in the meantime, men are persisting with their games of dominance, and nothing has really changed. Real social changes are possible only when our structures of dominance are demolished.

What I see happening now is that the Christian grassroots communities are helping the feminist movement to be more politically oriented, to find the roots of the tradition of sustained revolt within

Christianity. And women in the same groups, together with other Christian women, bring about an awareness that social change is impossible as long as we do not free ourselves from our original sin: stigmatization by a dominant, arrogant, patriarchal, colonial culture that rules, so it thinks, by the grace of God.

The grassroots movement has also opened the discussion of solidarity with Latin and Central America. In the Netherlands there now exist two great organisations of solidarity groups. SOLIDARIDAD is a group that has intensive contacts in Central America, including contacts with the guerillas and with the Eglesia Populare; CLAT, sponsored by many people deeply engaged with the Latin American issues, is aligned to the Christian Democrats in these areas. CLAT has been very popular in Holland, for members of our own groups as well. The discussion we have started about the position of CLAT, and about history in decisive moments such as these, is now going on and is very intense. CLAT is concerned with the extensive aggression against the government of Nicaragua. It gives a clear picture of the aggressor's position: they are exporting our frustrated Western European anti-Marxism to others. It is not the first time that we have exported a religion.

In mid-1983 we had a congress of grassroots groups from all the countries of Europe. The former Bishop of Cuernavaca, Mexico, Mendez Arceo, taught us that we do not need to be Marxist, but at least we do not have to be anti-Marxist. And he taught us that it was not enough not to be a capitalist, we have to be anti-capitalist. At the same time, a woman from the GDR, Ilsegret Fink, asked us to take the socialists seriously as discussion partners, without the bias that Christians are, finally, better than atheists.

This issue of this congress was "Liberating Faith in Europe". We no longer wish to carry with us the old frustration against socialism as a godless heritage. And at the very least, we refuse as Christians to use this frustration to polarise opposition to those who try to change their society, whether in Holland or in Central America.

The National Council of Jewish Women: A Study of the Los Angeles Section in Transition

Judith Aronson

I would like to begin with a traditional blessing:

You are blessed, for we bless You,
The one who has given us life,
Who has sustained us through our joys and tribulations,
And has brought all of us, together, to this day.

In thinking about this presentation, I realized that I would like to tell many versions of the same story through the eyes of the various participants, somewhat like the Japanese film *Rashomon*. The story of the Los Angeles section of the National Council of Jewish Women is one that requires us to see tradition and change from several different points of view. But since space does not permit intertwining all the various strands and stories I have heard, I will tell you the one I know best, my story. I think it is legitimate to begin here, for my relationship with the organisational dilemma that I will describe affects me as a woman, as a Jew and as an advocate for social change.

The NCJW was founded in Chicago in 1893 by Hannah G. Solomon, friend and contemporary of Jane Addams, over an incident in which Jewish men left Jewish women off the programme for the upcoming Chicago Exposition. The Council became an organisation that participated in all the great social issues of the day and promulgated, on a volunteer basis, the kinds of activities that eventually became the attributes of professional social work and political lobbying for women. But the National Council of Jewish Women *was* a traditional women's organisation, for it was a "delivery system" of doing for others, less fortunate. It is the gradual transformation of the NCJW from a service and charitable organisation to a wider and modern women's organisation that I want to discuss here.

My first formal learning experience was at a nursery school at a settlement house called Council House, in New York City, sponsored by the National Council of Jewish Women. My mother was part of the young mothers' club, and since this was during the Depression of the 1930s, she found there affordable and stimulating activities. In the book, *The Jewish Woman in America*, the social work of volunteer upper and middle class Jewish ladies is brilliantly described. These women were part of the National Council of Jewish Women, which has a long history of serving immigrant women in a multitude of ways. Although my mother was born in the U.S. and now holds two master's degrees, she was at that time without even a high school diploma. She was hungry for learning and limited in her access to it. Her parents had told her that she could not possibly go to college if she did not want to become a schoolteacher. Since schoolteachers did not marry, she opted for no education. Council House meant to her, and to her children, a place to grow and develop ideas. It was a place to begin, and we did begin.

Twelve years later, living in Hartford, Connecticut, I had my second contact with the NCJW. This time, I taught in a community Sunday school as a high school student. It was my first paid job in Jewish education, which was to become, many years later, my profession. It fulfilled the original motto of the NCJW, "Faith and Humanity". In 1949, I assisted in the outreach of NCJW into the Jewish community, educating children who could not afford Synagogue schools, as well as assisting in teaching English to the survivors of the Holocaust who had managed to reach the U.S.

My next contact with the NCJW came thirty years later in Los Angeles, California. When I arrived in Los Angeles in 1979, I was a transplanted New Englander from Boston, now in "Lotus Land". My connections in Jewish education circles and even a women's support group were available to me, but I had not found a place to hang my feminist hat. The gift of a year's membership in NCJW plunged me into the midst of a time of great change, which I did not quite understand until 1982, when I found myself in the centre of a small whirlwind.

In that year, I was invited as a delegate to a three day conference of NCJW in San Diego, as a prospective vice-president of the Los Angeles section, which has about 3,000 members. I was an experiment, since there had never been a full time professional working woman in a top-level volunteer position in that organisation, which expects volunteers to devote three days a week in their offices. At the convention, I discovered that the job of President of the section was being contested by two women, an unusual event, and that the outgoing President was under attack by her board for making changes that were exhilarating, but frightening, to the traditional members. One candidate supported the changes, the other rejected them.

I found myself, as a newcomer to the organisation, facilitating a session in which the issues and the anger of the preceding four years were addressed. During these four years, under the outgoing President, the organisation was changing to one in which the members became the "clients"—recipients of services, as well as the volunteer "deliverers" of services. How ironic it was that the feelings of the very leadership that had instigated these changes had not been dealt with. Council House had become a women's centre, called the Women's Centre at Council House, and the women involved in its leadership were terrified of the changes they had made. The very feminism they had expressed had succeeded in alienating them because they were afraid of its impact on them personally and on their interpersonal relations.

It is significant in this context that the Los Angeles Section of the NCJW does have a paid professional staff, as well as its volunteer staff, for it is an organisation which is financially self-sufficient and which supports itself through the work of seven successful thrift shops. The paid executive director is an economist with a strong background in labour management, who runs a smoothly functioning million dollar a year enterprise. The paid professional staff has followed the President's feminist path more easily than the volunteers and members. As a result, there has been an alienation of many members and some decrease in membership, while at the same time, the attraction of new members who are working women and political activists, changing the direction of the group in what I consider positive ways.

Section activities in NCJW stem from a list of national goals and priorities determined by a biennial national convention. Certain projects are simply national projects that gain local support, such as the Shippabox programme, maintained by primarily older women who gather weekly to sew clothing for indigent families in Israel and send their products for distribution there. Similarly, the NCJW sponsors a Research Institute for Innovation in Education at the Hebrew University and has pioneered in a project called HIPPY, the Home Instruction Program for Preschool Youngsters, as well as other projects for disadvantaged children in Israel and around the world.

Following this kind of concern, for many years the L.A. Section maintained an in-house Agency for disturbed adolescent girls. Although it was known that some of the clients of the Agcncy—always spelled with a capital "A"—were daughters of NCJW members, it was never publicly acknowledged or discussed. The distinction was always made between "them", the client population, and "us", the successful members. With the influence of the women's movement, that distinction could no longer be made, and women began to drop the facade that traditional middle class life in suburbia was perfect. On the contrary, within that middle class society, accelerating problems with drug abuse, divorce, emotional instability, identity crisis, and a myriad of health and economic problems began to be acknowledged. In view of all this change, Council House responded by refocussing on the needs of its own members, and in keeping with its tradition, on needs of women in the community in general.

I have not yet mentioned the particularly Jewish factor in the NCJW. Ironically, as in all other Jewish organisations, there is the conflict between the universal and the particular. In the transition of which I am speaking in Los Angeles, the pull was toward both the polarities. By that I mean that as the Women's Center at Council House opened its doors to women's groups in the general community that needed office and meeting space, so too did it develop an in-house department of Jewish affairs. One of its major achievements was the establishment of the Jewish women's resource library at Council House, one of two such facilities in the United States.

In opening out in the universal direction toward women's community work more generally, the Women's Center at Council House now houses such agencies as the California NOW, the Women's Substance Abuse Resource Center, the Committee to Ratify the ERA, the Coalition for Alternatives in Jewish Education, the Women Lawyers of Los Angeles, Women Against Violence Against Women, the California Women's Health Center, and others. These agencies trade programme input for office space. Many prosper and then move to their own space, while new groups are brought in.

All this activity has led to the establishment of a new in-house agency, WHW—Women Helping Women. This is a hotline, maintained by trained volunteer para-professionals, which will serve as a resource and clearinghouse for women in the community needing counselling in a wide variety of areas. While help is out there in the community, women often do not know where to turn to fill their special needs.

Council House also opens its doors on Friday night for a feminist drop-in centre. This Shabbat, or Sabbath experience, is for lesbians and straight women who seek a safe place to explore ethical and religious concerns. They annually sponsor a Passover seder for about one hundred women and children, providing a non-sexist religious experience for the whole community. Along similar lines, in 1983 the NCJW sponsored a conference in Los Angeles called "God, Prayer and the Jewish Woman," which explored feminist theology and problems of sexist language.

All of these provide a sense of the scope of NCJW activity. But the real issue here is, what happens to women when faced with social change. For many, the changes of 1982 meant fear and alienation. Many had liked things the way they were, with anonymity in the problem areas, and visibility in socializing and voluntarism. Their own identity, and perhaps their "cover" for problems, stayed intact. But others, like myself, felt liberation and exhilaration, and have plunged into the new areas with zest.

One example is Rose, a retired woman in her seventies who is a volunteer in the Center for Victims of Domestic Violence, a Shelter maintained in a separate building owned by the NCJW. Rose goes to the Center a few times each week and does a variety of jobs, such as teaching English as a second language and running children's programmes. She has become a friend, confidante and role model for women at the Shelter. Rose believes women should be, and can be, independent and secure on their own. She herself, as she puts it, has been divorced more years than she was married and has had a good life. Rose worked hard, raised her family alone, and now exudes a sense of pride in what many would consider her unconventional life. She is interested in life and the problems of living, and is willing to share herself, not as a lady bountiful, but rather as an understanding sister who knows that the route to independence for abused women is a slow, treacherous and painful one.

However, many younger women in the section find the kind of voluntarism of women like Rose to be problematic for themselves. In years past, young women patiently worked their way up the organisational ladder in NCJW as an adjunct to their private lives, perhaps as an outlet for their energy and ambition, or as their only opportunity for growth. Today many young women who are educated and working professionally, are impatient for success, even as volunteers. They aspire to and are capable of leadership roles without working their way up through the ranks. The problem is still unsolved, but I have been something of a model and test case, since I am the first vice-president to be employed full time. Drawn to NCJW because it gives me a chance to volunteer and feel part of the feminist and Jewish communities, I rely on my staff counterpart to handle the work of the department on an ongoing basis.

Here I have spoken of only a few aspects of a complicated organisational model for women. I should at least mention one of the most important political aspects of the NCJW—an extensive programme of political involvement which trains lobbyists in the techniques of influencing government. Our annual meeting, which was held last week, was a coalition meeting on disarmament and the nuclear freeze, aimed at facilitating women's action on these issues.

Prophetic Judaism has always advocated, "Dream dreams and see visions." From 1893 in Chicago to 1983 in Los Angeles, some Jewish women have taken the risks necessary to promote the causes of social justice and have begun to apply these insights and techniques to our own personal needs as well, so that all of us together might carry out Hillel's admonition:

> If I am not for myself, who am I?
> If I am only for myself, what am I?
> If not now, when?

Muslim Women and Social Change in Indonesia: The Work of Aisyiyah

Baroroh Baried

The Socio-cultural Background of Indonesian Women

In the history of Indonesia, over a long period, the position of women has been considered very important, especially in the area of politics. For example, in an 8th century Middle Java inscription a ruling son, King Sanjaya, mentions the previous rule of his mother as queen. The Sanjaya inscription was followed by the inscription of another queen, a Buddhist queen of the Sailendra, dating from the 9th century, while from manuscripts and stories of the Indonesian archipelago, queens do not seem to have been at all uncommon. Other traditional stories from Sumatra, Timor and West Java tell of women from whose bodies rice, fruits, coconut trees and bamboo could grow.

More recently, history records the rule of queens in the 17th century. Aceh was ruled by a queen for 30 years, Sultanah Tajul Alam Safiatuddin Johan Berdaulat, who was crowned to succeed her husband because they had no children. The coronation of a woman was approved by both government officials and Muslim scholars, and it turned out that her reign was very productive for the development of Islamic law, literature and science in the Aceh territory. Many schools were built for both men and women, because, according to the Queen, Islam commanded that men and women should gain knowledge together.

Another example from the 19th century was from eastern Indonesia, the South Celebes. Siti Aisyah We Tenriolle was an intelligent and strong-willed woman who became the Queen of

Ternate in 1856, inheriting the reign from her grandfather. She united three regions during her rule, composed an epic of seven thousand folio pages, and founded the first school for both women and men in Ternate.

While these examples show something of the great strength of the heritage of Indonesian women, it is also true that feudal and colonial life in Indonesia caused a weakening and decline of the status of Indonesian women, more generally, by the end of the 19th century. Women continued to have a strong role in agriculture and household economics, but, in general, feudalism and the backwardness and lack of education of middle class women made it easy for men to enslave them and minimize their great contribution. The beginning of the 20th century brought renewed and widespread change to women in Indonesia.

The New Emergence of Indonesian Women's Awareness

One of the first great women leaders of the modern period is Raden Ajeng Kartini, who lived in the late 19th century, and is recognized as the first Indonesian woman to declare her conscience and to resist the customs which diminished and imprisoned women. Kartini was intelligent and had the opportunity to study in a Dutch private school. She was able to mingle with a large circle of people, to read and communicate her ideas to the outside world. Kartini wrote letters which expressed her feelings, her experience, and her analyses of society. These letters became records of the Indonesian people's life, and a vast source of information. Her letters urged social change for Indonesian women—to improve their fate, to obtain their rights, and to realise their duties. According to Kartini, education was the key to women's progress. This became her first and primary struggle, and she started a school for girls.

In addition to the influence of Kartini, a second major factor contributing to social change for Indonesian women was the emergence of Islamic Reformism in the second half of the 19th century. The reform movement had as its main goal to purify the teachings of Islam, based on the Holy Koran, from the accumulation of local Indonesian teaching and custom. Islamic teachings alone should be the guidelines of every aspect of life. One of the Indonesian Islamic reform organisations was the Muhammadiya, founded in 1912 in Yogyakarta by Kyai Haji Akhmad (K.H.A.) Dahlan. He was a theologian, with a broad view of the future. He understood that Indonesian Muslims were in a crisis of faith and in need of guidance.

He founded the Muhammadiya for that guidance in the Muslim faith, and along with it envisioned the establishment of a women's department. For this purpose he chose a group of intelligent and active girl students to be trained to run the women's section. They eventually became the first board members of the new women's organisation, under the name Aisyiyah, a name derived from the Prophet's wife Aisyah. Officially, Aisyiyah was founded in 1917 in Yogyakarta.

In the beginning, the Aisyiyah was the instrument of the Muhammadiya for the purpose of developing Muslim women's understanding of the Islamic religion, so that they would know the ways of divine service to God—performing the five daily prayers, fasting, paying the religious tax, going on a pilgrimage to Mecca, etc. In addition, they would know the basis of virtue in the Koran and Hadith, and understand the prohibition against adultery, cheating, lying and so on.

In this first stage, Aisyiyah did not have its own statutes, rules or administrative directives; it was managed by the Muhammadiya. Gradually, Aisyiyah developed its own administration and equipped itself with its own staff members, and began to expand outside of Yogyakarta into other cities, at first as an adjunct of Muhammadiya, and then on its own. In the early years Nyai Akhmad Dahlan, the wife of K.H.A. Dahlan, would travel with her husband and gather the women in those places where he was organising the Muhammadiya.

In 1922, one of Aisyiyah's first important efforts was the founding of a mosque for women only in Yogyakarta. Afterwards, more and more places established such mosques. The mosques, called Musalla Aisyiyah, enabled women to gather to pray together (*jama'ah*) five times a day. They also provided meeting places for Aisyiyah women, and were the natural centres for religious courses, kindergartens and community activities, such as the distribution of food alms (*zakar fitrah*).

Although its organisational structure was technically a part of the Muhammadiya, the Aisyiyah became known and well-organised in society as a separate and self-dependent organisation, like other women's organisations in Indonesia. Therefore, in 1928, Aisyiyah, together with seven other women's organisations, formed an Indonesian women's organisation known first as the Perikatan Perkumpulan Perempuan Indonesia, afterwards changing its name to the Perikatan Perkumpulan Istri Indonesia (PPII). The federation of women's organisations which began there in 1928 is now known as the Indonesian Women's Congress, and includes more than fifty organisations.

This first Indonesian women's congress was an important historical event, for it marked the emergence of both corporate and co-operative awareness among Indonesian women. This awareness was built upon an awakening sense of nationality as well. At that time, women's unity in Indonesia was not feminist in the sense of being confrontationist, but a women's movement aimed both at the development of Indonesian women and the achieving of Indonesian independence.

The Activities of Aisyiyah

At first, Aisyiyah's efforts were devoted to religious courses, such as Koran reading groups for women, and to educational activities, such as the running of kindergartens. In the Koran reading groups, religious teaching is given to Aisyiyah members and other women in the community. In relation to this, religious articles, pamphlets and periodicals are published by Aisyiyah. In the area of education, the kindergartens participate in religious teaching, through songs, games and stories.

In addition to the kindergartens, Aisyiyah has other educational activities as well. Aisyiyah founded vocational schools for girls, such as home-economics schools, teachers' colleges and midwives' schools. These schools have helped to furnish the needed teachers in places where Aisyiyah operates and to provide midwives and nurses for Aisyiyah maternity clinics and hospitals.

Other social welfare activities of Aisyiyah include running mental health courses for adolescents, running family planning programmes, running boarding houses for girl students, running day-care centres, and assisting women to develop home industry and marketing skills in order to supplement family income.

In all of these activities Aisyiyah has brought about significant kinds of social change. First, Aisyiyah releases housewives from bondage to the household alone. They can leave their homes to spend time at Aisyiyah centres, tending to their own growth and education, and to that of their children. Second, in seeking knowledge and upgrading themselves, Aisyiyah women develop the ability to observe their environment. They understand what it means to be active in an organisation to improve the social environment, based on Islamic teachings. Third, they are conscious through Aisyiyah of the value of their role as mothers in bringing up the younger generation and implanting peace and order in society. Fourth, they begin to feel the subject, not just the object. They begin to feel they can do things. Finally, they are able to join in decisions about the problems they are facing, because they are conscious of being involved in something larger—the society.

Aisyiyah and Family Planning

I will describe somewhat more fully the social change in Indonesia brought about by the family planning programme initiated by Aisyiyah. Traditionally, family planning was thought of in a negative way in Indonesia. Religious people in general, and the Muhammadiya in particular, thought that birth control was forbidden in Islam. Aisyiyah followed suit. In 1957, when Aisyiyah's representative visited the U.S. as a member of an Indonesian women's delegation, she did not join the observation of the family planning activities, because family planning problems were still "taboo" among Indonesian Muslims.

When it became clear that a family planning programme would be carried out by the government in Indonesia, the Muhammadiya started to discuss Islamic teachings in relation to family planning in its forum on Islamic laws. That was in 1963. The discussion concluded that family planning was justified, when medical consultation showed the mother's health required family planning. In Islam there are also teachings involving family planning. For example, there is the teaching that the time span between one childbirth and the next should be at least 30 months; the teaching that parents should not leave their children in a state of negligence; and the saying that a strong Muslim is more loved by God than a weak one. Muslims should be strong people, physically, mentally, economically and educationally, able to observe the religious teachings well, in order to become strong members of society. Moreover, they should be able to provide for their children and descendents.

Since this time, family planning has been justified by Muhammadiya and by Aisyiyah, based upon Islamic teachings. One feature of family planning that is prohibited, however, is killing the foetus or abortion. Also, family planning should, if at all possible, make use of contraceptive equipment that does not do harm to the human body, as do tubectomy or vasectomy.

In 1971, during the Muhammadiya and Aisyiyah Congresses, family planning was adopted within the framework of guiding families and insuring family welfare. Since then, information on family planning, based on Islamic law, has been put forth by Aisyiyah. The programme has been centred at Aisyiyah's maternity clinics and hospitals. There, information on family planning is given and carried out under the supervision of Aisyiyah medical officials. Soon Aisyiyah began to realise the usefulness of family planning programmes, since they involved family welfare in a wider scope—including health problems, nutrition, education and skills for the reinforcement of family income. Also important were the problems relating to faith and religious consciousness as a whole.

The Aisyiyah Rural Women's Development Programme

In 1978, the Aisyiyah Congress put forward the Rural Women's Development Programme to intensify the efforts of Muhammadiya's general Family Welfare Programme. The new programme was to be implemented by using, and building upon, the traditional Koran reading group system.

The Koran reading groups traditionally have the following structure: first, the participants are not obliged to follow the course regularly; second, the curriculum is up to the teacher giving the lesson; third, there is no target or conclusion decided for every lesson; and finally, there is no general syllabus for every Koran reading group. The main purpose of these groups is to get women together for religious lessons relevant to them, at their own age and educational level.

In 1978, the Aisyiyah Congress decided to initiate its new programme in five areas, with ten Koranic reading groups in each area. Each of the 50 Koranic reading group sites was to have at least 40 Aisyiyah members, thus involving a minimum of 2,000 women. The emphasis would be on women between 20 and 35 years, i.e. those of childbearing age. The ultimate objective of the project was to provide information and training to rural women. In addition to the religious instruction of the traditional Koran reading group, these groups would emphasize (*i*) health education, (*ii*) nutrition, (*iii*) family planning, and (*iv*) home-economics, with the stress on skill training for income-generating activities.

During the first year of this three-year pilot project, the goal was to train 30 Aisyiyah leaders to implement the programme, to select the 50 Koran reading groups to participate, to encourage at least 55 per cent of the non-users in these groups to accept family planning by the end of the year, and to reach at least 10,000 followers of Aisyiyah with family planning information. The second year of the programme included an evaluation procedure, with means to communicate the results of the evaluation to the leaders of the Koran reading groups. The third year aimed to maintain at least, 2,500 women of childbearing age in the Koran reading group programme and to motivate at least 500 new women in this group to accept a family planning method. In addition, the programme aimed to attract at least 800 active family planning users by the end of the year and to reach at least 5,000 more Aisyiyah followers with family planning information.

Having carried out this programme, the Aisyiyah realised that utilising the Koran reading groups was a new and important method of rural education and development. Aisyiyah now wants to expand this programme from the five original areas to other provinces, including those outside Java. Through this programme, Aisyiyah is able to reach into rural areas and to teach members how to make their life better, as well as that of their family and community. Thus, in the work of Aisyiyah, it would not be incorrect to say that religion and social change have come together.

PART FIVE

DECIDING ON MORAL ISSUES: THE CASE OF ABORTION

Introduction

These papers make explicit one of the implicit themes of this book, the question of ethics: practical ethics, in that we begin with real situations of ethical conflict rather than with theories; comparative ethics, in that we discuss these situations alongside and in dialogue with people whose religious or ethical presuppositions may be very different from our own. Such dialogue includes not only Jews and Buddhists, but men and women.

Ethics has been implicit, of course, in much of what has been discussed. The values or ethics of a culture have to do not only with moral reasoning and acts of moral choice, but with the distribution of power, authority and decision making, and with social organisation. The Hindu term *dharma* makes this clear to us: it refers not only to ethical injunctions, but to the right-ordering of the whole of society. Therefore when we speak of the dis-ordering challenge of women's priesthood, or the re-ordering activity of women's organisations, we are talking about shaking the foundations of traditional values or ethics.

On what basis does one decide about moral issues, either those that arise within the family, or those that are truly worldwide? Who decides? And who decides who decides? How can we learn at least to see, if not to share, the point of view of others, and how might this enable us to see our own point of view more clearly? How might we work together on those issues that clearly transcend boundaries of nation, culture and religion?

One of the most difficult of such issues has been that of population policy, family planning, or fertility control, and specifically within this context, the issue of abortion. Here the need for dialogue is not only between people of different religious traditions, but between those of the same religious tradition who have very different views and opinions, between secular and religious people of the same culture, and even between men and women of the same culture. There is scarcely another issue that has been discussed and debated with more acrimony.

In the United States, the debate within the Christian tradition has been sharp; on one side are Christian anti-abortionists who defend what they see as the inalienable right of the foetus to life, who see that right as one to be protected by the state, and who therefore refer to their ethical position as "pro-life". On the other side are Christian proponents, not of abortion as such, but of the woman's right to individual choice in the matter of abortion, who refer to their position as "pro-choice". In her contribution, **Beverly Harrison**, Professor of Christian Ethics at Union Theological Seminary, looks at the significant relation between the rise of the women's movement and the rise of the anti-abortion movement. She discusses the limited concern for "sanctity of life" so often reflected in the pro-life movement, "We have a long way to go," she says, "before the sanctity of human life will include genuine regard and concern for every female already born." Beverly's book *Women's Right to Choose* (1983), is a thorough study of the abortion controversy.

Veena Das, Professor of Anthropology at the University of Delhi and a Visiting Professor at Harvard Divinity School, is a Hindu who is both reflective and analytical about her own culture and insightful about the culture of the West. In her paper, Veena raises clarifying questions about the U.S. abortion controversy. She discusses the presuppositions upon which both the pro-life and pro-choice advocates argue. The first is the theory of "rights," whether the rights of the foetus or of the mother. She questions the limitations of the theory of "individual" rights as the proper framework for the discussion of procreation and life, for to define the set of individuals (in-dividual or indivisible units) who have credentials for "rights" is impossible in the mother-foetus situation. Mother and child are neither two individuals nor one, so individual rights, emphasising the autonomy and separation of the individual, does not make sense. An ethic of *interdependence* would be far more relevant. Veena also raises serious questions about the emphasis on the primacy of "choice," underlined by the pro-choice position. And, finally, she points out the distortion of the semantic domain of "life," in the pro-life movement. One cannot construct a pro-life ethic on abortion which is disjoined from a pro-life position on rising military expenditures, declining social welfare programmes, or the wholesale slaughter of animals.

The presentation of **Carol Gilligan**, Professor at the Harvard Graduate School of Education, extends the discussion of the abortion decision to the wider issue of how we reason about moral issues generally. In interviews with American women who were considering an abortion, Gilligan found that they tended to cast their thinking about the decision, not in terms of abstract moral principles that would be applied to this one moment in time, but in terms of an on-going narrative—what has happened, what would happen, who would be affected, and how, by this decision. She speaks of what she calls a "different voice" in moral thinking, based not on a sense of the individual, autonomous self, reasoning according to the ethic of justice, but on a sense of the self as interdependent, reasoning according to an ethic of caretaking. Although both men and women do use both voices, Gilligan finds in her work that the emphasis on individuality and justice tends to be corrolated with men, and the emphasis on interdependence and care, with women. Carol Gilligan's book, *In a Different Voice* (1982), while limited to a sample of North American women, is a ground-breaking systematic attempt to hear what women consider a "moral conflict" to be, and how they make decisions regarding such a conflict.

The ethical discussion on abortion in the United States has been conducted in the context of a culture which has virtually arrived at zero population growth. The issue in the United States, then, is not population. The issues are many, among them whether society will take as active an interest in the welfare and rights of the born, as of the unborn; whether the real moral outrage is over the deprivation of the rights of the foetus, or the overall expansion of the freedom and choice of women in society; whether abortion issues are to be linked ethically with other issues involving life, such as the growth of public expenditure on instruments of mass destruction, such as nuclear weapons.

Even within the U.S., determining just how this issue is to be framed is difficult. On a worldwide scale, it is even more difficult. Outside the West, the abortion issue is inextricably related to the urgent necessity of population planning and birth control. The context is radically different from the zero population growth context of the United States. Along with the World Health Organization, the United States is the major funder for population control programmes in the world, and has begun to export control and a generally pro-life policy along with its funding for programmes in the Third World. However, culture-specific questions and the question of power in decision making are crucial in the population policy of any Third World country. Women from several contexts raise ethical questions to the West in relation to population policy. They question the tendency of western planners to consult only male-dominated government agencies. They question the absence of women at crucial stages in planning. They raise the suspicion that western industries sell untested and perhaps unsafe contraceptives to Third World countries. And they challenge the relentless insistence on the part of the West that the Third World must control its population, in the absence of any simultaneous recognition that the West must control its consumption. The framing of the abortion debate, then, is a sensitive matter. What *is* the ethical context in which this question is to be discussed?

A Theology of Pro-Choice: A Feminist Perspective on Abortion *

Beverly W. Harrison

Much discussion of abortion betrays the heavy hand of misogyny or the hatred of women. We all have a responsibility to recognize this bias, sometimes subtle, when ancient negative attitudes toward women intrude into the abortion debate. It is morally incumbent upon us to convert the Christian position to a teaching more respectful of women's history and experience.

My professional peers who are my opponents on this question feel that they own the Christian tradition in this matter and recognize no need to rethink their positions in the light of this claim. As a feminist, I cannot sit in silence when women's right to determine how procreative power is to be used is under challenge. That right is being withdrawn by the State even before its moral basis has been fully elaborated. Those who deny that women deserve to control procreative power claim the right to do so out of "moral sensibility," in the name of the "sanctity of human life". We have a long way to go before the sanctity of human life will include genuine regard and concern for every female already born, and no social policy which obscures that fact deserves to be called "moral".

I believe the human wisdom which informs our ethics about abortion comes from what earlier Catholic moral theologians meant by "natural law" more than from quoting the Bible alone. Unfortunately, however, natural law reflection in a Roman Catholic context has been every bit as awful as Protestant Biblicism on any subject that involves human sexuality, including discussion of women's "nature" and women's "divine vocation" in relation to procreative power.

*Reprinted by permission of *The Witness*, Vol. 64, no. 7 (1981).

Protestants who oppose procreative choice either tend to follow Roman Catholic moral theology or ground their positions in Biblicist anti-intellectualism, claiming that "God's word" requires no justification other than their claim that it (God's word) says what it says. Against such irrationalism, no rational objections have a chance. If Protestant fundamentalists do give reasons why they believe that abortion is evil, they too revert to traditional natural law assumptions about women, sex and procreation. Therefore, it is against the claims of traditional Catholic natural law thinking on the subject of sexuality, procreation, and women's power of rational choice that objection must be registered.

Any treatment of a moral problem is inadequate if it fails to question the morality of the act in a way which represents the concrete experience of the agent who faces a decision with respect to that act. Misogyny in Christian discussions of abortion is evidenced in that the decision is never treated as an integral part of the female agent's life process. Abortion is treated as an abstractable act, rather than as what it always is—a possible way to deal with a pregnancy.

Those who uphold the immorality of abortion are wise to obscure the fact that it is a fully living human female who is the moral agent in the decision. In the case of pregnancy, the woman's life is deeply, irrevocably affected.

Where the question of abortion might arise, a woman finds herself facing an *unwanted* pregnancy. Consider the actual circumstances which may precipitate this. One is the situation in which a woman did not intend to be sexually active or did not enter into the act voluntarily. Since women are frequently victims of sexual violence, numerous cases of this type arise because of rape, incest, or forced marital coitus. Many morally sensitive opponents of abortion will concede that in such cases it may be morally justifiable. I would insist that in such cases it is a moral good, because it is not rational to treat a newly fertilized ovum as though it had the same value as the existent, pregnant, female person, and because it is morally wrong to make the victim of sexual violence suffer the further agonies of unwanted pregnancy.

Another more frequent case results when a woman—or usually a young girl—participates in heterosexual activity without clear knowledge of how pregnancy occurs and without intention to conceive. A girl who became pregnant in this manner would, by traditional natural law morality, be held to be in a state of "invincible ignorance" and therefore not morally culpable. I once met a scholarly Roman Catholic nun who argued, quite seriously, that her church should not consider the abortions of young Catholic girls as morally culpable since the church was "overprotective" of them, which prevented them from understanding procreation and the sexual pressures which contemporary society puts on girls.

A related type of pregnancy occurs when a woman runs risks by not using contraceptives, perhaps because taking precautions is not "ladylike" or requires her to be "unspontaneous" about sex. However, when pregnancies occur because women are skirting the edges of knowledge and running risks, is enforced motherhood a desirable solution? Such pregnancies could be minimized by eradicating childish myths, embedded in natural law teaching, about female sexuality.

In likelihood, the largest number of abortions arise because mature women who are sexually active with men and who understand the consequences, experience contraceptive failure. Schizophrenia in this area is exhibited in that many who believe that women have more responsibility than men to practice contraception, and that family planning is a moral good, rule out abortion altogether. Such a split consciousness ignores the fact that there is no inexorable biological line between prevention of conception and abortion. More important, this ignores genuine risks involved in female contraceptive methods. The reason we do not have more concern for finding safer contraceptive methods for men and women is that matters relating to women's health and well-being are *never* urgent in this society. Moreover, many failures are due to the irresponsibility of the producers of contraceptives rather than to "bad luck". Given these facts, should a woman who actively attempts to avoid pregnancy be punished for contraceptive failure when it occurs?

Theological Context

In the history of Christian theology, the central metaphor for understanding life, including human life, is as a gift of God. Creation itself is seen primarily under this metaphor. In this context, it follows that procreation itself takes on special meaning when expressed within a patriarchal society in which it is the male's power which is enhanced by this "divine gift".

Throughout history, women's power of procreation stands in definite tension with male control. In fact, ancient historical evidence suggests that what we call patriarchy derives from the need of men, and later of male-dominated political institutions such as tribes and states, to control women's procreative power. We must assume, then, that many of the efforts at social control—including church teaching on contraception and abortion—were part of an overall system. The perpetuation of patriarchal control itself depended on wresting the power of procreation from women. Another critical point is that in the last four centuries, the entire Christian story has had to undergo dramatic accommodations to new and emergent world conditions grounded in the scientific revolution. As the older theological metaphors for creation encountered a new human self-understanding, Christian theology had either to incorporate this new reality in its story or to become obscurantist.

The range of human freedom to shape and enhance creation is now celebrated theologically up to the point of changes in sexuality or ways of seeing women's nature. Around these issues a barrier has been drawn which declares: *No Freedom Here*! The only difference between mainline Protestant and Catholic theologians is on the question of contraception. That Protestant male clergy are usually married does have a positive experiential effect on their dealing with this issue; generally they have accepted the moral appropriateness of contraception. Most Protestants and nearly all Catholics, however, draw back from recognizing abortion as a defensible exercise of human freedom or self-determination.

The problem, then, is that Christian theology everywhere else celebrates the power of human freedom to shape and determine the quality of human life, except when the issue of abortion arises. The power of *man* to shape creation radically is never rejected. When one stops to consider the awesome power over nature which males take for granted and celebrate, including the power to alter the conditions of human life in myriad ways, the suspicion dawns that the near hysteria that prevails about the immorality of women's right to choose abortion derives its force from misogyny rather than from any passion for the sacredness of human life. The refusal of male theologians to incorporate the full range of human power to shape creation into their theological worldview when that power relates to the quality of women's lives and women's freedom and women's role as full moral agents, is an index of the continuing misogyny in Christian tradition.

By contrast, a feminist theological approach recognizes that nothing is more urgent, in light of the changing circumstances of human beings on Planet Earth, than to recognize that the entire natural-historical context of human procreative power has shifted. We desperately need a "desacralization" of our biological power to reproduce, and, at the same time, a real concern for human dignity and the social conditions for personhood and the values of human relationship. And note that "desacralization" does not mean complete devaluation of the worth of procreation. It means that we must shift away from the notion that the central metaphors for divine blessing are expressed at the biological level to the recognition that social values bear the image of what is most holy. The best statement I know on this point comes from a Roman Catholic feminist who is also a distinguished sociologist of religion, Marie Augusta Neal:

> As long as the central human need called for was continued motivation to propagate the race, it was essential that religious symbols idealise that process above all others. Given the vicissitudes of life in a hostile environment, women had to be encouraged to bear children and men to support them; child-bearing was central to the struggle for existence. Today, however, the size of the base population, together with knowledge already accumulated about artificial insemination, sperm banking, cloning, make more certain a peopled world.
>
> The more serious human problems now are who will live, who will die and who will decide. . .

Alternative Reading of History

Between persons who oppose all abortions on moral grounds and those who believe that abortion is sometimes or frequently morally justifiable, *there is no difference of moral principle*. Pro-choice advocates and anti-abortion advocates share the ethical principle of respect for human life, which is probably why the debate is so acrimonious. I have already indicated that one major source of disagreement is the way in which theological story is appropriated in relation to the changing circumstances of history. In addition, we should recognize that whenever strong moral disagreement is encountered, we simultaneously confront a different reading of history. The way we interpret the past is already laden with a sense of what the "moral problem" is.

For example, professional male Christian ethicists tend to assume that the history of the morality of abortion can best be traced by studying the teaching of the now best remembered theologians. Looking at the matter this way, one can find plenty of proof-texts to show that *some* of the "church fathers" (as we call them) condemned abortion and some even equated abortion with either homicide or murder. However, when a "leading" churchman equated abortion with homicide or murder, he also *and simultaneously* equated *contraception* with homicide or murder as well. This reflects the then almost hysterical anti-sexual bias of the Christian tradition.

However, this anti-sexual tradition is *not* universal, even among theologians and canon lawyers. On the subject of sexuality and its abuse, many well-known theologians had nothing to say and abortion was not even mentioned. An important, untold chapter in Christian history is the great struggle that took place in what we call the medieval period, when clerical celibacy came to be *imposed*, and the rules of sexual behaviour rigidified.

By contrast, my thesis is that there is a relative disinterest in the question of abortion overall in Christian history. Occasionally, Christian theologians picked up the issue, *especially when those theologians were "state-related theologians"*, i.e., articulating policy not only for the church but for the political authority. Demographer Jean Meyer, himself a Catholic, insists that the Christian tradition took over "expansion by population growth" from the Roman empire. Christians only opposed abortion strongly when Christianity was closely identified with the State or when the theologians repudiated sexuality except in the reluctant service of procreation.

The "Holy Crusade" quality of present teaching on abortion is quite new and related to cultural shifts which are requiring the Christian tradition to choose sides in ideological struggle and to rethink its entire attitude to women and sexuality. No Protestant clergy gave early support for proposed 19th century laws banning abortion in the United States. It is my impression that Protestant clergy, usually married and often poor, were aware that romanticizing "nature's bounty" with respect to procreation resulted in a great deal of human suffering. The Protestant clergy who finally did join the anti-abortion crusade in the 19th century were racist, classist, white clergy, who feared that America's strength was being threatened because white, middle class, "respectable" women had a lower birthrate than Black and ethnic women. Sounds familiar?

One other point must be stressed. Until the late 19th century, the natural law tradition, and Biblicism following it, always tended to define the act of abortion as interruption of pregnancy after ensoulment, or the coming of the breath of God to the foetus. The point at which ensoulment was said to take place varied, but most typically it was at quickening. Quickening was important because knowledge about embryology was terribly primitive until the last half century. As a result, where abortion was condemned, it was understood to refer to the termination of pregnancy well into the process of that pregnancy after ensoulment. Until the late 19th century, then, abortion in ecclesiastical teaching applied only to termination of prenatal life in more advanced stages of pregnancy.

Another distortion in the male-generated history of this issue derives from failure to note that, until the development of safe, surgical, elective abortion, the "act of abortion" frequently referred to something done to the woman, with or without her consent (See Exodus 22), as an act of violence. Now, in recent discussion, it is the woman who does the "wrongful" act. When "to do an abortion" meant terminating a pregnancy against the women's wishes, grounds for moral objections were clear.

Furthermore, whether the act was done with or without the woman's consent, until recent decades abortion always endangered the woman as much as it did the prenatal life in her womb. No one has a right to discuss the morality of abortion today without recognizing that one of the traditional moral reasons for objection to abortion was concern for women's well-being.

Beyond all this, however, the deepest moral flaw in the pro-life position's historical view is that none of its proponents have attempted to reconstruct the all but desperate struggle by sexually active women to gain some proximate control over nature's profligacy in conception. Under the most adverse conditions, women have had to try to control their fertility—everywhere, always. Even when women are infertile, their relationship to procreation irrevocably marks and shapes their lives. Those who have sought to avoid sexual contact with males, through celibacy or through lesbian love, have been potential, even probable, victims of male sexual violence or have had to bear heavy social stigma for refusing the centrality of dependence on men and of procreation in their lives. Women's lack of social power, in all recorded history, has made this struggle to control procreation a life-bending, often life-destroying, one.

So women have had to do whatever they could to avoid too numerous pregnancies. In most societies and cultures, procreation has been in the hands of women's culture. Some primitive birth control techniques have proven rather effective. Increasingly, anthropologists are gaining hints of how procreative control occurred in some pre-modern societies. A woman often has chosen to risk her life in order not to have that extra child that would destroy the family's ability to cope or that would bring about a crisis unmanageable within her life.

We have to concede that modern medicine, for all *its* misogyny, has replaced some rather ghastly practices still widely used where surgical abortion is unavailable. In the light of these gains, more privileged western women must not lose the ability to imagine the real-life pressures which lead women in other cultures to submit to ground-glass douches, reeds inserted in the uterus, etc. to induce labour. The radical nature of methods women resort to bespeaks the desperation involved in unwanted pregnancy.

Nor should we suppress the fact that a major means of birth control now is, as it was in earlier times, *infanticide*. And let no one imagine that women made decisions to expose or kill new-born infants casually. Women understand what many men cannot seem to grasp—that the birth of a child requires that some person must be prepared to care, without interruption, for that infant, to provide material resources and energy-draining amounts of time and attention. It seems to me that men, especially celibate men, romanticize the total and uncompromising dependency of the newly born infant upon the already existing human community. This dependency is even greater in a fragmented, centralized urban-industrial modern culture than in a rural culture, where another pair of hands often increased an extended family unit's productive power. No historical interpretation of abortion as a moral issue which ignores these matters deserves moral standing in the present debate.

In drawing this section to a close, I want to stress that if present efforts to criminalise abortion succeed, we will need a State apparatus of massive proportions to enforce compulsory childbearing. In addition, withdrawal of legal abortion will create one more massively profitable underworld economy in which the Mafia and other sections of quasi-legal capitalism may and will profitably invest. The radical Right promises to get the State out of regulation of people's lives, but what they really mean is that they will let economic activity go unrestrained. What their agenda signifies for the personal lives of women is quite another matter.

An adequate historical perspective on abortion recognizes the long struggle women have waged for some degree of control over fertility and of their efforts to regain control of procreative power from patriarchal and state-imperial culture and institutions. Such a perspective also takes into account that more nearly adequate contraceptive methods and the existence of safe, surgical, elective abortion represent positive historic steps toward full human freedom and dignity for women. While the same gains in medical knowledge also open the way to sterilization abuse and to social pressures against some women's use of their power of procreation, I know of no woman who would choose to return to a state of lesser knowledge about these matters.

There has been an objective gain in the quality of women's lives for those fortunate enough to possess procreative choice. That millions of women do not possess even the rudimentary conditions for such a choice is obvious. Our moral goal should be to struggle against those real barriers—poverty, racism and cultural oppression—which prevent authentic choice from being a reality for every woman.

Notes on the Moral Foundations of the Debate on Abortion

Veena Das

Contemporary moral debate on abortion has been conducted primarily in terms of arguments that follow from rival premises about the nature of man and society. Although the premises are presented as examples of critical thinking, universalizable for all human societies, they are often mutually incommensurable. This seems to me the result of their epistemic status as "self-evident" truths. It may, therefore, be useful to examine these premises in order to determine how far their claims to the status of universal truths, arrived at through critical thinking on moral issues, may be defended as against the position that they simply constitute the philosophical presuppositions common to western cultures.

The Morality of Rights

The first argument that we may discern in this debate is conducted in terms of rights. Those who support the mother's unconditional right to abortion argue that it is possible to define a certain set, the members of which have a right to their own persons including their own bodies. This set is variously defined as a set of human beings, a set of persons, or a set of human beings with consciousness. Now a woman can be shown to be a member of this set, howsoever it may be defined. Since the embryo and later the foetus is part of her body, a woman's right to abort is included in her right to body-integrity. A woman's unconditional right to abort can only be supported on the condition that the embryo/foetus can be excluded from the set in which the woman is included. Hence we have a curious situation in which those who believe in the unconditional right to life of the embryo/foetus also base themselves on the same arguments as their opponents. They argue that since the embryo or the foetus is a potential member of the set of which the woman is already a member, it has an unconditional right to life and denying it this right amounts to a wanton act of killing.

This framework is not particularly suitable for discussing the moral aspect of abortion, for whichever permutation and combination of rights that we evoke, and whatever the credentials by which one comes to acquire these rights, there are bound to be border-line cases to which discriminatory criteria would have to be applied. For example, whether we define the foetus as a potential human being, a person, or a human being with the potential of acquiring consciousness, there is always room for debate on whether the discriminatory criteria have been correctly applied and whether the boundary should be shifted to either include new categories or exclude certain categories. If one denies the foetus the right to life on the grounds that only human beings with consciousness have a right to life, then one is faced with the problem that infanticide may also be defended by applying the same criterion. Similarly, people who have temporarily lost their consciousness may also be denied the right to life. On the other hand, if the foetus has the right to life because it has the potentiality to grow into a human being with consciousness, then one would have to extend the same right to categories of beings who show evidence of having consciousness, such as animals.

The point that I am trying to make is that the construction of a boundary by means of which one may carry on the intellectual process of inclusion or exclusion of categories of beings who have credentials for rights is a *social* construction. It is not something which is given in nature and hence can be indisputably recognized in our intellectual frameworks. The trouble with a concept like moral agency (constructed on whatever basis) is that it admits of variations in a manner that can be quite dangerous in the construction of a moral universe, smuggling in criteria of power from the back-door, as it were.

Due to the difficulties pointed out above, most philosophers tend to take a middle position on the right to abortion. They argue that a woman has rights over her body, and the foetus has rights over its life. However, due to the natural facts of conception and pregnancy, the rights of each may be seen to be constrained by the other. For instance, the whole debate on when the foetus becomes viable may be seen as an attempt to define that moment in the process of pregnancy when the woman's right to her body is completely subordinated to the right of the foetus to its life. Conversely, there are instances when the right of the foetus to its life may be seen to be completely constrained by the right of a woman to preserve her body-integrity. For example, many philosophers who take a middle-of-the-road position argue that a woman has an unconditional right to abort a foetus if it is a result of rape, for in this case her body-integrity has been so violated that the woman's right to her body takes precedence over the right of the foetus to its life.

If we review the theories which emphasise the mutual constraints exercised by the woman's right over her body *versus* the right of the foetus over his/her life and body, one common factor stands out. This is that the entire discussion is conducted in terms of the autonomy and separation of the individual. The individual is conceived in these theories, not only as an empirical agent of actions but also as the smaller isolate of human societies which is not further divisible and as a total moral universe in himself or herself. Literally "in-dividual". In this view, man is first placed in *nature*, and has natural rights over his/her life, liberty, person and possessions. Restrictions over these rights come from the process of bringing human beings into relationships with each other in order to form society.

One could postulate an opposite view in which man is first defined as a *social* or *cultural* being, having rights in common with members of social groups and acquiring individual rights only through a process of *individuation*. It seems to me, however, that the language appropriate for discussing the ethics of abortion, is the language of interdependence, taking the interspace between individuals as its basic isolate rather than their separation. It is not as if the foetus is drifting around the world and is then invited to come into the mother's body on the basis of contract! The relation between the mother and the foetus, I am emboldened to suggest, may be viewed as a natural symbol of interdependence and invites us to develop an ethics of interdependence that would be far more relevant to the modern world than ethics of the separation and autonomy of individuals.

The Morality of Choice

The morality of abortion has been given a new dimension by some who argue that the question cannot be framed in terms of the woman's right to abort. Rather, it raises the whole question of procreative choice. This position is consistent with the view that the individual is the final arbiter of his or her destiny. In the domain of sexuality and procreation, the individual is free to choose his or her mode of sexuality and the choice of whether or not to have children ultimately rests with the woman. The argument is made much more compelling by pointing out that abortion is sought most often by women who have been sexually abused, who have been deserted by their male partners, or who live in family situations where their financial and other responsibilities to present members of their families make them extremely apprehensive of taking on the fresh responsibility of a new child.

There are several strands in this argument which need to be separated. First is the conceptual importance of the category of *choice*. It seems to me that the most vocal supporters of a woman's unconditional right to abort on the grounds that the procreative choice rests with her, have paid insufficient attention to the problem that may be described as the inverse of the right to abort. This is the problem of exercising one's choice to have as many children as one wants. On the face of it, one might argue that a woman should have the freedom to have as many children as she likes. However, the moment we introduce problems of limited resources and obligation to future generations, it becomes clear that freedom to choose is limited by some notions of collective welfare, howsoever defined. In this case, the welfare of future generations who may have to face a depleted earth if present generations do not put a limit to their freedom to choose, may be at stake.

Thus the sanctity of choice may not be regarded as the ultimate principle by which a woman's unconditional right to abort may be defended. It is urgent that moral philosophers evolve a theory of abortion which includes the issues we have discussed here, for even when we accept the principle of limits to the freedom to choose, it is not at all clear as to who has the right to impose these limits. The obvious choice in an era of increasing intrusion of the State into the private lives of people seems to be the State, and yet a serious discussion is needed on the role of the State and the limits to State-power in order to make an advance into these issues.

The question of procreative choice is often discussed in terms of a dyadic pair, the mother and the foetus. Yet a discussion on the morality of abortion includes three, and not two pairs of dyadic relations. These are, the relations between a man and a woman as sexual partners, between the woman as genetrix and the embryo/foetus, and the man as genitor and the embryo/foetus. Those who emphasise the point of view that the question of abortion can be reframed in terms of the right to make procreative choice, deny that the foetus has a similar right to choose. They argue that the rights of the foetus have been historically invented in western Christianity and were an expression of the increasing misogyny of church authorities. While there may be some truth in the statement that the awareness of the right to life of an embryo has been connected with movements to restrict the rights of women the historicity of this argument cannot be evoked as grounds to disprove its truth. For, one can show that the rights of many categories of people including slaves, women and children have been "invented" in the course of history and were a result of altered socio-economic conditions.

It also seems to put an unfair burden on women to assume that the other pairs—that of a man and a woman as sexual partners, and that of a man as genitor and the embryo/foetus—need not be considered in the debate on abortion. The position that one takes on the question of who has the right to control fertility cannot be de-linked from the problem of defining responsible sexuality. Yet it is interesting to observe that in the debate on abortion, the sexuality and fertility of women are seen as linked but the sexuality and fertility of men are sought to be separated. In the Roman Catholic position, the absolute right of the embryo/foetus to life is linked with the obligation to observe pre-marital chastity. However, responsible sexuality is never defined in this tradition to include a celibate relationship *within* marriage, since that would contradict the modern western ideas about the centrality of sexual intercourse in the definition of conjugal love. It seems to me that the nature of celibacy needs a serious discussion and one need not be deterred by the definition of sexuality as the realm of play, spontaneity and pure communitas in the modern conceptions of marriage from which arises the suspicion of marital relationships based upon celibacy. One has to remember that modern definitions of a good marriage may be contrasted with other definitions that emphasise the importance of restraint in sustaining a marital relationship, as for instance in the writings of

Gandhi. The point is that when we consider the question of who controls a woman's fertility as *linked* with the question of what is responsible sexuality, we are led to enquire into the nature of the whole set of role-relationships that make up the domain of sexuality and fertility, and not only that of a single dyadic relationship therein. The category of choice plays such an important role in our thinking today that much of medical technology proceeds on the assumption that it should increase the choices available to the individual. For example, today a woman may choose not to enter into a heterosexual relationship and yet may go through the entire processes of conception, pregnancy, and childbirth through artificial insemination. Development of semen banks has made it possible for her to select the genitor of her child according to his IQ, athletic prowess, or racial identity. Similarly, a woman may decide in advance whether to go ahead with a pregnancy in which the child may be born with a congenital defect. She may even abort foetuses of a particular sex selectively. It seems to me that this increasing emphasis on choice has often resulted in heightening the tensions inherent in a given society.

Two examples may be given here. In societies in which parents feel a certain ambivalence towards girls, the availability of medical technology to abort foetuses of a certain sex selectively might tilt this ambivalence towards dislike. In Indian families this ambivalence towards female babies manifests itself in the following manner. On the one hand, a male infant is more welcome on birth than a female one. More resources in health and education are invested by parents in male children than female children. Yet as a daughter grows, she comes to receive affection and love, and may grow to occupy an important position in a profession or be given a fair share of the family's resources in the form of marriage prestations. Many anthropological descriptions of family relationships show that as parents grow older thay may feel themselves closer to daughters than to sons. This complex and delicate web of relationships may be severely disturbed when medical technology makes it possible to exercise choices in areas on which control was not earlier possible.

The second example that I would like to give is from medical research. If the foetus has no right to life and may be treated by a woman as part of her own body process alone, then she may have her pregnancy terminated by choice and may sell the foetus for medical research. Recent reports in newspapers have suggested that the foetus may be kept alive outside the mother's body and is sometimes used for research on cosmetics. This leads to a situation in which not only the foetus is brutalized, but also the mother. For the first time medical technology has made it possible for a woman to use her fertility as well as her sexuality for commercial purposes. It seems to me that increasing the alternatives over which one can exercise choice, and acquiring greater and greater control over one's sexuality and fertility may prove to be more brutalizing than submitting to a design, a *telos*, that makes human existence meaningful.

The final argument that we may consider here with reference to the morality of procreative choice is that the concrete conditions under which a woman has to make the decision to abort must be taken into consideration. The empirical studies on the condition of such women point to two facts. The first is that in a majority of cases the decision to abort a child is not taken casually. It causes considerable anguish. According to the work of Carol Gilligan, women see the morality of the decision to abort as embedded in the concrete contexts in which the decisions are taken rather than in terms of the application of certain abstract rules of justice, universalizability, etc. Incidentally, even when women are not very vocal in expressing their guilt and anguish at having to take a decision to abort, it would be a mistake to assume that guilt and distress are not experienced. I have noticed that difficult births in Punjab are sometimes attributed to the souls of earlier children who died as a result of a spontaneous or induced miscarriage, stillbirth or death in early childhood. Possession rituals, or exorcism is the means of silencing these inner demons.

The second point is that a child is born within a family which has a history and a continuity. Whereas moral philosophers treat birth as a single point event, women treat it as a part of the ongoing chain of events. The discussion on the morality of abortion would be far more meaningful if it were linked with the issue of providing supportive care for the new infant. If the family is to be solely responsible for child-care, then clearly its ability to provide care for the new infant will weigh heavily in a decision to continue a pregnancy or terminate it. If, on the other hand, the foetus has an absolute right to life, then we must define the agencies who are to be held responsible to care for the infant if the mother is unable to do so. It is a sad fact, that many who are concerned for preserving life in the womb have given scant attention to the question of quality of life of those who are already living.

The burden of my argument here is that we have been misled by modern philosophers into thinking that the morality of abortion involves strictly the relation of a *woman* to the foetus. In fact this dyadic relationship is embedded in a number of relationships involving not only the responsibility of a genitor to the embryo/ foetus, but also the relationship of adult men and women. Further, this arrangement of relationships involves the rest of society. Without a discussion of the responsibility of society (either through the State or other agencies) towards the embryo, the foetus and the infant, and also towards those who are charged for caring for them, a discussion on the morality of abortion is incomplete.

The Morality of Consequences

The final set of observations that we shall consider, relate to the consequences of permitting termination of pregnancy. The consequences may be to the foetus, to the mother, or to the wider society.

Much of medical opinion justifies the termination of pregnancy if there is a strong possibility that the health of the foetus has been impaired due to genetic or other disease. In many countries, amniocentesis is medically performed for determining the normality of a foetus in the case of older mothers. This is to ensure birth of normal children. Even the vociferous defenders of right to life often agree that it may be a more humane solution to abort a foetus who is likely to suffer from severe physical or mental defects rather than to allow it to live, since the quality of life it is likely to lead would be extremely poor. In this context, it needs to be pointed out that although the "quality of life" argument bases itself on the language of facticity, in fact it is not inscribed in the nature of things that a physically or mentally retarded individual should have a poor quality of life. It is the great value placed upon individual autonomy, intelligence and competition that makes it so self-evident to the modern world that an individual who is dependent upon others for his physical or other needs suffers from a poor quality of life. Surely it is not beyond the capacity of modern societies, with the great advances in technology that they have achieved, to devise means for ensuring a good quality of life to the physically or mentally handicapped. What this would require, however, is that technology orient itself less towards controlling the characteristics of a population and more towards facilitating life-styles that may be inconsistent with individual autonomy but may be consistent with other human virtues. The greatest danger I see in the quality of life argument is that it may open the door for eliminating other categories of "inferior" people, such as those with low intelligence, "undesirable" racial characteristics, or women.

The second kind of consequentialist argument focuses its attention on the impact of a pregnancy on the mother, rather than on the foetus. Thus termination of pregnancy may be allowed if the mother's life is in danger. According to some, the termination of pregnancy may be considered defensible only if the mother's life is in danger while others would extend this to the mother's mental health. Feminists of various persuasions argue that whatever the moral status of the foetus, it cannot be compared with the moral agency of a fully developed female person. Secondly, they argue, women have to often take recourse to abortion as a way of dealing with a pregnancy more often from carelessness in the production of contraceptives rather than just bad luck. Research, they argue, has failed to develop a hundred per cent safe contraceptive because matters relating to women's health and well-being are simply not taken as *urgent* matters. To this argument I may add that very little thought has been given to the development of contraceptives that take into account conditions under which sexual intercourse takes place in societies where the conjugal couple do not have the privacy and intimacy that western couples enjoy. Should women be asked to pay the price for the failure of the rest of society to develop appropriate medical techniques for their health and well-being?

Supporters of the right to life, argue that where a pregnancy can threaten the life of a woman, her obligation to protect her own life contradicts the right to life of the foetus. In this case we need to think of the woman as withdrawing life-support from the foetus in order to preserve her own life rather than as committing homicide. The common-sense view on the matter is that a new-born infant is not the centre of a support system of other people in the same manner as a fully grown female is. Hence the grief felt at the loss of a foetus cannot compare with the grief at the loss of an adult female person. To my mind, this raises the whole question of why we value the sanctity of life and under what conditions are we willing to deprive a person of his/her life. It needs to be remembered that in the Lockean system, on the basis of which many philosophers take the right to life as a fundamental right, a person had an obligation to preserve his/her life, since the desire to survive was an expression of God's will in man rather than his/her own personal wish. Thus the question as to why we consider the right to life an inalienable one cannot be disassociated from fundamental cosmological considerations that have been swept under the carpet by modern followers of Locke. It is time that we devote our attention to an articulation of these considerations, as well as to the formulation of alternative cosmologies. Only then can we provide a comprehensive framework within which these issues can be discussed.

Finally, abortion is sometimes defended as a technique of family planning. It is being extensively used in countries like China. When used as a policy instrument by the State or its agencies, the forcible termination of pregnancy raises questions about the right of the State to control the most intimate aspects of an individual's existence. It is the obverse of the right of the State to prevent individual women from demanding abortion. Both issues need to be discussed *together* within a framework of a theory of State. Yet the very people in western countries who legislate against the right of women to demand abortion, applaud the political will in countries like China in using abortion to control their populations.

Concluding Observations

It has not been my intention in this paper to defend or oppose particular theories of abortion. Rather, I have been concerned with trying to *understand* an argument. It is striking that the discussion on moral issues relating to abortion suffers from a fragmentation of the discourse. The discourse seeks to treat human beings as *locations* of decision rather than people whose lives have a narrative continuity. A satisfactory theory would involve the articulation of a cosmology within which questions about life, sexuality, fertility and control would be discussed. It seems to me that unless we shift our emphasis from rights and utility to a consideration of virtue, such a framework will elude us for a long time to come.

A Different Voice in Moral Decisions

Carol Gilligan

I have in my own work sought to represent the voices of contemporary American girls and women as they talked about moral conflict and choice, and to amplify and validate these voices by associating them with voices in the western literary tradition. When I entitled my book, *In A Different Voice*, I meant simply that: there is a voice different from the voices represented in the western intellectual tradition, different from the voices that have defined morality, the human condition, and women. My central point in trying to identify that voice, is that we must become curious about its origins and meaning, notice it, listen to it carefully, hear its presence not only in women, but also in men.

I want to stress the importance of not assimilating this voice too quickly to schemes of interpretation that repeatedly have both observed its difference, and then systematically left it out. In a sense the most honest statement we can make at this point is that we have *not* listened to the voices of girls and women, and therefore we probably do not understand these voices, because all of our categories of understanding and interpretation in the West have been based on the investigation, consideration and analysis of the experience of men.

Once one notices the omission of women, it becomes a long and complicated task to explore what the inclusion of women's voices might mean. To recognize women's voices as human voices means to recognize that women's experience might inform, even transform, our understanding of the human condition. To discover that over half the population essentially has not been studied is, in one sense, an enormous opportunity. It opens the possibility that there may be in that group, in our group, ways of thinking and knowing that have not been explored. There may be new ways of thinking about questions on which we seem to have arrived at something of a dead end.

I am a researcher and I confess I did not set out to study women. In a way, I was part of the very problem I want to present. I set out in my research with two questions. One was the question of the relationship between moral judgement and action. I was interested in how people think about real, as opposed to hypothetical, moral problems. The second question was the relationship of experience to moral development. How does one's actual experience of moral conflict and choice affect one's thinking about morality and one's view of oneself as a moral actor or agent?

In pursuing these questions I made a change in the traditional instruments of measurement, which was absolutely crucial to the subsequent findings of my research, especially to my findings about women. This I offer here as the single most important point of my presentation. The point of the change was to free the instruments of research or investigation, i.e. the questions that are asked, from presuppositions about what morality is, what a moral problem is, what moral conflicts are; what the nature of moral choice is, what identity is, and what the categories are by which we define ourselves. In the prevailing research instruments that are used in western psychology, the scales of moral development, the questions which lead to the responses that are assessed, and the scales of identity contain two central value presuppositions: first, that morality is basically justice, and second that identity is basically autonomy.

The first value presupposition goes back to Socrates: virtue is one and its name is justice. Jean Piaget, studying the moral development of the child, said all morality consists of systems of rules, and the question to be studied is, How does the mind come to respect rules? From this, he traced the development of the ideas of justice. Lawrence Kohlberg, setting out to study moral development in adolescents, sought to measure reasoning about justice in a sample of male adolescents. But the very questions that were posed in the investigation were premised on this particular, presupposed, definition of the moral domain.

In my research, however, I did not begin by posing a moral problem and then asking, How would you resolve it? Rather, I asked people how they would define what a moral problem is. What experiences in their lives had they construed as moral conflicts? Thus, the research questions were: Have you ever been in a situation where you faced a moral conflict? Have you ever had to make a decision where you were not sure what the right thing to do was? What was the situation? What was the conflict *for you* in that situation? It is clear that here we were shifting our starting point to allow the participant in the research to define the moral domain. What was conflict *for you*? What did you consider in thinking about how to resolve the problem? What did you do? Do you think it was the right thing to do?

With regard to the question of identity, we, the research team, began with the simple question, How would you describe yourself to yourself? Then we would ask such questions as, Is the way you see yourself now different from how you saw yourself in the past? What led to the change?

This shift in the questions asked made it possible to identify a different construction of the moral problem, that is, different from that presupposed in the psychological literature. Against the prevailing definition of morality as a problem of justice, and identity as the achievement of separation, morality emerges as a problem of care and responsibility, and identity the achievement of relationship.

It is important to remember that I began with the question of the relationship between moral judgement and action. I was looking for a real moral choice to study, and I selected a sample of pregnant women who were considering abortion. Obviously, choosing the abortion decision, I ended up with a sample of women, and I began to hear where it was that these women attached moral language to their consideration of the abortion problem.

The first question in the interview was, How did you get pregnant, and how have you been thinking about it so far? The goal was to map the decision-making process in the woman's own terms, and to see if those terms were moral terms. The responses of the women studied contrasted dramatically with the public discussion of abortion in America. The public discussion casts the conflict as one between the right to life and the right to choice. These women, however, articulated a different way of framing the issue. Whenever they used moral language—words like "should," "better," "ought," "right," "wrong"—I would ask, "When you say this would be the better choice, or the right choice, what do you mean?" The women identified repeatedly the moral problem as a problem of *responsibility*. If one is to be responsible for having a child, one has to ask, Is it possible to care for this child?

The whole view of choice, of the relationship between other and self, was fundamentally different. Choice, rather than being seen as an isolated moment, was a moment in an ongoing narrative of events, which in the abortion decision were specifically the events of relationship. There were the events that led to the pregnancy, and the events that would occur if the pregnancy were continued. Choice was not abstracted from the context, the story, the narrative of lives. Self and other, rather than being seen as separate and opposed, were seen as interdependent. This means that, for the woman, hurting herself was harmful to the developing child and hurting the developing child was harmful to herself. There was no way to separate self and other into a distinct opposition. So in this as well as in a variety of other conflict situations, women searched for an inclusive solution, for a way to avoid harm both to others *and* to themselves. Failing to find such a solution, the women in the abortion decision study tended to ask which alternative would do the least harm. They did not ask what was the ideal solution, even the "right" solution, but the least harmful solution for everyone involved. This different voice, then, revealed a different way of thinking about the self and the other, about the causes of conflict, and about the strategies for arriving at a "better" solution.

It was in identifying this voice that I began to notice its absence from western psychological literature on development. Here I simply want to add a note of caution to all those who have occasion to use western psychology. In making use of its conceptions of morality, its conceptions of identity, and its scales of measurement, one is borrowing a tradition that has been sustained by systematically leaving out women, by silencing women, and by eclipsing their experience in the definition of the human condition. But the omission of women also tells you that this is a tradition that has been blind to the facts of human relationship.

Let me cite Freud as an example. To say, as Freud did, that we have a theory of sexuality, a psychology of love, and that we know nothing about women is to reveal a psychology of love and sexuality that has very little to do with relationships. In 1926, Freud observed that, "The sexual life of adult women is a dark continent for psychology." To put it in this metaphorical language, to say that women's sexuality—a subject so central for Freud—is a "dark continent," is to imply that women's experience occurs on some continent *apart* from the rest of human experience, a continent that can be illuminated, somehow, without changing the rest of the map. This way of thinking is especially interesting to us here, for it obviously parallels the leaving out of so many cultures in our theoretical formulations about human society and human nature.

The question is, What has been missed by leaving out women, and how might the inclusion of women *change* the mapping of human growth? How might it challenge, revise, expand, or correct our current assumptions about morality, truth, conflict and choice, as well as our assumptions about women and men? The absence of women's voices in western moral and religious traditions, and relegation of women to ancillary roles in the central stories that have been told in these traditions, make it possible that women and women's thinking might inform these traditions in new ways.

There have been two strands to the western moral tradition. One focuses on contract, on enlightened self-interest, and on the extension to the other of the rights and claims that are one's own. This might be called a self-interested form of morality, and it is tied to the notion of social contract in its modern formulation. The second tradition is that of self-sacrifice, which is tied to the notion of altruism. For centuries, these two lines of morality have wandered through the western traditions, appearing in the contrast between reason and compassion, fairness and forgiveness, justice and mercy, and emerging repeatedly, although by no means exclusively, in the contrast between men and women. These distinctions implied an underlying division between thought and feeling, a separation between the process of discerning what is just, and the capacity for response. But the division between reason and compassion focuses a problem in this formulation, since the implication that women are thoughtless and men without feeling clearly cannot be sustained. Instead, there appear to be two modes of thinking, carrying differing implications of feeling and signifying different ways of perceiving others and of knowing oneself. However, to observe that this contrast has been framed within a tradition that has not itself included women's voices, is also to raise the question of how the inclusion of women's voices might change the very framing of the problem.

Listening to women talk about moral conflict and choice, and about themselves in relation to others, I have observed that women tend to translate the abstract language of moral discourse into the vernacular of human relationships. This is usually grounds for criticizing women's moral thinking, i.e. for saying that women confuse moral problems with problems of interpersonal relationships. But the very "confusion" is revealing. The two moral languages, of self-interest and self-sacrifice, came to be labelled as "selfish" and "selfless" by women. These were the recurrent words that I heard, interviewing American women, the word "selfish" always meaning bad, the word "selfless" always good. And the criticism of these two words, indeed a criticism of the very polarity of self-interest and self-sacrifice, is that they both exclude relationship. Selfish means excluding the other, and selfless implies excluding the self, which creates a special problem with moral choice, since there is then no self, actor, or agent in the situation of choice. In any case, both selfishness and selflessness imply an exclusion which destroys relationships. There is no relationship if others are not present in their own terms, or if the self is silenced.

Listening to women's voices as they spoke about moral conflict and choice raised the question as to whether women were calling attention to the extent to which both of the central lines of the western moral tradition are ways of thinking that diminish relationships, and thus limit the possibilities for care, love and response.

In identifying two different moral voices, I wondered whether these voices could be identified systematically in people's responses to moral questions. The answer was, Yes. Different observers reading the same interview, could agree about the distinction between these voices, and which considerations in thinking about moral problems belonged to which of the two domains. Systematically encoding this distinction then made it possible to investigate it in a series of studies across samples mainly composed of advantaged, western-educated men and women—a sample chosen deliberately to refute the "gender difference" hypothesis. In other words, the sample was chosen so that the women, whether Black or white, would be highly educated and have professional opportunities, since the absence of opportunities is generally cited as the explanation for differences observed in women's moral thinking.

Within the sample studied, most people, in thinking about moral problems, used both voices—that is, introduced considerations of both justice and care. This is very important, for it means that both ways of thinking are understood by both women and men. But in both men and women one voice tended to be more salient. That is, in deciding what are moral problems, in resolving moral problems, and in evaluating moral choices, people tended to focus their thinking either on issues of justice, equality, reciprocity and rights or on issues of care, connection, responsibility and response. One voice tended to be salient, suggesting that the two voices articulated two different organising perspectives. As major and minor modes appear in music, major and minor modes appeared in most people's thinking about moral decision.

There was a strong corollation in the population studied between the major mode of moral thinking and gender. Although neither mode of moral thinking was gender specific, and most people used both modes, the salience of these modes was gender related. Men in these studies tended to use "justice" as their predominant mode of moral reasoning and to define themselves as separate in relation to others. Women in these studies tended to use "care" as their predominant mode of moral reasoning and to define themselves as connected with others.

Psychologically, how can one explain the presence of these two different ways of moral thinking? By looking, I believe, at two different dimensions of human relationships, not by thinking of one mode of moral thinking as connected to relationships and the other as isolated from relationships. *Both* of these moral visions—of justice and of care—come out of experiences of relationship which are universal in human life. The first is the experience of inequality: as long as adults are larger than children, every person has experienced being in an unequal situation. This situation of inequality grounds a vision of justice, fairness, equality, rights. The second is the experience of attachment: since human survival depends on adults attaching to children, every person has experienced attachment and the consequent vulnerability to separation and loss. Attachment creates interdependence, and therefore it creates a vision of morality as caretaking—as perceiving, attending, and responding to need.

In a study of high school girls, I asked the question, What does "dependence" mean to you? All of us might think how we would respond to this question, and to the question, What is the opposite of dependence? Most Americans will say that the opposite of "dependence" is "independence," because that opposition is so firmly rooted in the American tradition. But adolescent girls often opposed dependence to isolation. For them, dependence meant: "Someone would be there when you need them," "Someone would listen to you, would try to understand." By opposing dependence to isolation, the girls conveyed the assumption that dependence is positive, that the human condition *is* a condition of dependence, and that people need to rely on one another for understanding, comfort and support. Therefore, dependence was *not* simply the condition of the unequal, the one controlled by someone else, the one who lacks independence. Dependence, rather, was created by choices to be there for others, to take care of them, to listen, to try to understand and to help. In this way, a whole range of activities which have been traditionally associated with women and linked with passivity and inequality become represented as active moral choices that create and sustain relationships of attachment. This vision extends from interpersonal to intercultural relations.

It is human experience—the experience of inequality, and of attachment—that gives rise to two moral visions. One, the social-contract vision of justice has been dominant in western thinking thus far. But these two ways of moral thinking reveal different perspectives on the relationship between self and others—as unequal or equal, attached or detached. As we listen more carefully to the moral voice that speaks about interdependence and the problems of detachment, a voice articulated more frequently by women, different ways of thinking about power emerge as well as different ways of understanding violence to others and to self.

The crucial questions this work leaves me with are these: First, in whose terms do we speak? Who is to define the terms of the discussion? Who is going to set the terms of the dialogue? Noticing that the terms have been set, in the past, by men we must ask how women's experience might change the very terms of the discussion. In the field of psychology, the discussion of attachment is always subsumed to the focus on inequality, and the "justice/autonomy" view of morality and self defines the mainline of human development. It becomes very crucial to reframe the questions.

How does one empower women to speak in situations where women have been silent? One way is simply to represent and to validate women's experience and vision, to articulate the order of women's experience, and to validate it as human experience. In my research, my focus is now on adolescent girls because of the observation that it is at this time in the life cycle that girls tend to become silent. At the time when thinking becomes interpretive, and one is taught to think through interpretive schemes that have not represented women's experience, or even noted its omission, it becomes very hard for girls and for women to render that experience coherent.

Finally, I would like to close with the suggestion that, in our age of nuclear weapons, international interdependence has become a reality of life. Autonomy, which has been taken as a premise for our sense of "identity," conversely becomes an illusion. And the images of winning and losing, in games and in making moral decisions, begin to appear as very dangerous images of relationship. For this reason, looking to our own experiences as women, and realizing that these experiences have not been systematically explored, we must look for different images of relationships, different ways of thinking about values and about development, and different ways of affirming our human interdependence.

PART SIX

BUILDING A COMMON FOUNDATION FOR SOCIAL CHANGE

Introduction

This final group of papers presents thinking on women and social change which is both grounded in a particular context and culture, and yet extends beyond that culture, helping us to build a common foundation for social change.

From many of the previous papers, "shared themes" have already emerged that seem to link many women in thinking and working, across the bounds of religion and culture. For example, Carol Gilligan's work on women's articulation of a distinctive **ethic of care** seems to strike a responsive chord in women from very different cultural contexts. Both Veena Das and Carol Gilligan stress **interdependence** as the context of moral reasoning. The lives of women and men, Jews and Arabs, Americans and Russians are profoundly interdependent, and moves toward change must recognize that relatedness. From many of these women comes an affirmation of **experience**, rather than ideologies or principles, as the place to begin thinking about difficult issues. There is also the repeated claim to **self-definition**, no longer allowing oneself to be defined and shaped by the images of women as presented in the minds, the scriptures, the laws and the institutions of men. There is an affirmation of intense yearning for **liberation**—from the prisons of South Africa, from the mental stamp of the passbook, from the economic and political oppression of Central America, and from constrictive images of womankind. There is the affirmation of both **particularity and universality** in the ethos of the women's movement. One can be a Jewish feminist, a Christian feminist, a Gandhian feminist. And yet to be deeply rooted in one's particular tradition does not, in our context, inhibit one's full acceptance of those whose deep roots are in another tradition. There is a distinctive **openness about religion**, with the sense that at its best, religion provides roots of nourishment, not boundaries or walls of separation. Here the traditional marginality of women in the dogmatic, orthodox, or ritual traditions of many cultures is in many ways a blessing, enabling a level of openness that is less common among those who have staked their claim in the interior of the tradition.

In the four presentations with which we conclude, a number of additional broad themes are given consideration. First, **Sissela Bok**, a moral philosopher, now Professor of Philosophy at Brandeis University, presents a vision of **practical non-violence**. Sissela is the author of two books on practical ethics, that is, ethics that are inextricably a part of our day to day lives: *Lying, Moral Choice in Public and Private Life*, and *Secrets: On the Ethics of Concealment and Revelation*. In her presentation here, Sissela considers the escalation of violence in the world, and relates growing militarization, by the spread of both nuclear and conventional weapons, to widespread conditions of poverty, especially where scarce resources are used to purchase arms. The issue of non-violence and violence has too often been cast in terms of its extremes: complete, principled, non-violence and complete, principled, belligerence. She suggests that women and men today can make a difference by steering an alternative course: identifying areas which we insist upon as violence-free zones, within and between people, families, communities and nations, and seeking to expand those zones toward the ideal of non-violence.

Sylvia Marcos emphatically underlines the word **rebellion**. Sylvia speaks from her experience in Cuernavaca, Mexico, with Procesos de Accion Communitaria, a psychotherapy collective which sees social and political transformation as part of the struggle for autonomy and dignity among alienated and marginalized people. She has published extensively in the area of psychology, most recently *Manicomios y Prisones* (1983), "Madhouses and Prisons". She presents us with cases of women from the marginalized poor near Cuernavaca, who have had the courage to run against the tide, as rebels. Her suggestion is that rebellion is what all of us have in common. But primary rebellion, the rage that turns us against the tide, is not enough. Sylvia insists that it is crucial that we move toward permanent rebellion, in which our rage or negativity is transformed into methodical, tireless work for change—knowing full well that the ideal may not be reached.

Nawal el Saadawi provides insight about the nature of **power** as something with which women must be concerned. Women cannot turn from power if we are to bring about change. Nawal is alert, however, to the ways in which power co-opts the religious tradition, and she cites the various leaders of all ideological stripes who came to be seen in Egypt as "relatives of the Prophet". She insists that claiming women's power begins at home, with work to change and to free ourselves; then extends to local and national networks for change; and finally to international, global efforts for change. Power does not begin at the international level, but rather is dependent upon organisation at the local level. Women must be able to see the linkages—between the oppression in the bedroom, in the nation, and on the international scene—and must work together to generate power. As Nawal puts it, "Now is the time."

Nawal is an Egyptian doctor and writer, formerly Egypt's Director of Public Health, until she was dismissed as a result of the publication of her book *Women and Sex* in 1972. She was imprisoned for her outspoken views during the last months of the presidency of Anwar Sadat. Some of her many writings on women have been translated into English, including *The Hidden Face of Eve*, on women in the Arab world, and *Woman at Point Zero*, a novel.

Finally, **Devaki Jain**, Director of the Institute for Social Studies Trust in New Delhi, speaks from the perspective of an Indian, who sees the relevance of Gandhian ideals to Indian feminism and to global feminism. Devaki has long worked in the area of women's employment and women and development. For India's International Women's Year she edited the book *Indian Women*, and has also published *Women's Quest For Power—Five Case Studies*. In this presentation, Devaki first argues for the importance of a universal ethic for women, saying that we cannot be satisfied with the easy answer—that feminism is culturally specific. As a second step, Devaki looks at some of the methods and approaches to social change undertaken by women in India, especially those that make use of religious institutions and values. One example is the use of *bhajan mandalis* or song-singing groups, in the initial organisation period of SEWA, the Self-Employed Women's Organisation of Ahmedabad. She speaks of the decision of women in some Gandhian institutions to refuse the special identification of untouchables, or Harijans, even to gain special State funds. She tells of the resistance of the women of Khirakot to a disruptive new quarry, and the use of

Hindu ritual gestures by women in Assam to halt the elephants who had been brought in to level their shanties.

All of these make use of fundamentally Gandhian perspectives, which Devaki sees as complementary to the core of many of the world's religions, and convergent with contemporary feminist methods. These include non-violence, self-reliance, fearlessness, and the capacity to care. For any liberation movement, **self-reliance** is perhaps the most fundamental of all: the empowerment of claiming "home-rule" on the very day one takes charge of oneself, and will no longer be either exploiter or exploited—at home or in one's work, in one's village, or in society at large. She suggests process, method, as the potential source of unity—the thread which can run through the differences and, like handspun or *khadi*, be women's instrument for change.

Toward a Practical Ethic of Non-Violence

Sissela Bok

I want to begin by talking about how one woman took a stand against violence. She linked the many ways in which it affects our lives and makes us take it so for granted that we become even more blind to suffering and even more tempted to avoid thinking about dangers to our collective survival. Astrid Lindgren is her name. She is Swedish, and a writer of children's books. Translated into many of the world's languages, her books about Pippi Longstocking and other free spirits have entranced readers everywhere. In 1978 she received the German Booksellers' Peace Prize.

Astrid Lindgren spoke out in her acceptance speech against the brutality that pervades so much of what children play with and read and see all around them. She had in mind the many war toys and the games in which mass killing is taken for granted; but also the concentration on violence in the media, the resort by world leaders to ever more aggressive rhetoric, and the drift toward a more and more militarized world, with modern weapons of mass destruction sold in ever greater volume, fanning wars, impoverishing nations, helping dictatorial regimes oppress the citizens of their own countries.

She ended with a story about a mother and her son. The mother had never gone along with the saying "spare the rod and spoil the child". Such dictates, she believed, merely offered parents false excuses for beating their children into submission.

But one day this woman's son had done something that made her lose patience. Deciding that he deserved a spanking, she asked him to go out to find some branches with which she might whip him. The little boy left and was gone a long time. At last he came back, weeping, and said: "I could not find any good branches, Mother, but here is a stone you can throw at me."

Then the mother saw herself with her child's eyes. The boy must have thought that since she actually wanted to injure him, she might as well do so with a stone. At that moment, she made a vow to herself: No more violence! And she put the stone on a shelf in the kitchen as a reminder.

We can all grasp the threat this boy felt, and share his mother's understanding of her own part in it. Indeed, we can grasp the danger to one child from the throwing of one stone much more easily than the infinitely greater threat of devastation to hundreds of millions of children, women and men in a nuclear war. We have all experienced the difficulty of facing such a threat—of thinking about it, reading about it, responding to it in any way—to the point that it has often blocked out, for many of us, all awareness of the danger.

Ask children today and many will tell you that they do not expect to live out their lives without a nuclear war; but they will often go on to tell you that they do not think much about this fact, since there seems so little anyone can do about it. This is an extreme form of the defence mechanism known as denial. It is, as one doctor has said about patients who cannot confront the possibility of serious illness or death, a "pulling down of the shades".

Doctors estimate that at least 20 per cent of all patients who are told about being at serious risk of death pull down the shades thus—to the point where, a few days later, they have no memory of having been told. Faced with intolerable anxiety, they have blocked out the information. For some, the blockage is but a temporary reflex allowing time to regroup their forces and to begin to take it all in. For others, the shades turn out to be permanently lowered.

We have witnessed a massive pulling down of the shades in the face of the danger of nuclear war and collective extinction. But there is nothing temporary about *this* process. The denial is relentless and pervasive. And it engages a far greater proportion than the 20 per cent of sufferers from serious illness who are unable to confront the risk of their own death. Whole populations have lowered the shades, and go about life as if the risk to human survival were not one that required immediate response. Government leaders pull down the shades too, and in the seeming dusk they play international politics as usual.

But in the last few years we have seen growing efforts to pierce through the collective denial while there is still time: to help raise those shades that are now so firmly drawn. Women have been in the forefront of these efforts in many countries. We are witnessing an extraordinary coming together of people from all walks of life, all opinions and faiths. It is as if more and more people had decided that they *can* do something about the danger—that giving in to a sense of powerlessness is not only self-defeating but profoundly unworthy of the ideals they hold.

Against these efforts—against the teach-ins and the vigils and the town meeting resolutions and the marches—strong voices were raised at first. Editorials castigated these efforts as romantic, confused, ill-informed, impractical. Scholars pleaded for a debate among experts, and above all for an avoidance of popular movements, demonstrations and marches. Critics taunted as sentimental anyone who dared to speak out without what they took to be the proper background and knowledge. One hesitates to think with what contempt they would greet a writer of books for children who presumed to take a stand against war and violence.

Those who called on us to leave matters to experts and to governments were asking us to draw the shades down again, and thus to return to the easeful state of collective denial we already know so well. They appealed to our fear of seeming naive, our awareness of how much we did not know, and our distaste for struggling against seemingly hopeless odds.

But without popular pressure, experts and governments will never feel the urgency of the current problems. They, too, struggle with denial, and with fears of confronting the reality of the nuclear threat. A generation ago, it was not until mothers and fathers and children protested the world over against radioactive fallout that the treaty banning nuclear tests in the atmosphere was finally signed. Likewise in our period, governments will not negotiate in full seriousness, full awareness, until individuals in innumerable groups bring home to them the urgency of doing so.

There are signs that the efforts to raise the lowered shades are succeeding. Many more individuals are now aware of what is at stake. Communities and church groups and organisations across the world are addressing the threat of nuclear war. Fewer experts now regard the work of these groups as merely naive and meddlesome. And governments feel the pressure; they can no longer count on being able to press the arms race without being held accountable.

The United States Catholic Bishops' Pastoral Letter is an example of an effort to inform, raise consciousness, discuss and advise both individuals and governments with respect to war and peace. To individuals it speaks on such matters as refusal of military service, working in armaments industries and in weapons research; to governments and policymakers and all citizens it speaks on the morality of nuclear deterrence and on that of aiming weapons of mass destruction at civilian populations. And it calls—for the first time in a document of this kind to the best of my knowledge—for a climate of opinion in the United States which will make it possible to express profound sorrow over the bombings in Hiroshima and Nagasaki.

Press accounts of the Bishops' Letter have often left out another side of what they said—one which they stressed as equal in importance to the emergency over nuclear weapons: the role of the arms race as what they call "an act of aggression upon the poor". War preparations on the present scale not only risk death, perhaps in the near future, to countless persons across the globe; right now they threaten jobs, health, food supplies and even the most minimal standards of living for many. The arms traffic is draining funds away from desperately needed social programmes in many countries. Some nations now forego vital imports of food, fuel, spare parts or medicine, according to the Brandt Commission's report entitled *Common Crisis*, because of vast military expenditures. And the weapons that governments acquire thus are often used to quell internal critics, as well as to do battle with neighbouring states. The poorest societies are often the most victimized in this militarization of large and small states.

Just as we have to struggle to overcome our reluctance to face the risks of nuclear conflagration in the future, so we must work to overcome a similar reluctance when it comes to the actual suffering that is the lot of so many right now. The task of making peace, as the Bishops point out, will be sidetracked if we concentrate on military strategies and on bargaining positions with respect to nuclear war alone. Peace is not merely the absence of full-scale nuclear war: it must include the absence of what is euphemistically called "conventional war" as well, and true security for the many who are the victims of oppression and persecution, even by their own governments or fellow citizens.

If any group can help others overcome the reluctance to confront both the future dangers and the present suffering, surely it is the women who can do so. Perhaps it is only by learning about concrete experiences on the part of such witnesses and participants that we can go beyond the statistics and fully understand and feel the conditions that they are working to change. Whether it be through hearing about such joint work as to try to save a village forest in India or to combat the labour patterns and laws that destroy families in South Africa or to strengthen the respect for human rights in the Middle East, these women have shown us *and* one another the subtlety and variety of their methods and the ingenuity with which they put them to use. It is by helping work of this kind to spread and to find new support that it will be possible to reverse the rule of poverty, fear and violence under which so many now live.

Much of their work is carried out with an expressed commitment to non-violence, but not all. And here is an area of enquiry which may benefit from collective experience, by helping to sort out what we understand by violence and to consider all the alternatives to violent means for achieving one's goals. It may also help us to agree more than we do now on whether there are times when such means are unavoidable. Finally, it may give us a chance to consider when methods that we might all regard as non-violent are nevertheless coercive and used in unjust causes.

Let me return for a moment to the woman in the story with which I began—the woman who put a stone on her shelf as a reminder of her vow: No more violence. We all know what she meant. Not that she could magically do away with violence in her own life, let alone her society or the entire world. Not that she might not defend herself or her child; if need be with the very stone she had put aside or some other weapon. But rather that she would not use violence to hurt, nor to punish when other alternatives existed; and that she would try anew to *perceive* violence in all its guises, work against it, and do away with it whenever possible.

Many critics of her position would caricature it to make it stand for complete rejection of all means of self-defence. Such a position can hardly work in today's world against heavily armed opponents, least of all in the international arena. Those who caricature the stance for non-violence thus often believe that, since they have defeated the weak arguments for complete abandonment of self-protection, they have thereby justified any amount of militarization and violence that they happen to support.

Such a conclusion hardly follows from their arguments, and it opens the door to innumerable excesses and abuses. It is only by taking a strong initial stance against violence that one can go on to examine exceptional circumstances under which it might nevertheless be justified, while remaining alert to such excesses and abuses, and while searching at all times for non-violent alternatives.

In this regard, I am most interested in the Gandhian alternative. Gandhi, far from denying the presence of violence in the world, meant to carve out spaces, territories in human interaction, where violence would nevertheless not be used: territories in the family, in the community, among friends and enemies, between governments and citizens. Once these territories have been thus carved out, they can be enlarged, extended, and become models for others.

This may be what is happening now, when individuals and professional groups and religious groups are rededicating themselves to the pursuit of non-violence. It may be what lies behind the force of geographical regions declaring themselves free from nuclear weapons, as many are proposing for Scandinavia and other parts of Europe and Latin America.

Such efforts strike some, once again, as quixotic and unrealistic. But I believe that they only seem so in that never-never land dreamed up by those who think of themselves as political realists—a land in which one has to choose between only two alternatives: an impossible ideal of complete non-violence on the one hand; and on the other hand a free-for-all of arms build-up and continued hostilities. We have to learn to perceive all the possibilities that lie in between: all the non-violent means short of that unreachable ideal.

William Blake wrote of how we take part in our own difficulties in perceiving: "If the doors of perception were cleansed, everything would appear as it is, infinite. Instead, man has closed himself up'til he sees all things thro' the narrow chinks of his cavern."

Those who would have us give up, or give over, our concern for peace would consign us to remain without a struggle in the condition Blake set forth. In the efforts to open those chinks of the cavern, and to see all as it is, infinite, everyone has a part to play—including writers of books for children, scientists, scholars, men and women from every region, every culture. Without them, there will be no permanent chance for making peace.

Toward Permanent Rebellion

Sylvia Marcos

The Case of Nora

Nora was born in Amaçuzac. At 13, she was raped by a passing man who forced her out of her hut. Her father and other men left her momentarily alone. She was, after all, a vulnerable female. Virginity is the moral myth of rich women. It is a myth, because almost no rich or poor Mexican woman now is a virgin when she marries. The process of change has been a speedy one. But Nora preferred to be a virgin. However, in the words of the men, *valiendo nada*, she was "worth nothing". In the words of the public, as they say of women raped, she was "thrown into an intolerable situation".

An incident such as Nora's rape is often a part of the early lives of Mexican prostitutes. When the adolescent servant girl was raped by her master, my next door neighbour, I heard Dona Popoca say, "The only way now is prostitution." For some, it seems the "only way". But there *are* different things one can do with a horrible situation. Choosing prostitution is the alienated solution. It is the way of least resistance; already people from the outside are telling a young woman, a victim already, what to do, imprisoning her in a role.

Nora was different. She imagined and chose another way. She started her life alone. She left the village, she worked in miserable conditions, but she did not accept the definition of herself imposed by others. She is the example of the rebel. There she was, thrown on the world all alone. She became a peasant servant, then a city servant. Then she travelled to find better work, sometimes robbing to survive. Nora became a tireless rebel. The incident of her rape was transformed into rebellion by her rage and by her refusal to conform. Her rebellion became a long term commitment to transform her world, my world and your world—a world that permits women to be raped, to be seen as "guilty" of rape, and to become the trash that society creates.

Nora is now a doctor. She is not an established MD, but a barefoot doctor. And she has been teaching the science of healing to many women like herself in the poor villages of Mexico. She grasps with immense lucidity how women's oppression in male-female relationships imitates other kinds of oppression in society. Nora will never stop her work, I am sure. I know her. But she could have ended up, as many have—the poor, alienated by-product of society in which rape is one of the many symptoms of women's oppression.

Our Common Rebellion

The thought that comes to one's mind when speaking across cultures is: "What can one speak of that will be relevant to many different women? What can one say that will cut across cultural and class differences?" At the time of writing, there were three women in my household. There was the peasant woman, very poor, from Chiapas: a mother with three children, left alone without a husband. And there was a young girl, from a little town outside Cuernavaca: a girl with a very traditional upbringing, taught to be a virgin and to be inhibited in the use of her body, and now living freely with her young boyfriend, not thinking of getting married. Finally, there was me: writing, going to various places, and lecturing to people in different parts of the world. What indeed could we three from Mexico have in common? And what do we have in common with all the others, from so many places? Suddenly, it came to my mind: rebellion.

Rebellion is what we have in common. I am a rebel, each one of us is a rebel. We are different types of rebels, but we are all rebelling against intolerable situations. I am sure if we go back into our own lives, we have all had moments when there was nothing else to do, when we felt totally oppressed or alienated, totally incapable of managing the situation, totally at the end. But somehow, something happened, and we claimed our capacity for rebellion. We took force and power from within ourselves, and we said "No".

We are all rebels. There are academic rebels who refuse traditional ways of thinking and dismantle sexist methodologies. There are social rebels, who refuse traditional ways of marriage, family and social life, and create new ones. There are religious rebels, who refuse the patriarchal ideas and structures of religion, and attempt a new creation. There are emotional rebels and bodily rebels, who refuse the constraints of well-mannered morality, are free sexually, and are thought of as a danger to society because they rebel. And there are socio-political rebels, who see economic and political oppression, such as the horrible killing of the people in Guatemala, and refuse the world of power that permits and condones such things. For us, rebellion is life. If we do not have this rebellion, there is no hope and there is nothing we can do.

Primary Rebellion and Permanent Rebellion

I want to distinguish, however, between primary rebellion and permanent rebellion. Primary rebellion erupts from the first horrifying realisation of oppression, as a Black, as a woman, as a Jew, as an indigenous or tribal person. Primary rebellion is the first wave of response, when you first say to yourself "I am a woman, and because I am a woman I have been confined and limited. I could not choose what I wanted to study. I could not go into research. I could not choose whether or not to marry. And when I married, I had to leave my work." In primary rebellion, one rebels against everything. It is now or never, and one wants change *now*.

Because of the sense of focus and urgency, primary rebelliousness, in individuals and in groups, has several characteristics. First, there is exaggerated aggression against the "enemy". Second, there is often extreme censorship of other individuals and groups. They will say, "She is not a real feminist, she is very male-oriented," or "No, she's not a real Black sister, she is very white-oriented." Third, in primary rebellion people are incapable of compromise and incapable of doing long-range work and planning. Thus, primary rebellion must become but a step toward permanent rebellion. If not, we as rebels end up destroying one another.

We must make the step to permanent rebellion. As a permanent rebel, like Nora, one is capable of methodical and systematic commitment. At times this may mean something very boring. We all know too well how tiring it can be, and how difficult it can be to keep up hope. It is difficult to commit ourselves fully to something we will never fully attain. But this is the secret of permanent rebellion. We have to work, knowing that we will never completely attain the ideal that we seek. It does not and will not exist as we are visualising it. We must be able to sacrifice the complete attainment of the goal and be able to work toward it as a value that orients our life. This is not compromise, it is permanent rebellion. Such rebellion requires that we work tirelessly, methodically and systematically—"having hope against hope".

There are three essential dimensions of permanent rebellion. They are values that characterise permanent rebellion for women. First, the value of the body, and the affirmation of the body. Second, the value of action, and the necessity of being activist. Third, the value of spirituality and the sustaining energy of the spirit.

The Difficult Dynamics of Change

As we consider the move from no rebellion at all, to primary rebellion, to permanent rebellion, we must think both of individuals and groups. There are the dynamics of change that are inter-subjective: group dynamics. And there are the dynamics of change that are intra-subjective, that involve a struggle of self with self. The inter-subjective and intra-subjective dynamics are not separable, but in the process of change they are constantly intermingling and interacting.

For example, we as women have the patriarchal man inside ourselves. We have taken into ourselves the oppression of women in society, and we internalise the image of ourselves which society has taught us. We internalise restrictions, limitations, and even when we are victims of society's violence, as are the victims of rape, we internalise the definition of ourselves as guilty, as trash.

This exaggerated conformity I would call alienation, for such women are alienated from a sense of themselves and their value. Alienation is the mental over-adaptation of an individual or a group to socially determined conditions of existence. First, this over-adaptation limits the capacity of a subject to conceive of herself in conditions other than those in which she has been placed. Second, these conditions seem to her to be normal and justified. Third, she is characterised by an inability to imagine and to define real social alternatives.

If we take these characteristics, we see the classic non-rebellious person. She will say, "I don't understand what you are fighting for. What is the problem? I am very happy with my husband. I am very happy to cook and clean for him." In South India, at Kanyakumari, I met an Indian woman who lived in South Africa. She said to me, "We don't know why there is such trouble about apartheid in South Africa. You know, the whites are very nice to us. They let us work and earn our living." To these non-rebels, conditions that are oppressive to themselves or to others seem normal and justified. Even those directly affected by oppression often cannot imagine another situation. They are incapable of seeing a way out in terms of concrete action. In Nora's situation, another woman would have ended up a ten peso prostitute because she would not have been able to conceive of anything else.

There are other characteristics of this exaggerated conformity, other ways of thinking that shape this non-rebellious alienated consciousness. There is the rationalization of the dependency situation, accepting it by understanding it, giving the reasons for it. There is the atomization of social conscience, considering oneself and one's oppression as unique and individual, and not part of the wider systemic oppression of a whole group like oneself. And there is the tendency to conceive of oneself in symbiosis with the dominant. This symbiosis in relation to the dominant, the oppressor, means one wants to be like him. The goal is not to change the structure, but to be in his position. This is the dynamics of symbiotic oppression. It is not so evident as saying that women want to be like men, or Blacks want to be like whites. It is more subtle. It means we want the dynamics of the male situation, the white situation. When this happens, the last hope vanishes for internal change, real change, social change.

The Case of Emma

I began with Nora. Let me conclude with the story of Emma, the initiator of an association of women house servants in Latin America. Emma was conscious of herself as a woman and conscious of the particular sufferings she had to undergo just because she happened to be born a woman. Her husband left her, without support. He was tired of trying unsuccessfully to meet basic needs for his family. Emma, like the appalling majority of peasant women, became the head of the household. So it is in peasant villages, where 48 per cent of people live in households headed by a woman. Emma became mother and father, male and female, cleaning her house, nurturing her children, but also cleaning and nurturing for payment. She became a servant.

As her responsibility changed, her consciousness changed. Emma became intensely aware of herself. She had been left alone, with all the pains and responsibilities of family. And she also became aware of and concerned with her role and work as a servant, her servant self. She did not understand why she must liberate her mistress from dirty and tiresome work, accept a dungeon to sleep in, accept scraps of food to eat, and accept work without time limits. She started speaking to other women servants when they were out at the rubbish heap throwing away the house trash.

In this meeting place, paradoxically beautiful, the rubbish heap, a sense of community started to grow. They started meeting and discussing, trying to wipe away from their inner selves the symbiotic relation with the dominant, the belief and acceptance that this arrangement was God-given or Nature-given. Why should they model themselves and their aspirations in the mistress image of the lady of the house? In doing so, they legitimized the order of things in their own minds. This internalisation of the order of dominance was their main enemy, and it was *in them*, not in the dominant alone. The power of the dominants they would face later, but the very idea that there are masters and servants and that masters have more value than servants was ingrained deep inside, in their perception of themselves, of the order of the universe, and of their place in the universe as women, and as poor people. La Asociacion des Trabajadoras Domesticas was born. Its fruits are now maturing.

The process of these women was both inter-subjective and intra-subjective. They are all poor women, most of them alienated from themselves, with deeply internalised self-devaluing images. Their process of change has been typical of the psychological and sociological dynamics of many groups trying to transform their reality. Their struggle against an external oppressive enemy has turned at times to internal conflict, growing out of their own multiplicity and their different stages of rebellion. Oppressed groups struggling for liberation often have to face, as the first enemy, their own inter-subjective interactions and conflicts.

For some in the oppressed group, there is overwhelming apathy, tiredness, and melancholy. In Latin America, especially in Mexico, this apathy or fatalism is very often the result of the mingling of chronic malnutrition and discouraging personal experience: "How can you believe that this time it will work and things will change, when we have the appalling facts of past experience?" In addition, they have also interiorised and absorbed into the inner self, an image of oneself as worthless. This image is not only restrictive, limiting, but fully pathological. Any psychodynamic or psychoanalytical theory includes it. The fear of failure is almost certain.

And finally, of course, there is the suspicion of anyone in a position of power. These women in La Asociacion des Trabajadoras Domesticas were suspicious of any woman of superior status. They rejected out of hand every bourgeois woman who came to help, not finding any common bond with them as women. The experiences of workers parties and leftist parties is similar to that of women's groups and minority groups. The suspicion of the other is a classical first step in the group's dynamics. There are suspicions of the "other", not necessarily superior or inferior, just other. There is suspicion between members of political parties. There is suspicion between feminists. There is suspicion of anyone who has power, including themselves, especially themselves, as they gain power. Finally, destructiveness, bitterness, mistrust and painful institutionalised envy result from the inter-subjective interaction of the group.

In this case, the other women thought Emma worked because she wanted power for herself. She did too much, they thought. She must be wanting something else. The weak and unpowerful accept only a recognized superior to concentrate power. An equal, never. They would have to recognize their envy and their suspicion by self-reflection and continued growth. Emma survives. The association survives. But the questions Emma's experience raises for us are critical. Why do we continue to repeat the patterns of oppression in our very effort to win freedom? Why do we turn against one another, like the slaves of former times? How can we free ourselves of internalised oppression? And how can we, as women, move together from primary rebellion to permanent rebellion?

Toward Women's Power, Nationally and Internationally

Nawal el Saadawi

Social Change: A Personal View

Let me begin with an example of my own experience of social change. My mother, before she married my father, never saw him, in spite of the fact that she was from an upper-middle urban class in Cairo and was educated in a French school. But she never saw my father, except from behind the shutters. I myself, when I married, married three times. I divorced two husbands. So you can see how much change there has been in one generation! My daughter, who is now 25 years old, is deciding not to marry at all.

We are changing, and we are changing very rapidly and radically. Of course, there is struggle and conflict that comes with change. There are powers that try to pull society backwards. But the powers that push society forward are greater.

Again, if I look at my own life, there is change—just in the past decade. I was in prison in 1981. I lost my job in 1971. I was censored from 1971 until the 1980s. Now, in Egypt, I am free and I am writing. I am not in jail. And my books are reprinted and republished in Egypt. This is change. I have been specific here, with concrete examples. We do learn something from generalisations, but when we think about specific examples, then we really see what is happening to our lives.

Now, what about Islam? And what of the other great religions? When we think about "religions" in general, it seems to me that, more or less, they are the same. They all have a general human call for the equality of people—regardless of colour, race or sex. One finds this conception of equality in all of the religions, as well as in Marxism or existentialism. But when we come to the specifics, when we come to the daily lives of men and women, rich and poor, one race and another, this general sense of equality does not seem to be in evidence. Here we find oppression, including the oppression of women. So we must not have illusions about religion, because religion is used, and it is used often by those in power.

Religion, Social Change and Power

Let me cite an example of religion and power in Egypt. When I was young during the time of King Farouq, before President Nasser, all the religious institutions in Egypt said that King Farouq was the descendent of the Prophet Muhammad. He was not, in actual point of fact, but the religious establishment tried to make a link, an extended blood-relation, between our King and the Prophet Muhammad. This would give the King sacred authority, complete authority over the people. This happened with President Sadat too. He named himself "The Believer". Nasser was called "The Militant Fighter". But Sadat named himself, "The Head of the Family," and "The Believer". This gives us a sense of how religion is used politically.

Why is it that most religious institutions try to make a sacred link between the President or King, and God or the Prophet? Religion, in this sense, is very flexible, at times, one would say, manipulable. Just as Islam made the link between King Farouq and the Prophet Muhammad, so all sorts of political and economic policies—even the British colonialism of Egypt—were interpreted by Islam as something good. When Nasser came, he started to launch socialist reform, including the nationalisation of the Suez canal and the nationalisation of the banks, in order to have some economic independence. And what happened? The religious authorities and institutions started to say, "Well, socialism is Islamic." And they started to pick up words and verses from the Koran emphasising socialism. And they attacked King Farouq. Yesterday, when he was in power, Farouq was a relative of the Prophet Muhammad. Now he is the devil and he is corrupt.

When Anwar Sadat came to power, his political and economic policies isolated Egypt from the Arab countries and made Egypt dependent upon the West, economically. We lost our independence. We lost many battles during the time of Sadat. He started the Open Door Policy, which meant that he stopped the national industrialisation and the nationalisation of the banks. He started to invite foreign banking and foreign capital.

Anything foreign during the time of Sadat was much more respected than the national—even the human being. This made me furious. And this, finally, sent me to jail, because I defended my identity as an Egyptian, as an Arab. I was charged with "publishing articles critical of President Sadat's policies". Everywhere I went during the time of Sadat, I felt that I was not placed on a level with the foreigner. The money of the foreigner was almighty. Sadat even created new laws for foreign money and foreign banking. And how did the religious establishment respond? They started to say, "Well, capitalism is Islamic!" They might even have found the Open Door Policy to be Islamic.

These examples show us one of the main problems of religion—it is flexible, sometimes to the point of being manipulated by power. In many ways, of course, flexibility and change are good. That is life. And if life is something changing, and religion is something fixed, then there is a problem. But if life is something changing, and religion is something changing, then it is possible to *use* religion, as our government has.

Change, in relation to society, is one of the main features of Islam. Such change is regulated by *ijtihad*, "interpretation". *Ijtihad* opens the door for flexibility and change within society. However, our questions must be, "*Who* changes religion? And *how* does it change? Who is responsible for *ijtihad*?" Because, too often, religion simply changes with power. Those who have the power change religion according to their own interests, not according to the interests of the people.

Women, Social Change and Power

Several women have raised the question, "Can we move toward a universal women's movement and philosophy?" We need it. For we women are excluded from religion, from philosophy, from politics and economics. We are outside these realms, and we must develop our own philosophy and our own power as women.

How can we generate our own power as women, regardless of countries or boundaries? This is an important question, and it is the kind of question that goes to the roots. Can we create a universal philosophy as women? Can we unite, and generate power, both nationally and internationally?

Without national power, we cannot have international power. We have to build our national power; but we also need to work internationally. In the Middle East, we have started by forming the Association of Solidarity Between Women. This is a pan-Arab association for women's rights. We are trying in Arab countries to work nationally, and then to extend to pan-Arab women's power, and then to develop an international movement.

We begin with change as individuals. We have to start with ourselves. If I had not liberated myself from my first oppressive husband, I could not have spoken of liberation to others. We have to start with the self, with ourselves. Then we have to start at home, together, in our own countries, and build our solidarity and base of power there. Then we are also able to build our power internationally. These go hand in hand—liberating ourselves, and organising nationally and internationally.

Now is the time. Unless women come forward and assume power nationally and internationally, we will never have peace or justice. Women, as half of our societies, have never had real political power. Never. And when I wrote in Cairo that women should start a political party, everybody was angry, even the Marxists. They said that it was unheard of for there to be a political party for women. But the real struggle in our world is political. If we women are pushed into welfare work, into social work, we will get nowhere.

Any feminist should be a political activist in its real sense. I am an activist, although I am not a member of any political party. Most of the parties are not really politically active. Politics is a game. I will shut my shutters and write a book rather than waste my time in meetings with such political parties. But nevertheless, women should organise and have political power, based on economic power, on self-awareness, and on a new philosophy for women.

What might such a philosophy of women include? We women have learned a lot from each other. We have learned to see some of the linkages between the world's problems. For example, I have learned a lot from women in the West who have written about patriarchy, and who have written about the relationship of patriarchy to imperialism, capitalism, Zionism, and so on. Political dictatorship is related to a society where the father is a dictator. All of us have begun to see the relationship between those powers which oppress women, and those powers which create massacres everywhere. We have to continue to make the link between this international oppression, and the exploitation and the oppression of women. Unless we see such links we are not going to be able to form our philosophy and our strategy.

Part of our strategy may be to use religion. I am not against religion itself. But I am against religion if it is going to be used against women. I want to live, and I want to enjoy life, and I want to give life my ideas, and to take from life. If religion is going to stop me, I am going to stop religion. This should be the character of women: to stand up and to rebel if we must.

But we are brought up to be non-violent, even when people are violent against us. This is inequality. If we are indifferent with regard to our rights, we encourage exploitation. I think that we women are ourselves responsible for war, for massacres, if we ourselves do not fight for our rights. We should fight. We should not compromise with our rights. We should not turn away from our own power.

Change, Identity and the Veil

I would like to speak about one issue of social change with regard to Islam, the question of traditional veiling among women in Egypt. It has been described as "Islamic dress," having to do with a new sense of Islamic or national identity. What do we mean by national identity? And what has it to do with dress? If I change my shoe or my dress, do I change? Many political powers try to direct our attention to superficialities—to what we wear, not to real identity. The essence of my identity does not change, whether I wear a robe, or tight trousers.

While some say there is an "Islamic dress," I say, there is nothing called Islamic dress! There is nothing called Islamic identity, because Islamic identity itself is changing. My mother's identity as a Muslim woman, in a general cultural sense, is not my identity, nor the identity of my daughter as a Muslim girl. So our identity is not fixed. It is changing. Identity has more to do with how you think your thoughts and ideas than with how you dress. So my point about the issue of "Islamic dress" is how we can transcend such conceptions and fashions that attempt to imprison us in the name of identity.

The powers that try to exploit us in the Third World are subtle, quite subtle. Even in the West we hear now that we should pay attention to our identity, pay attention to Islam. The West, in a sense, encourages Islam—not its most progressive aspects, but its most reactionary and superficial aspects, such as the veil. Political and economic struggles are interpreted as religious, although they are not really religious at core. This often diverts attention from the real issues of liberation which are at stake. Even the revolution of Muhammad was against the rich, the upper class, the Quraish people. It was not religious, but ecomomic. But in the Third World, when there are economic revolutions, they are quickly understood to be religious—not in the progressive sense, but in the most reactionary sense. That is how the West wants to understand them.

In the fifties, during the Nasser period, when I was in the Faculty of Medicine in the University of Cairo, there was not a single veiled woman in the University. And during the seventies, after twenty years, during Sadat's period, the veiled women started to appear. Why? That is the question. I would say that often, when a politician develops reactionary policies, he uses religion and emphasises religion. And he might even name himself "The Believer". Thus, during the seventies in Egypt, Islamic groups were encouraged and financed. And Saudi Arabia played a large role. The richest country in the world, affiliated with the most capitalist country in the world, seemed to work together to revive the most reactionary aspects of Islam. I met a girl in Jordan, a poor girl who was wearing a veil. I asked her, "When did you start wearing this veil?" And I discovered that somebody paid her money to put on the veil.

Many people think that the oppression of women in Egypt and the Arab countries is related to Islam, and that the veil originated in Islam. This is not true. If we look to the origins of patriarchy and the story of Adam and Eve, Eve is said to have represented the body and Adam the head. Women were considered bodies without heads, so they should be ashamed of their incomplete nature, and hide their heads. Therefore, the veil is part of Judaism, Christianity and Islam. More widely and significantly, such forms of restricting the freedom of women are rooted in the class system and the patriarchal system.

My grandmother lived in a village, a poor village, in rural Egypt. She never wore a veil a day in her life. She worked in the fields. Recently, I visited her village and found my cousin Zeinab, with no veil, with her thighs even naked, because she was working in the fields and irrigating the land. She was working, and totally unaware of her body. I have never seen a single woman veiled in my village. The veil, historically, did not start with Islam and, socially, it is related to an urban middle-class sector of society.

Religion, Economics and Change

In my books, I do not usually attack Islam as such, because I think this is a lost battle, in spite of the fact that from my experience in my village the masses are not religious. The masses are poor and they are so occupied with their daily bread and work that they never think of religion, even if they go to pray once a week on Friday. The younger generations do not even do that. The economic crisis, the unemployment, is so difficult that they do not have time or energy to think about religion or the veil. The masses are pragmatic. They are poor. They need to eat. They are working for their basic needs. When they have met their basic needs, when they have eaten and rested, then they think about religion.

Many people say that the masses are religious and that, therefore, we should respect and honour religion. I think this is not true. When Nasser started to distribute land under a programme of socialism, and when he gave the poor peasants a piece of land, they never thought of religion. When Nasser started to abolish the economic and political base of religious institutions in Egypt, no one worried about a threat to religion. We have to be careful lest we overemphasise religion. The majority of people become aware of religion when they have all their basic needs, and most of the people in my country and in Asia and Latin America do not have their basic needs yet. Politicians do, however, make them aware of religion, and try at times to convince them that they should fight for religion, not for bread and food.

Conclusion

I would like to end with a few remarks based on the specific experience of Egypt, but relevant to much of the Third World. We are fighting an unequal battle—the First World and the Third World. The more we develop subtle resistance, the more the First World develops subtle ways of oppression. How are they bringing about this oppression? Perhaps most powerfully with mass media. How can we fight the technological revolution of mass media?

Another subtle form of oppression is the creation of a dual society. This is what multinationalists are doing in our countries now. They are creating an elite society which is modernised, with fashionable clothes and fashion-consciousness—in order to consume the goods which are being sent to us. Who is going to consume American shampoos and cosmetics, unless they create these elite groups in our countries to consume these goods? Who will help external powers to exploit us? A class must be created. They are created to be the allies of the West, and to them is preached the message of modernism, pseudo-modernism, based on consumerism. But to the majority is preached the message of traditional, or even reactionary, Islam. They are encouraged to have the national, traditional dress and "identity" of the veil.

How can we resist as women? We change, and we rebel. We claim whatever power is ours already. We discover the sources of support that are already with us in society. For example, we have in Egypt, the most backward marriage and divorce laws of all Arab countries. But in practice, we Egyptian women practice divorce. And we are freer than Tunisian women, for instance, even though in Tunisia they have the most progressive marriage and divorce laws. A woman in Tunisia can divorce her husband; in Egypt she can't. But in Egypt, in spite of the law, a woman can divorce her husband. I divorced two husbands, without the law. This is the tradition; and we live more by traditions than laws. This is why, all my life, I have scarcely participated in campaigns to change the laws. For we have to change many, many things, and not only the laws.

In Islam and the Arab world, and in all our cultures, we must claim those things that are positive, and discard without hesitation those things that are negative. In Egypt we have a long tradition of women of power. For thousands of years, for example, we have had the Goddess Isis, and her tradition. Thank God, thank Goddess, we still have her spirit with us!

Gandhian Contributions Toward a Feminist Ethic

Devaki Jain

The question I want to raise is, What shall we do with religion? It is there. It tugs at women; often it hurts them. Its powers are on the increase, especially in the newly liberated countries. Religion both unites and divides the world. At times it seems that religion is immutable—enormous, difficult to manage, frightening, and yet influential, since each of the religious traditions claims some ancient, deep and sanctified root. We must find a way into religion and out of it, because traditions of religion are powerful and because women's lives are interwoven with them. I am using "religion" here in the wider sense, that is in the sense of deeply held values, which would include traditional values, social values and cultural values.

Thus it is that we must ask not only what religion can do for women, but more importantly: what can women do with religion? In other words, how can women use religious traditions and values to their advantage? How can we meet traditional values half-way, so that the tradition can help change society?

This paper is in three sections. In the first, I argue for the importance of a universal philosophy or ethic for women. In the second, I illustrate how religion has been used by women in India and suggest something of the Indian contribution to a universal ethic. In the third, I try to suggest what the common ground for such an ethic might be. My hope is that we might first work toward a common view, and then work backwards into our individual traditions to see where we might draw power and empowerment from them for women.

From my experience with women and development during the past ten years, as a woman activist and a social scientist, I am beginning to see the need for a better understanding of religious traditions and the relationships they create in society. I also see the significance of learning to use the traditions for creating a just and peaceful society.

Women all over the world, and especially in the developing countries, have been the primary bearers of religious and cultural traditions. Some may give negative reasons for this, i.e. that women are motivated to resort to tradition by fear, superstition, ignorance, or lack of power. However, we also find studies suggesting that women, speaking in general now, tend to be more sensitive to moral or ethical questions, more responsible and responsive to human needs, and less dominating in relationships. The evidence for such a psychological assessment comes from a wide range of research and writing. It also comes from looking at the kinds of issues in which women participate, in great numbers and with great commitment.

For example, the majority of those who take part in peace movements and are activists in non-violence seem to be women. In India and elsewhere, women have come out in large numbers against particular injustices, such as the confiscation of land, the shooting of dissenters, the cutting down of forests, etc. Providing security has been so much a part of women's historical experience that it has become a part of women's ethic: to care.

Is there some connection between these characteristics of women and their attachment to tradition? Most religious traditions do talk of spirit, some in norms of goodness, such as honesty, compassion and the universality of mankind and womankind. It is also true that religious organisations have tended to become alternative sources of power, and have often perpetuated discrimination and inequalities. Is it possible that the religious valuation of compassion, in some way, has "touched" women more than the religious valuation of power?

Against this background of questions, I would like to look at the linkages between that aspect of Hindu thought which stresses individual autonomy leading to self-realisation; Gandhi's stress on self-reliance and self-control; and the universally recognised foundation for women's liberation, namely autonomy, a sense of one's own self. In all, autonomy is a positive value. Hindu thought sees its spiritual content; Gandhian thought underlines its social content, i.e. the fact that self-reliance and autonomy do not mean isolation of the individual, or individualism, but rather, autonomy and self-reliance linked to the family and society. Women's thought points to its global possibilities as an element in a universal ethic for women.

The Need for a Global Vision

The first step for women is to identify goals, and then to draw out of the fabric of religious tradition, those threads that seem strongest to use in creating the society we seek. But what are these goals? Are they common to all women, or must they be culture, religion, class, race specific? Is there a kind of feminism which can be a universal ideology for women, or must there be several feminisms?

It is too easy to say that feminism is both universal and group specific. It is also too easy to say that feminism is completely group, religion, or culture specific and that the issue of women and religion will have to be approached independently, in each tradition, with no common denominators. What is more difficult, but to my mind more important, is to accept the challenge of identifying a critical core which is universal to all women, and then mark out the boundary areas which may be different.

Let us take the Indian case, with reference to the Hindu Code Bill, for example. The women's movement in pre-Independence India wanted a general civil code which would apply to all religions. Kamaladevi Chattopadhyaya, a leader of the movement in pre-Independence India, put it this way: "There is one thing these brilliant Indian women have done, and that is to show in their own personalities how alert their respective organisations are, and how little of substance there is in the English delusion that Indian life must continue on a Communal Basis; in fact, it was ever so ordered. Hindu, Muslim and Christian on the same platform, colleagues and comrades pleading the same cause, demanding a common citizenship so that a true national spirit may develop and woman may take her full share of civic responsibility, make a deep impression."[1] Kamaladevi goes on to record the dismay among these women when, in fact, separate civil codes were granted, especially due to the pressure of conservative religious groups. Thus, today in India, Muslim women have a different civil code from the Hindus. The voices heard most loudly continue to be those of religious leaders,

[1] Kamaladevi Chattopadhyaya, *Indian Women's Battle for Freedom* (1983), p. 103.

primarily conservative men. And today, the voices of women raised to support a universal civil code, are few. Even women's groups are sometimes reluctant to press the issue, lest they be accused of communal aggression.

If certain issues can be identified as impinging on all women irrespective of religion, then it would be possible to overcome this accusation. Indeed, in pre-Independence India, the women leaders did have a common ideology, and persisted with it when designing their demands. Today, however, there is no common platform, hence articulation becomes "culture specific" with all the divergent and divisive elements of such splintering.

The history of the civil code issue in India illustrates the point that women, coming from particular religious or traditional structures, *can* help each other by bringing out and exchanging the most advantageous aspects of each of their cultures, but we can do so only if certain goals and aims, issues and strategies, are identified as common to all women.

In essence, I think that most religious traditions are *liberating*. Fundamentally, through religious traditions men and women free themselves of mental and physical bondage, and find spiritual illumination. Such illumination provides a kind of liberation, a release, from the earth. In this respect, religious traditions are remarkably similar. It is in the *establishment* of structures of religion, however, that religious traditions have become distinguished, one from another. What we must find, therefore, are the dynamics of liberation within each tradition which move people beyond the establishment into freedom.

Contributions from India: Toward a "Gandhian Feminism"

As in most societies in the world, in India there is a tradition of group singing and dancing, especially by women. The singing can be directly religious as, for example, the singing of *bhajans*, or hymns. But the singing can also be merely suggestive of religion, as in the case of folk music, theatre, or dance. Villages and neighbourhoods often have what are called *bhajan mandalis*, "circles of song singing," in which women gather to sing *bhajans*, either informally or in a more institutionalised way.

Such *bhajan mandalis* are a live and strong form of women's grouping among Hindus in India today. It is an important fact that

SEWA, the Self-Employed Women's Association in Ahmedabad, used the *bhajan mandalis* as an entry point to get to know the poor self-employed workers of Ahmedabad. SEWA extension workers joined the *bhajan* groups, sang with them, had discussions after the *bhajans* were over, and thus introduced themselves into the neighbourhoods where working women lived.

After this introduction, the SEWA workers were able to do a household survey on the economic condition of these women workers. They then could analyse the survey, discuss it with the group at any *bhajan* session, and enable the women to find a course of action. The women themselves then went into action, and, as is well known, formed a larger and larger association.

Bhajans continue in SEWA today. In fact, every meeting of SEWA, whether at the level of the extension workers or at mass meetings, begins and ends with the singing of *bhajans*. This is consistent not only with the women's culture of SEWA workers, but also with Gandhi's style of collectivity. And SEWA, of course, springs from Gandhian roots.

It is well known that Gandhi always began his day, his meetings, his fasts and his activities with prayers in the form of song. Such prayers included many Hindu *bhajans*, such as the familiar "*Raghupati Raghava Raja Ram*." Other prayers were Muslim or Sikh in origin. They communicated the message of solidarity, equality and the universality of religion. Gandhian ashrams, such as Radha Bhatt's Lakshmi Ashram, continue this tradition; SEWA has drawn upon this tradition as well, bringing women from the *bhajan mandalis* into trade unionism.

A further illustration of the indirect use of religion for social change also comes from Gandhi and what, in a tentative way, might be called "Gandhian Feminism". My comments here emerge from three workshops with 15–25 women involved in various forms of Gandhian "constructive work". The first workshop laid bare, in very poignant terms, how the philosophy of Gandhi had drawn these women away from conventional roles in class, caste and family and into activist work in Gandhian social institutions. And yet, even within the movement, they were sometimes inconvenienced, subordinated, and even harassed by men who shared their own ideological framework.

Each of these Gandhian women revealed how, from childhood, she had shown her difference from the rest of her family in wanting to respond to poverty, misery, injustice and inequality. Sometimes this was expressed by teaching neighbouring slum children; by sharing food with others stealthily; even by leaving home and joining a Gandhian ashram community. Later, there were struggles for education, for choice of partner in marriage, or for the choice not to marry and lead the life of a social non-conformist.

In adulthood most of the women present were workers of one kind or another in Gandhian institutions. Here they experienced the usual tensions between domestic and professional roles, usually with men who expected women to first fulfil their domestic responsibilities. They also experienced the criticism that they were "over-playing" the "women's issue". It was even suggested to them that there was no such issue in Indian society.

Looking back, while these women could see a common thread in their struggles as women, they could also recognise that in some important ways they were not interested in joining the more vocal sex-based "women's movements" in India. They were still primarily motivated by Gandhian issues, giving priority to the poorest of the poor.

One such issue is that of the treatment of untouchables, or Harijans, the "children of God," as Gandhi called them—those castes which had been "outcasted" by the caste system on the basis of their ritual "impurity". During the freedom struggle, Gandhi had taken the line that the Harijans should be integrated into Hindu society, and therefore no separate identification, socially or politically, should be made. Gandhi felt that if special reservations of seats or positions were made for them as "handicaps" to help overcome their historical deprivation, they would always remain stigmatised. He believed in an appeal to caste Hindus to open their minds and hearts to embrace all colours, castes and creeds and to shed the discriminatory perception of the Harijans.

Gandhi also attempted to change the reason for the stigma, which was that untouchables engaged in impure and odious tasks: carrying night soil, flaying animals and working with leather. He insisted that work may be odious, but people are never impure. Therefore he demanded that every Gandhian worker clean his or her own toilet. In the ashrams, the workers themselves cleaned the night soil, not only of the villagers, but of the castes which were employed to do so!

Dr. B.R. Ambedkar, an untouchable colleague of Gandhi, had a different view. He felt that these castes, which came to be called "scheduled castes," would never attain equality unless they had asserted themselves separately. Indian policy today uses positive discrimination in favour of the scheduled castes and tribes, so that they are given both identity and privileges in exchange for revealing that identity. These privileges have created the basis for a new, positive self-consciousness.

This debate between those who see separatism as an obstacle to equality and those who see separatism as a means of attaining equality has some universal dimensions. The Black power movement made blackness, which had been the basis of stigma, a positive value and made a bid for solidarity on the basis of blackness. This made mobilisation across class lines more possible than it had been in the integration movement.

However, in the Gandhian Women's Workshop in Bangalore, the women were united in their support of the Gandhian view, especially with regard to the Harijans or scheduled castes. Caste is different from race or gender, in that it does not carry a visible mark, but the policies of separatism retain artificial barriers, and their attendant stigmas, within the community.

At the workshop, Radha Bhatt described, for example, how such policies hurt the homogeneity of Lakshmi Ashram. When the Inspector of Schools used to visit the school, he wanted to check how many children there were from these stigmatised castes, to make certain that the scholarships or grants given to her school for these children were being properly used. These girls hated to be identified as scheduled. In fact, they found the school a haven of peace precisely because they did not have to carry with them the caste tensions of their village, and could see themselves as part of one unified community. During the inspection, the scheduled caste girls broke down in front of the Inspector. As a result, Radha Bhatt has come to refuse these special grants in aid, so that she would never again have to make those children stand up and expose themselves.

While the Gandhian women at the workshop appreciated both aspects of the issue, there was agreement with Gandhi's view, which emphasises the "means" to equality, not just the "end". It is this that might be described as the basis of Gandhian feminism: an insistence on the means, rather than the ends alone. Durable achievements demand dedication to the method, the process of revolution. If the means, the methods, build on human goodness, then a genuine change of attitude and durable results can be achieved.

The Gandhian presupposition here is that man is essentially good, not nasty and brutish as some philosophers would have us think, nor born with original sin. The human soul is part of the infinite soul, the Brahman, and is already linked to the divine. All that is required is to foster and stimulate these basic, and good, impulses.

Another example of an emerging spirit of Gandhian women's work is also from the area around Lakshmi Ashram. Khirakot is a village down the hill from Kausani in the hills near Almora. Several years ago, an enterprising man from outside the village started to quarry limestone from a deposit in the hills near Khirakot. To carry it to the road, he had to pass through the outskirts of Khirakot and cross the fields, crossing several times the narrow footpaths which are used by the people of the village whenever they go to cultivate their fields, to bring water, or to fetch fuel and fodder for the cattle. The man initially transported these limestone loads by human labour. He found the business so remunerative that he decided to set up a power-mill. The mill, in turn, had a capacity which demanded much larger volumes of stone from the quarry. This led to the use of donkeys as pack animals. Convoys of donkeys used to go from the quarry to the road, occupying the narrow footpaths used by the local population, especially the women.

Initially, the villagers accepted the man's activity with their usual tolerance. If a man could find a good source of livelihood, they should not stand in the way. However, as his activities increased, the women found they sometimes had to stand for hours with heavy loads on their heads, waiting for the donkeys to pass, as the narrow paths could be used by only one person or animal at a time. Also, the outsiders were a threat to the community, since many young girls had to go to school using the same paths. The women decided the man's packing must stop.

They appealed to the men of the village, who claimed that they had talked to the miner and that he had refused their request: he had permission from the government for quarrying, he said. The women then tried to obstruct the pack trains by narrowing the footpaths so that the donkeys could not walk on them. The miner responded by registering a case in court against the women's obstruction. But the women intensified their obstruction by physically occupying the paths. The miner further increased his protest through the courts.

The men were ready to give up, as they could not see themselves fighting a legal battle. There was no money for litigation, they said, and they could not see the legality of their case, as the miner was supported by the government in his activity. But the women would not accept this position. They insisted that the case be fought on the grounds of trespass and causing public nuisance. They raised the money from their own resources and savings, and fought the case for nearly two years until they won, and the digging at the quarry stopped.

The success of such resistance fired the self-confidence of the community and made women assume leadership roles. It brought other women into the movement. The village has now decided to replant the quarry with trees. They see their resistance to this kind of destruction of the environment as part of their movement to preserve the ecology of the Himalayas. The Chipko Movement of the wider Himalayan hills area had already given the people some idea of the power of resistance, for by "hugging the trees" ordinary women and men were able to halt the spread of deforestation.

Another example of this kind of experience is that of the women of Kumarikatta in Assam. Here, some tribals had long occupied an area of land and were cultivating it. Periodically, the legality of their claim upon the land was questioned and initiatives were taken to evict them. Each time, somebody had intervened on their behalf, and the status quo continued. One time, however, the intervention failed. The authorities went so far as to give notice of eviction and arrange for a herd of elephants to trample down the huts of the tribals.

The elephants came, and the tribal village people gathered outside the huts. There were moments of tense silence and stillness. The social workers who were working with the tribals could see no way of protecting the "squatters". It seemed inevitable that the finale would have its own momentum.

Suddenly, without any previous discussion, the women rushed forward out of the crowd of those to be evicted and embraced the trunks and legs of the elephants, constantly chanting the prayers that they usually chant on the particular *puja* day for the worship of the elephant God, Ganesha. It is customary on that day for women to rub sandal paste, *kumkum* and flowers on the elephants and to stroke them with devotion. The women now imitated the same ritual, with full ceremony. The elephants seemed to respond, in turn, by refusing to advance, accepting this worship with their conventional grace. No one—neither the authorities, nor the social workers, nor the male squatters—could do anything. The elephants turned back, and the tribals returned to their huts.

Both these episodes illustrate the ability of women, not only to identify their common problems, but to perceive a common solution, which usually involves steely courage, great risk and the conviction of the non-violent method. All that seemed necessary in these situations was a link to some source of self-confidence. The women needed simply to recognize their own inner strength—they did not need to be told how to organise, or how to overcome their difficulties. They seemed simply to need this crucial link to Gandhiji's philosophy of non-violent action. Such a life-line is provided by the work and inspiration of institutions like Lakshmi Ashram. Both the knowledge of what needs to be done and the power to do it are already there. The outside worker needs only to become an insider—to be with the people, as Gandhian workers are, for example, in the *padyatras*, the "walking journeys" they take through the hill villages. The communication of love, care and interest is precisely the life-line, the mobilising force, that such villagers need.

Love as a central value is common to many religious traditions, but the Vaishnava tradition of Gandhi's family adds to love a certain earthliness. In this love, life is not rejected but embraced. Simplicity in consumption is not based upon self-denial, which makes for a harsh puritanism, but self-control, which makes for strength in working in society. This is a way of love, not for the ascetic who withdraws from the world, but for the one who lives, with others, in the world, as did Gandhi.

Gandhi's this-worldly approach to revolution was especially appropriate to women's experience. He demonstrated this during India's freedom struggle. Women were significant participants in economic struggles—the boycott of foreign goods, such as textiles, and the Salt March. Women took the message of the spinning wheel seriously. Even today, at the Gandhian women's workshops, the *message* of *khadi*, as distinct from simply the *commerce* of *khadi*, is a real commitment. For women in the Independence Movement, spinning meant self-reliance, and identification with the unskilled and unemployed.

In their biographies, many women leaders of pre-Independence India have described how Gandhi's call to *satyagraha* (literally "truth force"), opened the door to them for their own liberation from oppressive social modes. The code of his ashrams included simplicity in dress and reverence for women. The rules of the ashrams made it possible for women to "come out" of the narrow worlds of their homes to participate in a wider community.

In a sense, Gandhi met the Indian tradition half way. He directed it away from its establishment "structures" and toward its changing "dynamics". It was just this capacity to meet the tradition half way that facilitated the emergence of women from the grip of the orthodox tradition. However "reformist" or "middle-path" such an approach may seem, it is tactically effective, because it provides vehicles and options for change.

Toward a Feminist Ethic

Where do we go from here? In this section we will try to knit, rather loosely, the experience of women into a possible ethic, derived largely from Hindu thought as interpreted by Gandhi. The growing documentation on women worldwide—our economic roles, our behaviour, our attitudes, our aspirations—has begun to reveal some interesting facts.

First, for example, is women's overwhelming *desire for peace*, our support of movements for peace, and our rejection of the accumulation of arms.

Second, there is women's sense of *responsibility* as well as *care* for each other and for the survival of the whole. This may be expressed in the poignant commitment of a woman from a lower resource household to making any sacrifice, however physically dangerous or devastating to health, in order to keep the family alive. Or it may be expressed in the kind of caring that women do in other social situations, whether in working together as women's groups or in generating different work styles at their own work place. A sense of *care* seems to stand out

Third, there is a *rejection of hierarchy*. Women prefer to work in styles of equality and in situations of what we might call "tentativeness"—the capacity to be moved and to change.

Fourth, there is an appreciation of the small-scale, which fosters the *capacity for self-reliance*. In the developing world, especially in its traditional sectors, be it agrarian or urban, women find themselves functioning in either subsistence households or in the self-employed sector, at least in non-socialist countries. In socialist countries, production for self-consumption is found in the "kitchen garden," a part of all peasant households whether in China or Vietnam. Such kitchen gardens seem to account for 40 to 60 per cent of the household's food consumption, and these gardens reveal a higher productivity rate than the collectives. In other words, women are still in the household sector, both for production and for self-consumption.

In industry, even though large parts of the economy are "organised" in the developed countries, women still play a role in the household sector; whereas in the developing world, which does not have the dominant organised sectors, women predominate in the small autonomous micro-production/consumption units.

Finally, there is a *sense of tradition*. Cultural and religious roots influence women. Traditions of carrying on the culture prevail. Women have links with the tradition, sometimes deriving strength from it through their own women's networks. Through this they maintain some autonomy as women. At times, also, women suffer with the traditions.

The question is, Can we build on the tradition, and if so how? Can we draw upon women's own experience in moving toward the future? Can we find a philosophical, moral and ideological base for a feminist ethic? In my opinion, work in women and development has suffered from the lack of such an articulated base.

The Basis of a Feminist Ethic

What would be the basis of feminist action for social change? To my mind, the basis would have to be the development of individual autonomy and self-reliance. Many theologies of East and West have reflected on the question of individual "autonomy". But the idea of self-development and self-realisation as the basis for a moral society is not the popular idiom of the day.

Today the collective ethic is predominant. Terms like "organisation strategy" and "consciousness raising" really suggest the submersion of the individual. Whether we consider communes in socialist or liberal countries, or whether we consider such institutions as trade unions or the family elsewhere, the boundary is the group, not the individual. Ethics is asked of the group, not the individual, which has tended to erode the individual's sense of responsibility.

Women, however, still assume and face responsibilities as individuals, *in* the family. Women's traditional ethical norms are neither individualistic, nor group-centred. Rather, women seem to consider the individual in the context of the group. It should again be stressed that Gandhi's ethic of self-rule and self-reliance was *not* rugged individualism, but rather individual responsibility in the context of the community. Thus, a focus on individual morality, with its self-consciousness and self-control, would replace the aggregation of irresponsible individuals with a moral aggregation of responsible individuals. It would draw more of society into the kind of moral behaviour which women already follow in relation to their families.

For me as an Indian, familiar with the Hindu way of life, this emphasis on individual autonomy, with the goal of self-realisation, does not appear strange. This way of thinking provided the base for the non-violent freedom movement launched by Gandhi. While his use of non-violent resistance to liberate India is well known, his economic and political strategies, which he saw as part of the freedom struggle, are relatively less known.

I should elaborate on this, since the paradigm of a feminist ethic I am considering draws inspiration from Gandhi's views. For Gandhi, freedom from the British was only one step towards overall freedom. To him, self-reliance meant not only liberation from foreign power, but liberation from internal domination of one another by classes and castes. The freedom struggle was the struggle to build self-reliance—from the individual level right up to the nation.

Swaraj ("home rule") was linked with *swadeshi* (the use of "self-made goods"), and *swadeshi* was linked with *swavalambh* ("self-reliance"). Self-made goods became Gandhi's platform, linking political with individual freedom. One should prevent not only exploitation by foreigners, but also exploitation by the owners of domestic capital. Gandhi stimulated consciousness among all classes of people that their interest lay in making India independent of British rule. But he did not limit himself to the simple phenomenon of separating British from Indian sovereignty. He tried to enable society to liberate itself from various forms of bondage—those imposed by outsiders, and those imposed by ourselves.

In relation to women, Gandhi saw straightaway that the roles assigned to them were due to the ignorance and lack of imagination of men. Women should not be in the kitchen, but in the forefront of public life. Women, according to Gandhi, have a highly developed sense of morality and responsibility, which should be used in national development.

To begin to change the position and status of women, Gandhi urged them to shed ornament, saying that the ornamentation they wear is part of men's conspiracy to make women into ornaments and possessions. He also suggested that food habits be simplified, including simply cooked or uncooked vegetables, hand-processed grains, and milk. This would reduce cooking, one of the tasks which holds women in bondage the world over. In this, Gandhi's ashrams went further than the kibbutz community in Israel or the communes of China, both of which have community kitchens. Gandhi emphasised simplicity in food habits, reducing unnecessary time for cooking.

Concerning men's unreflective use of women as workers, free labour and sex-objects, Gandhi went so far as to urge women to refuse to participate in sex, as a form of non-violent resistance to subordination by men. An entire generation of women who fought with him took a pledge of celibacy, just to prove this point. They were not nuns, who are also celibate, considering themselves married to God. Rather they lived among men, and with men in cohabitation, but rejected their sexuality.

Some of these ideas may seem extremist and old fashioned, but Gandhi was reacting to what he felt was the terrible fact of Harijan and female subordination, in a caste-ridden, hierarchical and diverse society. Though many of his statements on women may seem jarring when read today, Gandhi seems to have been intuitively attuned to them, and to have seen women's potential more clearly than any other political or religious leader in any part of the world. He perceived women as equal, but different. In their difference, Gandhi himself identified with women. He took up women's ways and issues—such as the prohibition of liquor, self-reliance through spinning *khadi*, and production for self-consumption.

In short, the ethic of self-reliance seems to have several related principles. First, that of bread labour: that each individual should work daily for bread, producing as much as he or she needs to consume. Second, simplicity in life style, minimising one's wants and recognising that acquisitiveness is often the basis of aggression and injustice. Third, identification with the poor, visibly demonstrating by the simplicity of one's life a solidarity with the poor and a willingness to distribute resources, however scarce, evenly. Fourth, discipline of the mind and body, preparing in every way for the hardship and potential deprivation of a non-violent struggle.

Gandhian education, called "Basic Education," was based on the cultivation of such self-reliance. Children learned how to work, and learned through their work. They learned to grow food, to spin and weave cloth, and to clean toilets. An essential part of their schooling was to learn the elimination of inequality between the castes and the sexes.

On a larger scale, Gandhi's social vision was based on decentralisation—in social, political and economic units. Decentralisation fosters self-reliance. It avoids the perpetual trend toward dependence by postulating a production pattern which has at the starting point self-consumption on the demand side, and an available set of locally accessible materials on the supply side. Consumption would be controlled to suit the production possibilities of those who have low resources and/or low skills. This seemed to Gandhi a viable place to begin generating greater equality without centralisation.

Finally, in considering the implications of Gandhian thought for a feminist ethic, let us remember his sustained and continuous reflection on the question of method, that the consonance of means and ends is crucial. It is this *way* of working that can be of great significance for us. It is clear from our discussion that a women's united platform need not be completely issue-based, but could well be methodology-based. Issues, by necessity, vary between classes, regions and cultures. For example, a crisis in the lives of the poorest women might be the immediate need for nutrition, wages, or water. In another class, the priority issue might be the right to divorce. Elsewhere, one hears that lesbian rights have become a frontal issue. The affluent in the developing countries may be looking for legal protection, property rights, better divorce laws, or equal opportunity in holding top decision-making posts. For the poorest, the issue may be how to prevent technological displacement from work, or how to prevent eviction.

Thus, particular issues which are very important for mobilising at the micro-level, and which provide the focus for building up women's solidarity and women's consciousness, do not necessarily provide a base for bringing women together from a wide diversity of areas and classes.

Methodologies, or *ways* of bringing about change, on the other hand, do provide some common territory. First, for example, the way of non-violence: the means of achieving an end must be consonant with the end. Peace cannot be secured by war; justice cannot be gained by trampling upon human rights. Thus, non-violent techniques and forms of peaceful resistance are the preferred method for developing a world of peace and justice. Second, the way of simplicity, expressed in the ethics of consumption restraint, redirection of consumption patterns and the limitation of the field of wants and desires. Third, the way of self-reliance, expressed in individual, local and community-based self-reliance, as well as in wider policies of decentralisation.

It is here in such a methodology that Gandhian thought, feminist consciousness, and real progress toward development converge. The building of this consciousness has to be an integral part of the development process.

APPENDIX

VIOLENCE AND NON-VIOLENCE: A DISCUSSION

(*Note*: This discussion took place after two full days of case-study presentations and discussions, followed by an evening public panel at the Kennedy School Forum on "Making Peace: Women in the Midst of Conflict." The Panel participants were Sissela Bok, a moral philosopher; Radha Bhatt, the head of a Gandhian women's ashram; Jean Zaru, a Palestinian Quaker from the West Bank; and Helen Caldicott, founder of the Physicians for Social Responsibility. This discussion, building on what went before, was chaired by Sharon Welch of the Harvard Divinity School.)

Sharon Welch (U.S.A.): I want to begin this morning's discussion on violence and non-violence by suggesting that we examine specifically the adequacy of these terms for understanding the issues that have been raised so far. Let us consider some specific examples, and think about what the terms "violence" and "non-violence" reveal, and what they hide. Drorah and Sissela will begin the discussion, after which we should hear first from those who have not yet had a chance to speak to this issue.

Drorah Setel (U.S.A.): I think a feminist ethic begins with the notion of interrelation. So in looking at violence and non-violence, we do not see them as either/or alternatives, but ask what elements of both are implied in making any ethical choice. One question that has been overwhelming to me in these past days has been that of being a Jew, and knowing that the Jewish people have been both oppressed and the victims of violence and, in the eyes of many here, now the oppressors and perpetrators of violence. We can't say that Zionism is either totally evil or totally good. It has been both. Similarly, talking with women here about the renewal of the church in Latin

America, I am both supportive of the church's role in liberation and pained to hear that there has been a simultaneous increase in anti-semitism. Let us not try to use the language of violence in too general a way yet, since there are violence-s.

Sissela Bok (U.S.A.): It seems to me that there are two types of coercion: one has to do with power and the other has to do with language. When power is used to make other people do what they do not want to do, and used unjustly, we often call that violence. And when language is used to mislead other people, to make them do or think what they do not want to do or think, we call that lying. When they are used unjustly, either power or language, I think we can use the terms "violence" and "lying," but the problem comes in determining what is unjust. We must ask, however, what if I use power to injure another in self-defence? We may or may not want to call that violence, and that is something I want to open up for discussion here. I think it might be wrong to decide that words are so complicated that we cannot use the terms violence or lying. Even in taking a clear and strong position against violence or lying as I have defined them, then still we must ask if there are times when force or words should indeed be used in such a way as to liberate people from oppression. On the other side we should be wary of terms such as non-violence, for even if I take a stand for non-violence, that does not necessarily mean that everything done under the banner of non-violence is "good" any more than every word spoken truthfully is necessarily "good". You can speak truthfully to destroy people's integrity, to undercut someone's self-confidence. Just because you have decided to try not to lie does not mean you should pour forth all the truthful statements you know. Similarly, just as you may have decided to use violence as little as you can in your life and relationships, it obviously doesn't mean that you should do everything else with a free heart just because it happens not to be violent. A non-violent act can be deceptive. A non-violent act can be tremendously unfair. Again, with respect to both violent and non-violent acts, we have to ask about the moral principles. One of the great dangers both for people in power and for people deprived of power is that they decide the time has come to forget asking about principles.

Sharon Welch: I would like to provide some examples of some of these ambiguities and difficulties, and begin by saying something about the violence of capitalism. In teaching courses on theologies of liberation, I find that many students find it difficult to understand the reality of structural violence as it exists in, for example, Central America. They can identify quite easily as "violent" acts of resistance in which people are armed. But for them to identify as "violence" an economic system in which poor people are killed, through starvation, is more difficult for many to understand. The violence here is impersonal; it is the violence of an unjust economic system. Violence is more than the simple act of inflicting physical harm on another person.

A corresponding ambiguity exists in the understanding of non-violence, and I was especially struck by this when I was teaching in Memphis and a person came to the school to advocate the establishment of a Peace Science programme. As an example of the value of Peace Science he talked about how in labour-management relations it is important for management to learn ways to respond to conflict non-violently. The reason management should respond non-violently was, in his view, not to bring about justice but to diffuse the protest, and that by giving token responses to protesters and engaging in dialogue, one could prevent violence. But one could also prevent justice. So I think it is very important to articulate the principle, the spirit, that is part of violence and non-violence, so that we can see non-violent suppression of justice and can see indirect forms of violence.

Brigalia Bam (SOUTH AFRICA): Are we in agreement that one can use violence to liberate, to destroy structures that are unjust? Are we in agreement on that?

Sharon Welch: I think it is important to be clear, when you say "violence" there, what kind of acts do you have in mind?

Brigalia Bam: The most common usage is what we now term "revolution" and I will use my country, South Africa, as an example, because I know that best. South Africa has structures that go through Parliament, that are legalized, so they have all the respectability of the Constitution. But these are structures that are deliberately designed to keep the majority of the people, the Black people, in bondage. The Law is that Black people, because of colour cannot vote. That is a Law. And it is the Law that if you are Black you cannot own land. That is a Law. Now if I want to own land in my country, South Africa, then I will have to use whatever means are available to me. How do we deal with these realities? My method would not be to persuade them to change. I would kill, finally, to get my land back.

Sharon Welch: How do you see the difference between the kind of violence involved in killing to get your land back, and that involved in killing someone to take land away?

Brigalia Bam: I brought this up because this is an ongoing current debate, where, as women, we have not taken a position. We as women are brought up thinking we can always use methods of persuasion, that we must transform, change attitudes, and so on. But when all these attempts at transformation, persuasion, fail... then what do we do?

Sissela Bok: Here I would like to introduce something of the controversy surrounding the film *Gandhi*, for the criticism of this film in this country has come from both the right and the left. Some on both sides have said that it may have worked to use Gandhi's methods in a country such as India and against an opponent such as the British, but how would those methods work in a country like South Africa where injustice seems to be permanent and those in power unresponsive? The counter question that must be raised, I think, is if you use other methods, if you go so far as to kill to get your land back, then will the whole enterprise be corrupted? Then one has to look at some other African countries, and ask how well have violent methods worked? And beyond that, the question—what happens to us as human beings when we use violent methods? I would very much like to hear what the Gandhians here have to say on that.

Radha Bhatt (INDIA): What she is asking is in two parts, to my mind. First, how may we break down the structure which is making such injustice? To my mind, non-violence shows a way and a different spirit. If you put a seed in the ground, the outside husk in time falls away and the shoot will come through. But if the shoot is not strong, the outside husk will not fall. Non-violence works in that way to my mind. If the people are strong, the structure will fall down by itself. I think that is what happened in India. I don't think it is that the British people were kind or not-kind, but I do think they wanted to keep their rule in India. But the people, who were oppressed and had no strength inside, and had really lost their power, discovered in the non-violence of Gandhiji that they could be powerful. They could be fearless. And non-violence also gave the British a chance to change. It was good for those coming up, and good for those who were falling down. Now second, you say that you have been deprived of your land. That really is a crime. But what should be the method? I think it should be non-cooperation, when I think of my own experience and the work of Gandhi. There was a law against making salt, for example, and yet thousands of people saw this was unjust, and they broke the law. The same was true of the taxes on the poor in Bardoli. They broke an unjust law.

Nawal el Saadawi (EGYPT): First of all, how did they take your land? Violence started in history, because a few people wanted to have the rights of the majority. And when you are a minority, when you are one, and you want to have the rights of ten thousand, you have to use a gun. You can't use logic. Violence started in human history when exploitation started. The minority were victorious over the majority by violence. Violence started physically, and then technologically. So, how can the majority take their rights facing this technological violence? If you say we need power from inside, to me it sounds as if when you invite two persons from Cairo to come here, one delegate takes an airplane and you ask me to use my legs in coming here. It's the same. I think we have to define goals, and not methods. And this is not against ethics, morality. What is morality? Should I kill to get my rights or not? We define it in a deceptive way. When you carry a gun, is it a crime regardless of your goal? And this power from inside: it is like asking me to develop my legs to walk very quickly in order to compete with the airplane. I have to develop my spiritual power in order to compete with the power of the gun? I think this is injustice. We must really discuss this.

Peggy Cleveland (U.S.A.): I think in discussing South Africa, especially with reference to Gandhi and the independence struggle in India, we need to remember one very important difference: the Boers are not going home; in their minds they are at home. There is a very long history of non-violent struggle in South Africa, which has tried the patience of a good many people, most recently in Soweto in 1976. A time comes when the methodologies that have been tried are no longer appropriate because the equations are so radically different. Now we are talking about direct economic support from the United States for the South African government, and there was a time, when that support wasn't so strong, that there was some hope for non-violent methods being used. In any case, I think it is important not to draw too close a parallel between the Indian and South African situations, for they are quite different.

Susan Bruno (U.S.A.): It seems to me that if we are going to look at this question from a feminist perspective, we have to ask—Is the power and principle of female bonding such that it can supercede the coercive forces of particular religions, national and cultural interest? If we ask that question then the whole business of violence and resistance takes on another dimension. Let me give a simple example. I am willing to use violence to protect my children. I will kill to do that, without qualification. As a white western woman, am I willing to use my power to resist an ideology that will kill that woman's children, even though she is a Palestinian and I am a Jew? We can talk about historical violence, but we are talking about that violence within patriarchal ideological structures, which we all buy into, when, for instance, we talk about killing to retrieve our land. But if I say, if I am bonded with that woman and we both want land, am I willing to kill her children so that my children can have land?

Elizabeth Amoah (GHANA): I have a slightly different point, really a question. In many societies, such as my own in Ghana, respect for parents or elders is considered an important moral principle. My question is about discipline: Do you consider using "the cane" on a child as violent or unjust?

Sharon Welch: Do you see it as violent or unjust?

Elizabeth Amoah: If you put it in its context, I don't think so. It is up to the parent to bring up the child in the right direction.

Sissela Bok: I would say that, of course, there are times when parents must use force with children. When a child is about to hurt himself or herself, for example. There are times when one doesn't reason with two or three year olds. One just has to take action. Nevertheless, throughout the world parents, as well as governments and armies, have indoctrinated children to believe that certain things are right, such as hating neighbouring countries. I think that one should be wary of indoctrination, whether physical or mental, and there women have so much to do with the attitudes of children. In areas where children have grown up with war and violence, it has been shown that they often start out with a real understanding of all sides, and then gradually develop the prejudices and violences and self-righteousness of the society. They get drawn in, in their early teens. Those who train young men in the armies know that it becomes increasingly difficult to train young men to kill after the late teens. But if only we could preserve the questioning of children . . . As a philosopher once said, Blind obedience creates tyrants. This is important to remember, and there is a real role for women here.

Shulamith Koenig (ISRAEL): I want to talk on violence and non-violence, and the "just war" from the perspective of the Israeli-Palestinian issue, because in one lifetime my people have had to face all of these dilemmas. Constantly, every day. We had a poem when we were children that said: "You who want to be righteous and just, be strong, and you will be righteous and just." And when we said it as six year olds in the thirties, we meant "morally strong," and this was how I, as a Jewish girl in Israel, was brought up. But then, as injustices occurred on both sides, the righteousness became self-righteousness and the justice became moral superiority. In the forties there were stories of our young people going out in the underground against the British, and a woman would come in front of the Britisher holding a child in her arms so we wouldn't shoot. We used to speak of what we called the "sanctity of arms," which meant that you only use arms to defend yourself. We went through this whole process, calling ourselves a "defence army". And this is the question: When are you an army and when are you a terrorist? When you carry a gun, as I have done in my teens, you always have to ask, When do you shoot? And we all said, The only time you shoot is to protect life. And then, from 1967, from defenders we become offenders.

And then we come to the situation we know today. The men and women of the West Bank are serving us daily in our streets. They are cleaning our latrines, they are working in our hospitals, they are working in the plastic factories, they are building the homes of the settlers who have taken their land. And I come and say to my Arab friends, to my Palestinian friends, Stop serving us. This is what you were saying, Radha. Stop serving us, and the structure will fall by itself. We will have to work in our own factories and clean our own latrines. And people then say to me, That is all very well for you to say this. You are an engineer, you don't have to worry. But those people have to eat. But when I saw the movie *Gandhi*, one thing I hoped was that I could show this movie to two million Palestinians. They can eat the grain they have on the hills; they can share what they have between them. They won't have to do it for a whole year, not for as long as the Indians did it. One month, two months. We will realize in Israel that enough is enough. But here is the question: When are you an oppressor, a defender, an offender?

Nancy Falk (U.S.A.): There is well documented literature about the tendency of violence to perpetuate violence. In the literature of child abuse, the child abuser is more apt to be the one who has experienced violence in his or her own family. That is on a micro-scale. Those who have experienced abuse are likely to carry it on. And this can be seen in the dynamics of nations as well, as is clear in the Middle East. Once a people has been corrupted by violence, that violence is apt to be self-perpetuating. Another point: It is a terrible mistake to confuse non-violent resistance and persuasion. Gandhi's movement was not one of persuasion, but resistance. Eighty-five per cent of South Africa is Black? If 85 per cent said, We die before we serve, there is no way that apartheid could be perpetuated in South Africa.

Beverly Harrison (U.S.A.): I think I agree with what you said, Nancy, except for one thing. We again need to be careful of the particularity. It has been said before, but I simply want to call it to our attention again. The British Empire was crumbling at the time of India's struggle; the South African Boers are sitting on diamonds and gold. Eighty-five per cent of the Blacks in South Africa, if they rise up, will be shot. And if we do not understand that, then we do not understand the particularity of apartheid and its structures.

Now, it is the moral task, the task of women, to build those zones of persuasion and non-coercion. But, unfortunately it is precisely the particularity and embodiedness that we as women often speak of that also reminds us that there is a material base to oppression. I think we have not heard enough about that.

Veena Das (INDIA): We have become very used to hearing that if the British were not so nice, non-cooperation would never have worked in India. It was because they had a conscience that we could succeed in making them withdraw, and in any case the Empire was already crumbling, so they would have got out anyway. I think the one thing people tend to forget is that India had not only the non-cooperation movement, but also the simultaneous violent nationalist movement. In the part of India from which I come, in Bengal, it is not Gandhi who is the hero, but Subhas Chandra Bose who is the hero. I think it is important, however, to remember that non-violence, moral courage, or whatever, was not something that just came naturally. It was something that had to be learned.

I must be one of the few Indians who could not bear to see *Gandhi* since I lost most of my family during the Jallianwala Bagh incident, but my fourteen year old son came back and said, "There was this whole crowd, why couldn't they simply attack General Dyer?" It was difficult to explain to him that it was very important not to attack General Dyer, because that is what led in the next round to say that no issues were confused. There was not a single Indian who raised a hand against General Dyer. This is something one has to remember—that non-violence had to be learned every day.

The other thing I want to say is that I have great envy of those who can talk about violence very easily, for in India even after the Partition we were all taught that this was not a talkable thing. Women who had been raped, people who had lost their whole families—they did not talk. I never knew even a "picture" of my mother, because it was not talked about. It was kept aside.

That brings me to my next question, which refers back to Julia Esquivel's witness from Guatemala, and that is, what kind of languages have been created in this world which allow a man to rape a woman eighteen times and then go home and be a good husband and a good father? Now I have looked into these languages, and there is one very important language that is being used and that is the language of Sacrifice. We say that we do "kill" during sacrifice, but we kill that victim and purge ourselves of a social evil.

The Japanese pilots on suicide missions used this language of sacrifice. We have the traditional languages of feud as well. And we also have the modern language of vivisection, namely that the person is being killed, against whom there is this violence, is an object, not a human being. I would like to draw your attention to this particular form of violence, because it is the prevalent mode of violence.

The power of non-cooperation is that if one is to die, one will not die being a willing victim. Gandhi was very upset about the Jewish concentration camps, surely because in some cases they died producing things for the Germans or they died digging their own graves. I know that it sounds callous to talk about internal power, but I also know that it is not something that comes easily. It is something that one has to learn after very disciplined efforts, and I want to remind you that Gandhi withdrew his movement again and again because he felt that people had not learned to be non-violent. A final point about Gandhi that I think has been completely missed is the fact that his was a feminist ideology. Gandhi often said, Don't call me Father, call me Mother. And his technique of non-cooperation and fasting is a technique which women use every day in Indian families. It is the power of the weak, in a certain sense. I will not cooperate with this system which has been built for me.

Devaki Jain (INDIA): I think it is good that this issue of violence and non-violence is important in the training of Gandhian cadres. The ethic of self-control is an amazing thing; the ethic of simplicity is part of it. The way you dress, how much money you take, how you eat. Maybe it looks a bit monastic, like Jesuit training for those who know the Christian idiom, but I think there was something else also. They were trained as in monasteries, but then released into social action. And Gandhi, as Veena said, always drew them back if he felt they were not ready. This kind of self-discipline and self-control also builds self-confidence—a kind of detachment from "ends". It is crucial to know how we feel about this issue of means and ends.

Now Sissela was asking us to consider the empirical evidence of what has happened in the other African countries, and Bernadette asked me when we came the first day, what would have happened if Gandhi had remained in South Africa. This relates to one other question, and that is the question of the scheduled castes, the Harijans, in India. Peggy Cleveland asked us to remember that the Boers in South Africa were not about to go home; they felt they belonged there. Now, the Boers in India would be us, the Brahmins, the upper middle class. We are they. We are sitting there still, exploiting, outcasting the Harijans. So we have in India the live example of a colonial group—us—sitting over another—the scheduled castes.

In India today there are two movements: the Gandhians and the Dalits, the scheduled castes who have been organised. And the Dalits believe in violent struggle, they deny Gandhi. They say that

Gandhi let us down by not making the scheduled castes a separate group; we want to identify ourselves as scheduled castes and have our own political party. But as we discuss this Dalit issue in India, the central question in my mind is: What are the processes we release in the methods we follow? Methods release processes. Where the gun has got liberation, as in Burma, the gun continues to defend liberation. When Susan asked what she called the feminist question: I would kill to save my children, so would I also kill to save a Palestinian mother's children? The question is, are we willing to kill? As feminists are we willing to kill, even to save our children? Granted, as Nawal said, there are many kinds of violence. But that final violence, where we take life: are we as feminists willing to do that? Are we willing to release processes which are going continuously to keep society on edge, processes in which we reap killing? Since so many of these fundamental differences have come to mind, I thought I would try to sharpen them. To me, self-training is a pre-condition for non-violence; and the vision to see what processes we release is the next step.

Julia Esquivel (GUATEMALA): I do not wish to give an argument, but prefer to give a testimony. This question of violence or non-violence is not really a question for us. It really doesn't interest us to discuss this, and we do not have time to talk about it. Because by means of a process, a long process of peaceful struggle to defend life, the most minimal right to life—to eat, to think, to have a roof over one's head, even just a small shack—has been taken from us. Therefore violence or non-violence is not the question in Central America. It is, rather, can we live or not? We are either going to live or be exterminated. This is the question for us. In other words, we don't have an alternative. We are like the woman who has to use every means possible to save herself and her children, or else be exterminated. I would like to tell you, with sincerity, that our people organised to use all non-violent means, legal means, juridical means, demonstrations, dialogue—all methods—and the response to all these methods has been death.

We have learned from past experiences, not only non-violent ones. People have seen the film *Gandhi*, and have made more perfect their own methods. But the sons of darkness are often smarter than the sons and daughters of light. Therefore I would like to say that for us in Central America—for the people of Guatemala, for the people of El Salvador, for the people of Nicaragua—the capitalist system is a project of death. It is death. We say this from experience—not from having read things, but from experience. There are many ways for justifying killing people for the accumulation of capital. It is an economic project—to count bills, to fill the banks, to have "national security"—and these things cost lives. They cost thousands of lives. In twenty-nine years, 100,000 people have been killed in Guatemala. And in forty years of the Somoza regime, how many thousands? We see military power which defends capitalism as a system of domination, of extermination. And I would like to remind you of the words of Jesus: Those who govern the people and dominate the people and use the people—this is mammon, this is the "god" of the devils, this is the father of death. This is a mystery. It is not a question of ideas. Facing this power, Jesus offers another way to deal with power. It should not be like this. But those who are truly great should serve others.

This is what they try to do in Nicaragua against all forces of evil. I would like to ask a question: Where are the indigenous people of this country, of North America? I would not like my people to disappear. We don't have the opportunity to think about violence or non-violence. Our question is to live or not to live. And what does independence mean? Why are we independent? To continue to be part of this system of death? We have to understand that we are fighting against a system of organised death, and for it there is a complete system of national security. And for this we have interiorized a terror of communism. I speak from Central America, from our experience in Guatemala. And in this sense, as Christians, there are many women, priests, pastors, lay people struggling with our people to live. For we want our people never to disappear.

And now a few questions. How was independence achieved in the United States? How has progress been made in this country? Violence is something that we all have inside of us. In all of us, there is a struggle of life and death. That is a reality, and it is a mystery.

Jean Zaru (WEST BANK): I would like to make just a brief remark to make the atmosphere more peaceful. I think we should pursue the subject of violence and non-violence without the patronising attitude that we are forcing choices on people. I have been concerned with the study of violence/non-violence for social change with the World Council of Churches and I know the reaction of many people: that we are too often addressing the powerless. Where their dignity of life has been denied—the choice must be theirs. Non-violence is a religious conviction for me. I am a Quaker. So I am not speaking for violence. But we must not tell the powerless how they should seek change.

Another point, rather than always addressing the powerless and giving them strategies, as Shulamith was suggesting a few minutes ago, we should address the people in power. Both of them are victims of violence. Shula has made strategies for the Palestinian people, but she did not say what strategies she would suggest to the Israeli government, or the Israelis in the army, or the Israelis that build settlements, or confiscate land. We spoke about strategies for the South African Black population; but why don't we speak of strategies for the people in power in South Africa, or the transnational corporations that exploit the South African population? We should really be very careful. If we are concerned about non-violence, then we should be concerned to raise consciousness about the evil in our world, wherever it applies. But, I know the images: it is always the powerless that are called terrorist, revolutionaries, and you give them strategies to work on. But you never discuss the violence that is legalized by governments, by states, and so on. So I hope we won't patronise each other and be insensitive to each other with our discussion. Address injustice wherever it lies, and then empower people to work in a non-violent way.

Bernadette Mosala (SOUTH AFRICA): Before we close the session this morning, I just want to say something more about the South African situation. I respect the information that people here in the West have about the South African situation, but I do not believe they fully understand the complexities, the subtleties, and the intricacies that are involved. While one wants to accept the empathy that comes forth, those who say "Why don't you stand up and say no!" one comes to the complex level of things. In South Africa there are people clinging for dear life to South Africa, for if they are pushed out they have no place to go. Another thing: that I cannot give you an adequate account of the strength of South African Blacks. That they can still smile takes a lot of courage.

Now the problem we face is not only the massive onslaught of arms from the western world, but of investments as well. We have organisations that have been set up—such as Women for Peace, which came up in 1976, soon after Soweto. It was set up in order to co-opt the Black woman into this body. And there are Black women in that organisation. And the organisation can talk and say, "Our

Black women say this or that. . ." To diffuse the spirit of resistance, or revolution, so that investors can feel comfortable about investing in that country.

I would like to move in the direction of Susan's question: That is, are we prepared, at all times and in all ways, as feminists, to identify with the suffering Black women of today. You talk of defending your children if anything threatens their life. Rural women in South Africa have to watch their children die. What is violence? In Soweto I live in a violent situation. We live in a violent situation, day in, day out. The question of violence is a difficult one. If you push me, I will retreat. And if you push me more, I will retreat some more. But the minute I reach the wall, I can't retreat any more. Self-preservation comes up. Even if it means pinching, biting with my teeth. Susan's is an important question, and I would plead that we move the discussion in that direction.

NOTES ON CONTRIBUTORS

Julia Esquivel is a primary school teacher, a poet, and a theologian. In 1980 she was forced into exile from Guatemala by repeated threats to her life from the ruling generals. In exile she has carried on her work on behalf of her people as the director of the Committee for Justice and Peace (Comite pro Justicia y Paz). She has published, in Spanish and English, a collection of her poetry, *Threatened With Resurrection*.

Elsa Tamez teaches at the Seminario Biblico Latinoamericano in San Jose, Costa Rica, and is a staff member of the movement of the poor for liberation in Central America. She is the author of a book entitled, *The Bible of the Oppressed*.

Brigalia Bam of South Africa, like Julia Esquivel, comes as one in exile, now unable to return to South Africa. From 1973–79 Brigalia served as director of the programme on Women in Church and Society at the World Council of Churches in Geneva. Since then she has worked in Geneva with the international YWCA and with an international union.

Bernadette Mosala works with the South African Council of Churches which has become an important voice for Black South Africans and, as a result, a target of harassment and continual investigation by the government of South Africa. Her portfolio in SACC is Director of Home and Family Life.

Jean Zaru has lived her entire life in Ramallah, originally Palestine, and since 1967 a part of the militarily occupied West Bank. She is an Arab, a Quaker, and a Pacifist. She has been a member of the Central Committee of the World Council of Churches and is a Vice-President of the World YWCA.

Shulamith Koenig is an Israeli, and works as International Coordinator of the American-Israeli Civil Liberties Coalition, and the Israeli organization, Kol Kore, "The Summoning Voice," concerned with civil liberties and democratic action in Israel.

Masako Tanaka teaches anthropology at Meijo University in Nagoya, Japan. She received her doctorate from the University of Rochester with a thesis on *Kinship and Descent in an Okinawan Village*. Her papers in anthropology include work on maternal authority in the Japanese family.

Elizabeth Amoah teaches religion at the University of Ghana in Legon.

Fatima Mernissi is a sociologist, working at the Research Institute of the University of Rabat in Morocco. She has written widely in Arabic, French and English on women in North African Muslim culture, and is the author of *Beyond the Veil: Male-Female Dynamics in a Modern Muslim Society*.

Elisabeth Adler is the Director of Evangelische Akademie, a lay church academy in Berlin, in the German Democratic Republic. Elisabeth has had a long career in international work with churches, including work with the World Council of Churches Program to Combat Racism.

Judith Plaskow a Jewish feminist theologian is a Professor of Religion at Manhattan College. Her book *Womanspirit Rising*, edited with Carol Christ, is a landmark in feminist thought.

Sandra Wilson is an Episcopal priest. She is the rector, or priest in charge, of St. Mark's Episcopal Church in Bridgeport, Connecticut. She is the first woman rector in the diocese of Connecticut and the first Black woman ordained to the priesthood in the churches of the Anglican communican in the world.

Daphne Hampson earned a doctorate in History at Oxford, followed by a doctorate in Theology at Harvard Divinity School. Daphne is now a Lecturer in Systematic Theology at the University of St. Andrews in Scotland.

Chatsumarn Kabilsingh is Assistant Dean of the Faculty of Liberal Arts at Thammasat University in Thailand. She has recently started the *Newsletter on International Buddhist Women's Activities* to link Buddhist women throughout the world by providing information on Buddhist women's activities and on the current worldwide status of the Bhikkuni Samgha.

Kumiko Uchino is a Japanese scholar, with a doctorate in Sociology from Keio University in Japan.

Radha Bhatt has worked since 1952 in Lakshmi Ashram, a Gandhian ashram for girls and women in Kausani, in the Almora district of the Kumaon Hills in the foothills of the Himalayas. For the past ten years, Radha has been the leader of this ashram community.

José Höhne-Sparborth is involved in a grassroots movement for social change, loosely called the "basic community movement" or the "grassroots movement". For twenty years, José has been a member of a Catholic congregation of religious women, the Sisters of Providence. For the past seven years she has lived in a Dominican community of women and men, called "Giordano Bruno," after the Dominican who was executed for alleged "heresy" in 1600.

Judith Aronson is with the National Council of Jewish Women, a United States organisation launched in the late 19th century.

Baroroh Baried is a Professor at Gadjah Mada University in Yogyakarta, and President of the Indonesian Muslim Women's Organisation, Aisyiyah.

Beverly Harrison is Professor of Christian Ethics at Union Theological Seminary in the United States. Beverly's book *Women's Right to Choose* is a thorough study of the abortion controversy.

Veena Das is Professor of Anthropology at the University of Delhi and a Visiting Professor at Harvard Divinity School. She is the author of *Structure and Cognition: Aspects of Hindu Caste and Ritual*.

Carol Gilligan is a Professor at the Harvard Graduate School of Education. Her *In a Different Voice* is a ground-breaking systematic attempt to hear what women consider a "moral conflict" to be and how they make decisions regarding such a conflict.

Sissela Bok a moral philosopher, is Professor of Philosophy at Brandeis University. Sissela is the author of two books on practical ethics, that is, ethics that are inextricably a part of our day to day lives: *Lying: Moral Choice in Public and Private Life*, and *Secrets: On the Ethics of Concealment and Revelation*.

Sylvia Marcos works with Procesos de Accion Communitaria, a psychotherapy collective in Cuernavaca, Mexico. She has published extensively in the area of psychology, most recently *Manicomios y Prisones*, "Madhouses and Prisons".

Nawal el Saadawi is an Egyptian doctor and writer, formerly Egypt's Director of Public Health. Some of her many writings on women have been translated into English, including *The Hidden Face of Eve*, on women in the Arab world, and *Woman at Point Zero*, a novel.

Devaki Jain is Director of the Institute for Social Studies Trust in New Delhi. Devaki has long worked in the area of women's employment, and women and development. For India's International Women's Year she edited the book *Indian Women* and has also published *Women's Quest For Power—Five Case Studies*.

Mary Daly

Beyond God the Father

In this brilliantly argued book, Mary Daly analyses the causes of women's oppression over the last 3000 years. From Genesis to the writings of contemporary theologians, she exposes the misogyny at the core of the Judaeo-Christian religion, a misogyny which continues to flourish in Christianity's modern secular manifestations.

Originally published in 1973, *Beyond God the Father* was immediately recognised as a milestone in the history of feminist thought.

'A brave, visionary, unforgettable book' Robin Morgan
'It is truly the first philosophy of feminism' Adrienne Rich

NON FICTION £4.95
ISBN: 0 7043 3993 5

Mary Daly
Gyn/Ecology

The Metaethics of Radical Feminism

A truly revolutionary feminist text that examines the forces that have bound the minds and bodies of women in this and every other culture through the centuries, and liberates language itself with the exhilaration of its thought.

Gyn/Ecology is a book unlike any other. It invites us to acknowledge without forgiveness or collusion those forces which have shaped our lives. Recognising them, we may move beyond them to cherish and develop that strength in ourselves which is surviving the centuries of gynocide: the ritualised, *actualised* mutilation, burning, mind-binding and torture of uncounted millions of women on pyres in India, tottering on stumps in China, hanging from witches' stakes in Europe, genitally mutilated in Africa and the Middle East, lying on psychiatrists' and gynaecologists' couches all over the Western world.

'Outrage, hilarity, grief, profanity, lyricism and moral daring join in bursting the accustomed bounds even of feminist discourse' Adrienne Rich

NON FICTION £5.95
ISBN: 0 7043 3850 5

Janice Raymond
A Passion for Friends

Female friendship is a much neglected area of scholarship. Indeed, we live in a society which does not even always acknowledge its existence: women together are often seen as women alone, that is without men.

In this groundbreaking and deeply philosophical work, Janice Raymond, author of *The Transsexual Empire*, examines the reality. She rediscovers for us the lost historical traditions of friendships between women, ranging across the world from the Beguines of Europe to the Chinese marriage resisters. The conclusions she draws have contemporary meaning: that, though for both lesbian and heterosexual women, female friendship may indeed involve betrayal and disappointment, the vital importance of the love, passion and affection that women feel for women demands recognition in our lives.

NON FICTION £5.95
ISBN: 0 7043 3997 8

Angela Davis

Women, Race and Class

One of the most brilliant and courageous women of our generation brings her passion and scholarship to confront issues that have haunted feminist history for over a hundred years, and issues a challenge to women now to recognise *in action* once and for all that the struggle for liberation is indivisible.

Angela Davis draws on new and still embyonic research into the lives and achievements of black women under slavery, and into the lives of black and white women workers under industrialism, to show that both sexism and racism are deeply rooted in class oppression; and that neither can be eradicated without destroying the dominant patriarchal economic system.

NON FICTION £4.95

ISBN: 0 7043 3892 0

Nawal el Sa'adawi
Memoirs from the Women's Prison

Cairo, 1981

Translated by Marilyn Booth

Nawal el Sa'adawi is a leading Egyptian feminist, sociologist, medical doctor, novelist and author of the classic on women in Islam, *The Hidden Face of Eve.*

Her career, as Director of Health Education in the Ministry of Health in Cairo, was a distiguished one. But in 1973 she was dismissed from her post as a consequence of her political writing and activities. Worse followed, for in 1981 she was arrested for alleged 'crimes against the state', to be released only after the assassination of President Sadat.

This book is her powerful account of those months in gaol, describing both her own experiences and her encounters with other women prisoners, some of them political activists like herself, other veiled Islamic conservatives.

NON FICTION £3.95
ISBN: 0 7043 4002 X